# William J. Glackens and Pierre-Auguste Renoir
## Affinities and Distinctions

# William J. Glackens and Pierre-Auguste Renoir

## Affinities and Distinctions

NSU Art Museum Fort Lauderdale

Essays by
Avis Berman
Bonnie Clearwater
Martha Lucy
Barbara Buhler Lynes

SKIRA | NSU ART MUSEUM FORT LAUDERDALE

*Front Cover*
William J. Glackens
*Hallie Knitting in Red Hat*, c. 1920, detail (pl. 55)

*Back Cover*
Pierre-Auguste Renoir
*Seamstress at Window* [*Ravaudeuse à la fenêtre*], c. 1908–10, detail (pl. 25)

*Art Director*
Marcello Francone

*Design*
Luigi Fiore

*Editorial Coordination*
Emma Cavazzini

*Copy Editor*
Doriana Comerlati

*Layout*
Evelina Laviano

First published in Italy
in 2018 by
Skira editore S.p.A.
Palazzo Casati Stampa
via Torino 61
20123 Milano
Italy
www.skira.net



Printed and bound in Italy.
First edition

ISBN: 978-88-572-3950-7

Distributed in USA, Canada, Central & South America by ARTBOOK | D.A.P. 75, Broad Street Suite 630, New York, NY 10004, USA.
Distributed elsewhere in the world by Thames and Hudson Ltd., 181A High Holborn, London WC1V 7QX, United Kingdom.

This exhibition is organized by
NSU Art Museum Fort Lauderdale
One East Olas Boulevard,
Fort Lauderdale, Florida 33301

*Sunny Kaufman Senior Curator*
Barbara Buhler Lynes

**NSU Art Museum Fort Lauderdale**
October 21, 2018 – May 19, 2019

**Hunter Museum of American Art, Chattanooga, TN**
June 21 – September 21, 2019

This exhibition is made possible by major funding provided by Sansom Foundation, Hudson Family Foundation, David and Francie Horvitz Family Foundation. Additional support provided by Kolter Hospitality/Hyatt Centric and 100 Las Olas, Mercantil Bank, and Ponant Yacht Cruises & Expeditions. Research and development for this exhibition was supported by the Terra Foundation for American Art.

Exhibitions and programs at NSU Art Museum Fort Lauderdale are made possible in part by a challenge grant from the David and Francie Horvitz Family Foundation. Funding is also provided by Nova Southeastern University, Hudson Family Foundation, Conni Gordon, Wege Foundation, Community Foundation of Broward, Broward County Board of County Commissioners as recommended by the Broward Cultural Council and Greater Fort Lauderdale Convention & Visitors Bureau, the State of Florida, Department of State, Division of Cultural Affairs and the Florida Council on Arts and Culture. NSU Art Museum is accredited by the American Alliance of Museums.

# Contents

# Acknowledgments

In 2001, NSU Art Museum Fort Lauderdale inaugurated a wing dedicated to American artist William J. Glackens (1870–1938), fulfilling the wishes of the artist's widow Edith Dimock Glackens (1876–1955), who envisioned establishing a permanent home for her late husband's work. The bequest, which was made by the couple's son Ira, and the Sansom Foundation that he and his wife Nancy established in 1950, includes over 1,300 paintings and works on paper that span Glackens's entire career, the work of some of his best-known colleagues John Sloan and Maurice Prendergast, and archival materials. As the largest repository of Glackens's work, the museum has undertaken and encouraged research, exhibitions and publications that enrich the understanding of Glackens and his art. This exhibition takes another step, shedding new light on Glackens, his work, and his role as an advocate of modern art in America.

I extend my deep appreciation to the members of the Sansom Foundation Board and its President, Frank Buscaglia, for their generous financial support for this exhibition and to Howard Shaw, Hammer Galleries, New York, who greatly facilitated loans of works by Renoir. I also wish to thank Avis Berman for her guidance on the exhibition and catalogue.

I extend my thanks to the museum's Sunny Kaufman Senior Curator Dr. Barbara Buhler Lynes for her dedication to coordinating all aspects of this exhibition and publication and to others in curatorial: Christopher Albert, Aleesha Ast, Diana Blanco, Gabriela Gil, Charles Ross, and Paloma Nuñez.

In their essays, Lynes, Berman and Martha Lucy have provided exceptional insight into Renoir's influence on Glackens, and the significance of both artists' work in the United States, for which we are most grateful. We thank Aude Viart, Director, and Saskia Ooms, Curator, Musée de Montmartre, Paris, for hosting and participating in the convening meeting for this exhibition. Also, we are grateful to Virginia Anne Sharber, Director, and Nandini Makrandi, Chief Curator, Hunter Museum of American Art. Our deep appreciation goes to the private collectors and institutional lenders to this exhibition, who loaned so many essential works. Thanks also go to Skira for editing and publishing this stunning catalogue.

Sponsorship from Sansom Foundation, Hudson Family Foundation, David and Francie Horvitz Family Foundation, Kolter Hospitality/Hyatt Centric and 100 Las Olas, Mercantil Bank, and Ponant Yacht Cruises & Expeditions generously provided funding for this exhibition and catalogue, and research and development for it were supported by the Terra Foundation for American Art.

I also wish to recognize the museum's Board of Governors, chaired by Dr. Stanley Goodman, and Nova Southeastern University and its President and CEO, Dr. George L. Hanbury II, for their essential support.

*Bonnie Clearwater*
Director and Chief Curator
NSU Art Museum Fort Lauderale

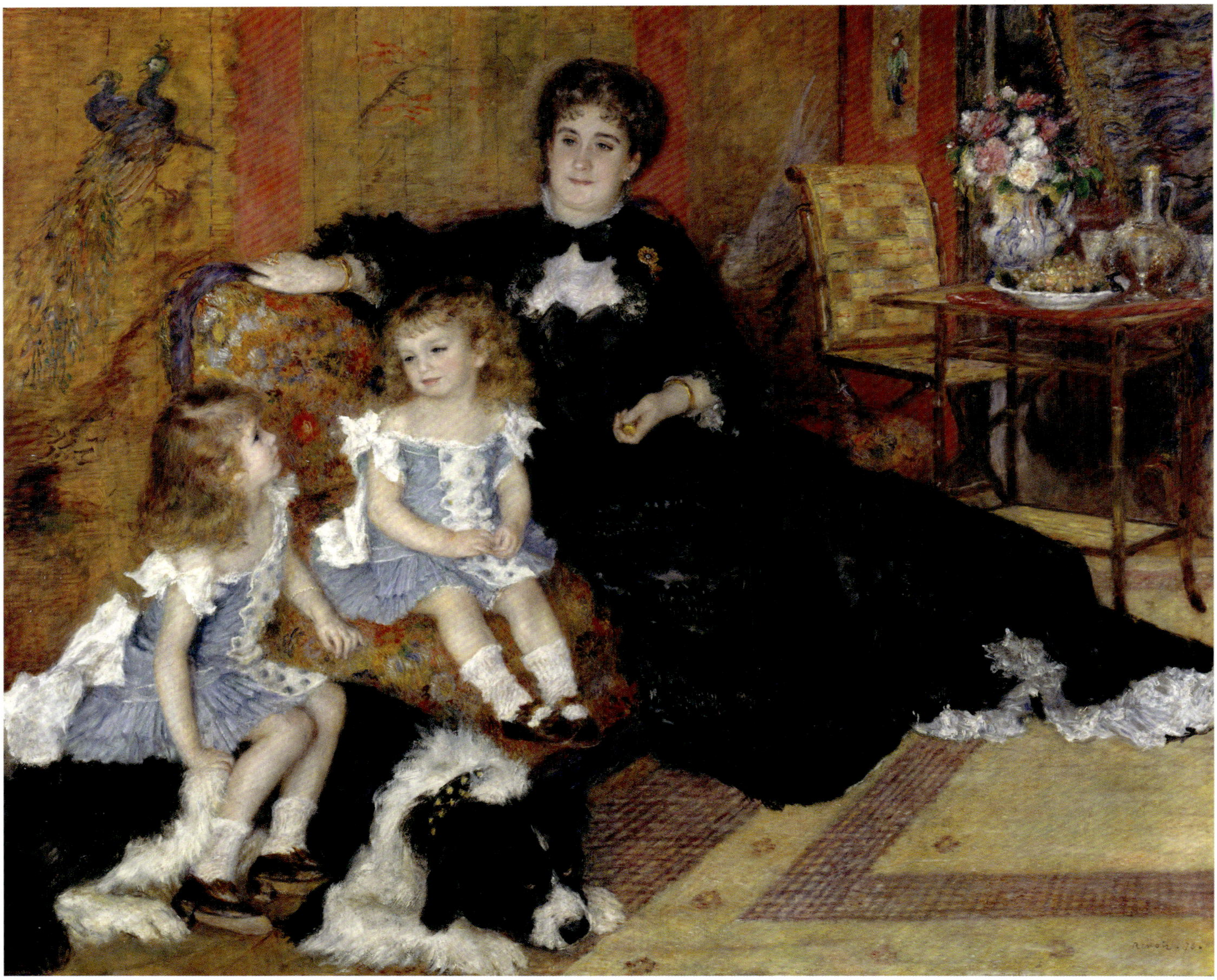

# Renoir, Glackens, and American Taste

*Bonnie Clearwater*

During a visit to the Impressionist and Post-Impressionist galleries at the Metropolitan Museum of Art, New York, a few years ago, I was struck by the abundance of Pierre-Auguste Renoir paintings on view. Although I did not count them, they seemed to outnumber paintings by any other artist. The experience led me to ponder as to why there were so many Renoirs in the collection. The Metropolitan owns 73 Renoir works, many donated by some of the country's most prominent collectors, beginning with the 1929 bequest of the Henry Osborne and Louisine Havemeyer Collection, followed by Sam A. Lewisohn, Stephen C. Clark, Robert Lehman and, most recently, the Walter and Leonore Annenberg bequest in 2002. Even before receiving these donated works, the Metropolitan made a major commitment to Renoir in 1907 by purchasing one of his masterpieces, *Madame Charpentier and Her Children*, 1878 (fig. 1), championed by the museum's curator of European paintings and influential tastemaker, Roger Fry.[1] I was curious as to how the Renoirs there and in other American museums reflected the taste of these collectors and curators, what inspired them to collect his work, and what it meant to a general audience and artists to see such a bountiful display of his works.

Other American museums could also boast large holdings of Renoir's paintings, the largest being the Barnes Foundation in Philadelphia with its 181 works acquired by Albert C. Barnes, always on display, followed by the Sterling and Francine Clark Art Institute, Williamstown, Massachusetts, with its 39 Renoirs owned by Sterling and Francine Clark. The scores of Renoirs in U.S. museums are the result of the enthusiastic response to the French artist's work by American collectors and curators in the late-nineteenth and early-twentieth centuries as detailed by Avis Berman in her essay for this catalogue. It was greatly due to the American appetite for these works that Renoir could finally support himself by 1890.[2] His dealer Paul Durand-Ruel described the American collectors as "less ignorant and less conservative than our French art lovers."[3] Renoir also garnered critical acclaim from American art critics, among them Walter Pach, whose interviews with the French artist were published in *Scribner's Magazine* in 1912. He wrote in the introduction to these interviews, "To have attained the famous three-score years and ten, and be producing work which surpasses that of his youth and middle age, to have seen the public change its attitude from hostility to homage, to be one of the best-loved of living painters: such is the lot of Pierre-Auguste Renoir."[4]

Barnes's unique approach to his collection played a role in shaping the appreciation of Renoir's painting in the United States. Barnes neither lent works from his collection to other museums nor permitted color reproductions of his holdings. (It was not until 1993 that the Barnes Foundation allowed the first color reproductions of its works.) Consequently, the restricted access to the largest concentration of Renoir, and especially his late work (c. 1890–1919), also limited the opportunities to study his oeuvre in depth. The Barnes Foundation's Renoirs could only be viewed either in black-and-white photographs, obviously

Fig. 1. Pierre-Auguste Renoir
*Madame Georges Charpentier (Marguérite-Louise Lemonnier, 1848–1904) and Her Children, Georgette-Berthe (1872–1945) and Paul-Émile-Charles (1875–1895)* [*Madame Georges Charpentier et ses enfants*], 1878
Oil on canvas, 60 ½ x 74 ⅞ in. (153.7 x 190.2 cm)
The Metropolitan Museum of Art, New York, Catharine Lorillard Wolfe Collection, Wolfe Fund, 1907 (07.122)

lacking the high-key palette that was essential to the overall impact of the paintings, or by visiting the Barnes Foundation located on the outskirts of Philadelphia, in Merion, Pennsylvania (opened in 1925). Moreover, as the Barnes Foundation was registered as a teaching institution, the number of visitors, other than students, was limited to 500 per week. Those who made this privileged pilgrimage were confronted with Barnes's idiosyncratic presentation, in which modern art was juxtaposed with Native American pottery; ceramics, metalwork and sculpture from Mexico, China, Africa, Greece, and Italy; Southwestern textiles; works by self-taught artists; German folk drawings; and Pennsylvania German decorative furniture (as opposed to a chronological, stylistic, or monographic arrangement, or according to categories distinguishing art from craft and design). Significantly, though, Barnes's late Renoirs could be viewed in conjunction with paintings by sixteenth- and seventeenth-century artists who had influenced him (Peter Paul Rubens, Tintoretto, El Greco); paintings by his contemporary, Paul Cézanne, whose works similarly exhibited a strong tactile quality; as well as paintings by artists whom Renoir had directly influenced, including Pablo Picasso and Henri Matisse, who greatly admired the elderly artist early in their careers for his rejection of Impressionism in favor of reinvestigating the Old Masters as a way forward for modern art. By the time Matisse, at age 48, befriended Renoir in 1917, he had collected four paintings and additional prints, while Picasso had purchased seven of his works by this date, all from the late period (one of which, *Bather Seated in Landscape Drying Her Foot*, also called *Eurydice*, c. 1895–1900, inspired Picasso's *Seated Bather Drying Her Foot*, 1921). Renoir's influence on the two younger painters could be seen in Picasso's classical nudes of the early 1920s and Matisse's early masterpiece *The Joy of Life*, 1905–06, in the Barnes Foundation.

Although students, artists, and the general public made the trek to the Barnes Foundation in its original home in Merion, attendance swelled to well over 230,000 annually after it relocated in downtown Philadelphia in 2012. Since the 2017 launch of the on-line collection catalogue, color images of the largest holdings of Renoir's late paintings in the United States finally have been widely viewable.

The permanent installation of the Barnes Foundation collection also provided an informative context for work by American artist William J. Glackens, who is represented by 48 works on view. In 1912, Glackens, who had been friends with Barnes since high school,

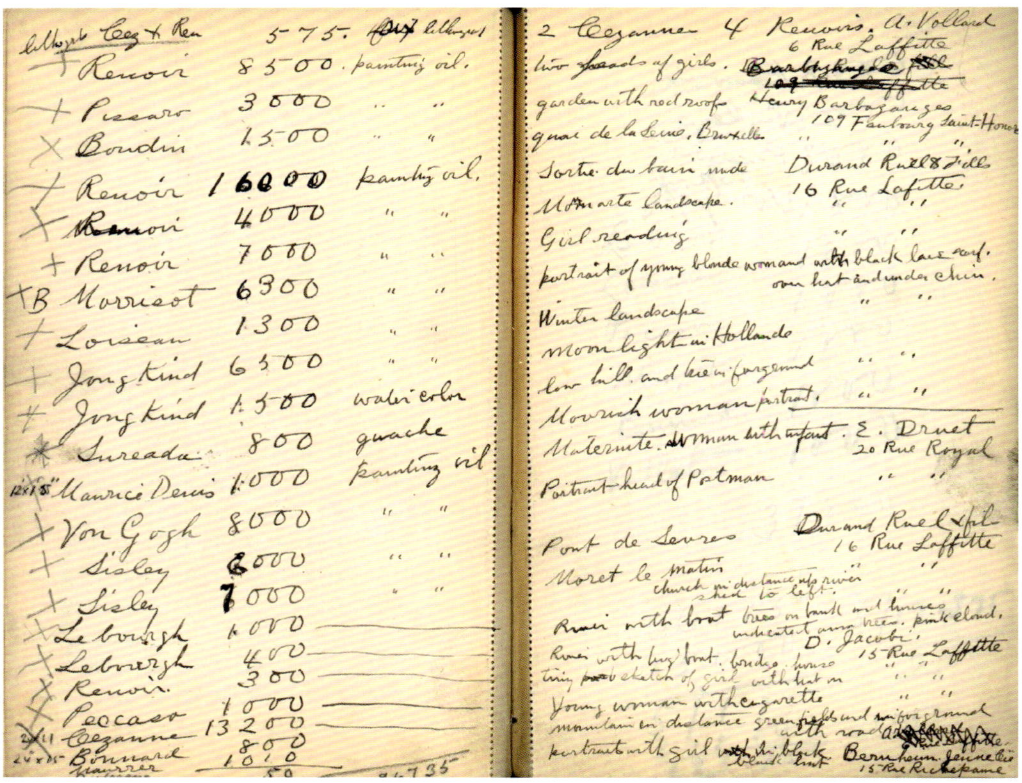


Fig. 2. William J. Glackens
*Sketchbook*, 1912
List of works of art and their prices in Paris
Charcoal on paper
8 ¼ x 5 ¼ in. (20.95 x 13.33 cm)
NSU Art Museum Fort Lauderdale; Gift of the Sansom Foundation, 92.57

was tasked by Barnes to travel to Paris to purchase art that would launch his collection (fig. 2). Works by Renoir were on Barnes's wish list. The 33 works Glackens purchased for $20,000 included paintings by Cézanne, Maurice Denis, Vincent van Gogh, Berthe Morisot, Picasso, and Camille Pissarro, among others, as well as the first five Renoirs in Barnes's collection.[5] These acquisitions, which were far more advanced than those on Barnes's original list, suggest the important role Glackens played in expanding his friend's newly minted taste for modern art.[6]

Of the 181 Renoirs Barnes collected, 145 are from the late period, including many nudes. Renoir's late nudes were especially monumental and fleshy in the tradition of Rubens and Titian, as well as outright flirtatious and erotic in the vein of his forerunners of eighteenth-century France, Jean-Honoré Fragonard, Jean-Antoine Watteau, and François Boucher. These lusty scenes ran counter to the mores of the late nineteenth- and early twentieth-century puritanical American collectors and public; and by the mid-twentieth century, abstract art superseded figuration in general. Moreover, Renoir's nudes also rankled contemporary viewers who were critical of this genre of Western art for objectifying and exploiting the female body. What becomes evident, though, when viewing late Renoir nudes is that this subject provided a reason for the artist to revel in the pleasure of the act of painting. Despite the relatively modest dimensions of Renoir's late works, his voluptuous figures almost fill the entire picture field, so much so that the subject nearly disappears, upon close viewing, into abstract dabs, swirls, and gestural strokes of paint. His nudes might have been among the paintings that Abstract Expressionist Willem de Kooning had in mind when he famously remarked that "Flesh is the reason oil painting was invented."[7]

The robust women in Renoir's late works were not mere concoctions of an old man's fantasy. In most cases, they were the models he had at hand, especially the nursemaids of his younger children (his plump wife, Aline Charigot, who modeled for him early in his career, was also represented later), and therefore were as much nourishing souls as erotic subjects. Renoir also enlisted his young children as models, and his paintings pairing a woman with a child or children held wider appeal for American collectors and museums than his nudes (the Metropolitan, for instance, owns only one nude and the Clark, just four). While most of these paintings idealize motherhood, the odd 1910 portrait of Madame Thurneyssen, wife of a German patron, and her daughter in this exhibition (pl. 26) suggests that Renoir was sympathetic to the complexities faced by modern women. In the tradition of the Medieval subject of the Nursing Madonna (*Madonna Lactans*), Renoir depicted the solemn seated Madame Thurneyssen with her left bosom slightly exposed and eyes focused forward, while her daughter (clearly too old for nursing) sits on her mother's lap and stares in the same direction, like the Christ-child, facing an inevitable fate.[8]

The reputation of Renoir's late paintings ascended in the years following his death. According to art historian Michael C. Fitzgerald, the penchant for Renoir's Neoclassical compositions (like those of Picasso's from the 1920s that were exhibited at Wildenstein & Co., New York, in 1923) was spurred on by "the desire to affirm traditional values" after the disruption of the first World War.[9]

The American museums' love affair with Renoir's work continued through the twentieth and into the twenty-first century, with major exhibitions presented in 1985–86 (*Renoir*, Boston), 2003–04 (*Renoir and Algiers*, Williamstown and Dallas), 2007–08 (*Renoir Landscapes 1865–1883*, Philadelphia), 2009–10 (*Renoir in the 20th Century*, Philadelphia and Los Angeles), and 2012 (*Renoir, Impressionism and Full-Length Painting*, New York), drawing large audiences.[10] These exhibitions were countered by a deep-rooted disdain for Renoir expressed by some American artists and critics of modern and contemporary art. When a group of anti-Renoir protestors demonstrated in front of the Museum of Fine Arts, Boston, in October 2015, even the *Boston Globe*'s art critic Sebastian Smee could not muster a defense for the artist, writing: "Is it worth getting worked up about Renoir? . . . He is an artist I detest most of the time. Such a syrupy, falsified take on reality."[11]

What Sebastian Smee and other viewers see as Renoir's "syrupy, falsified take on reality" is, upon closer consideration, surprisingly naturalistic. Renoir, perhaps more than any of his contemporaries, shows the viewer what love really feels like: how it feels to embrace a beautiful woman (or for her to hug her partner), what a mother's love looks like as she nurses her infant, and how to experience the depths of his adoration for his children. By closely cropping his subjects he brings the viewer right into the midst of these intimate scenes. Renoir's type of naturalism, and even his use of close-ups, were usurped by the new medium of film. His son, the renowned filmmaker Jean Renoir, credited his father for his cinematic approach, and critics have noted how father and son share a "humane realism."[12] Although we may feel reluctant to give into our emotions standing before a painting, most of us seem willing to be moved by the love stories and melodramas enacted in movies. We become absorbed in the naturalism of film and its ability to develop believable emotional situations. We tend to empathize with the characters in films, recognizing in their faces and gestures the emotions we have felt. The least bit of stylization in film would destroy the illusion. Our familiarity with the naturalism of film has, in effect, diminished our ability to react to the emotional charge of Renoir's paintings, which to our eyes may look overwrought. Moreover, since the 1960s, art that is expressive of emotion, especially the sentimental kind associated with Renoir, has generally been held suspect. The generation of artists who followed the Abstract Expressionists, including Frank Stella and Roy Lichtenstein, were seen as making a break from the emotional claims artists such as Mark Rothko espoused for their paintings. Never mind that many of the postwar artists either never disavowed the emotional in their work or recanted such propositions later in life, overtly emotional art was clearly out of favor in mid-twentieth century America.[13]

There is a thin line between love and hate. This is especially true in the art world, where the hot artist of one moment is often the pariah of the next. The marginalization of Renoir's reputation and corresponding rise of Claude Monet's late paintings (1914 to 1926) in the United States since the mid-1950s, is often attributed to the opinions of the influential American critic Clement Greenberg, who aimed to shore up the merits of the American Color-Field artists, including Clifford Still, Barnett Newman, and Rothko, by linking them to Monet's late water lilies paintings as a historical precedent. Greenberg's omission of Renoir from the trajectory of modern art that he outlined in his 1955 essay "American-Type Painting"[14] may have led some to conclude that he held Renoir in little regard. Art critic Donald Kuspit in his review of the Renoir late-painting exhibition at the Philadelphia Museum of Art in 2010, for instance, quotes extensively from Greenberg's earlier critique on Renoir (1950), citing many of his most disparaging comments, such as describing the late paintings as exhibiting "a suffocating kind of decorativeness."[15] However, Greenberg's essay was far more nuanced and even suggests why he and others have had difficulty evaluating Renoir's paintings. The American critic admitted to waffling in his opinion: "One day I find him almost powerful, another day almost weak; one moment brilliant, the next merely flashy; one day quite firm, another day soft."[16] He analyzed his dilemma in depth, concluding that "perhaps we are still too close to Renoir to fully appreciate his uniqueness." On the one hand, he realized that his admiration for Renoir's work was shaped by "the current notion of what constitutes paint quality and highly finished painting," as seen in the Abstract Expressionist painting he admired, which "derives very largely from his [Renoir's] art."[17] On the other hand, he recognized that he had a hard time separating Renoir's "method of high-keyed modeling" from the academic modernism that he disdained.[18] After grappling with his conflicting responses, Greenberg concluded that it was necessary to abandon preconceptions about Renoir's painting. He even opened up the possibility for an impartial assessment in the future, stating, "What perhaps we still do not appreciate correctly is the essential vision that animates Renoir's technique, the vision behind his vision of the aims of art."[19] Contrary to commonly held assumptions, Greenberg actually extolled Renoir's late paintings for having overcome "his desire to please," and for his "abandonment of preconceptions about 'good' or even polite painting."[20] This was

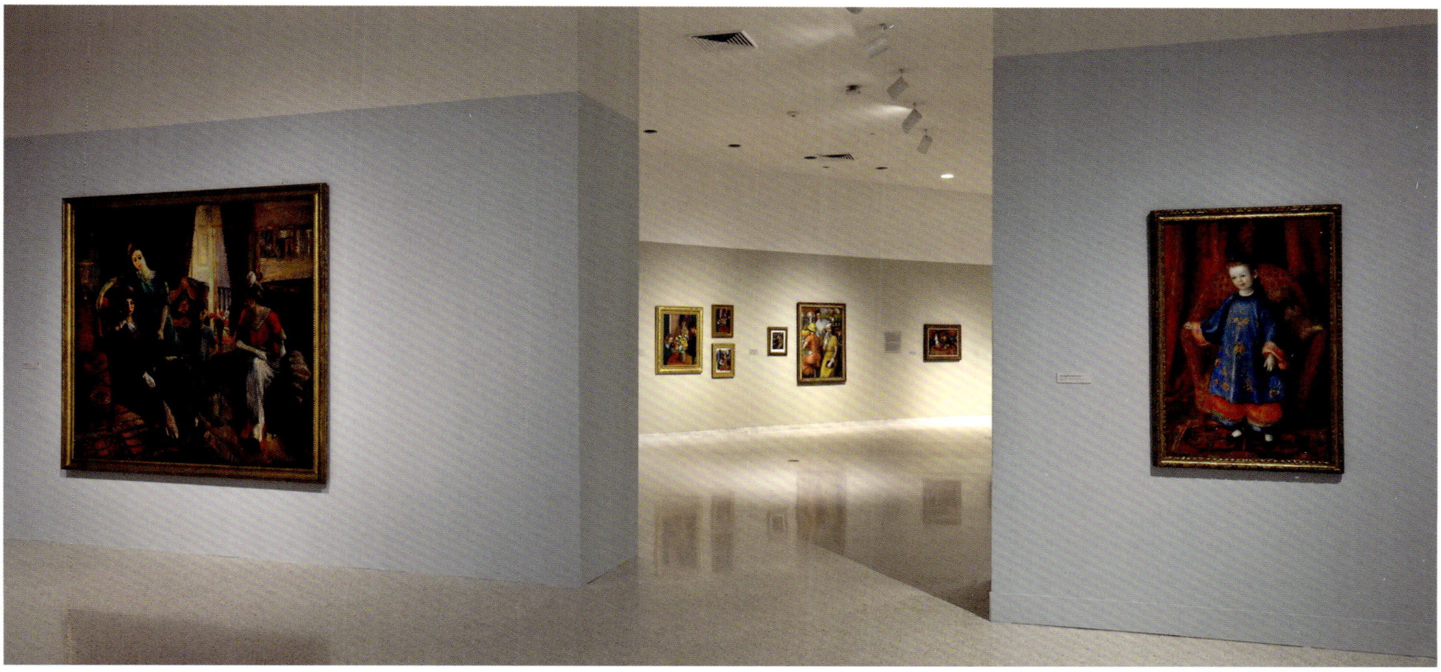

Fig. 3. Installation view of *William Glackens* exhibition, NSU Art Museum Fort Lauderdale, 2014

perhaps his most insightful observation. If this was indeed Renoir's intention, then we can trace to him the lineage of twentieth- and twenty-first-century art that includes the paintings of Francis Picabia, Albert Oehlen, Martin Kippenberger, Julian Schnabel, and basically all other contemporary painters who deliberately circumvent the standards of "good" and "bad" taste.[21] Greenberg was prophetic in declaring that he was too close to Renoir's work to fully evaluate it, and that it would be the task of future critics to assess its merits.[22]

The association of Renoir's painting with academic modernism, which was out of favor in the United States for most of the twentieth century, also colored critical opinion of his work. But by the time of the Philadelphia Museum of Art's late-Renoir exhibition in 2010, which opened at the Galeries Nationales du Grand Palais, Paris, in 2009 and then traveled to the Los Angeles County Museum of Art, critics were more receptive to the significance of Renoir's renewed fascination with Old Master painting, which influenced works from his late period. By the time of this exhibition, Greenberg's modernist criticism itself had fallen out of favor, primarily as a consequence of the rise of postmodern criticism in the late 1970s and 1980s and the embracing of images and styles from all periods of art history and popular culture, as seen in works by such artists as Schnabel and David Salle. In his review for the late-Renoir show, Kuspit wrote that perhaps Renoir "realized that newness quickly became oldness, which didn't mean lastingness." Instead, Renoir may have "wanted an art that would last beyond [his time], and continue to be of interest when the modern had become another old tradition, like Old Master art." Kuspit pointed out that Renoir was a "postmodernist" long before the term was coined.[23]

Renoir is once again in the spotlight in the United States in 2018, thanks to several new re-evaluations of the artist's work and influence (and as a prelude to the centenary of his death in 2019), including the release of a biography by Barbara Ehrlich White, this exhibition, as well as the recent *Renoir and Friends*, at the Phillips Collection, and the one dedicated to the relationship between the painter and his son, the film director, Jean Renoir at the Barnes Foundation.[24] This last prompted the *New York Times* reviewer to laud the curatorial "reassessment" of the painter's work, especially his late paintings.[25]

The rise and fall of Renoir's reputation in the United States may have also shaped opinions about the work of Glackens, who was known even during his lifetime as "the American Renoir."[26] The 2014 exhibition *William Glackens*, the first major survey of the artist's work in nearly 50 years, shed new light on his work (fig. 3). Organized and presented by NSU Art Museum Fort Lauderdale, the Barnes Foundation, and the Parrish Art Museum

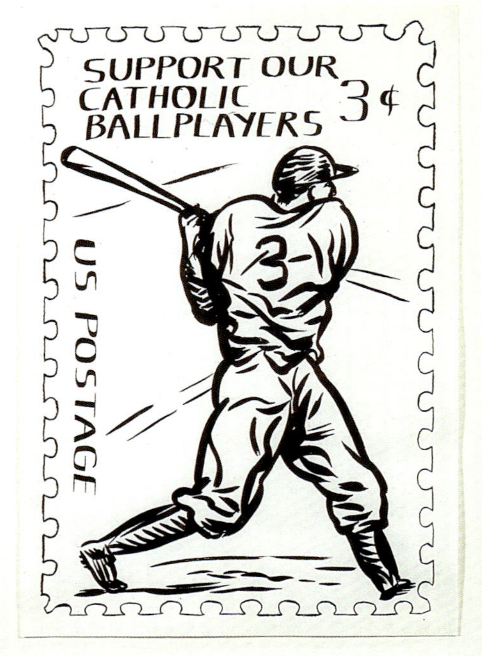


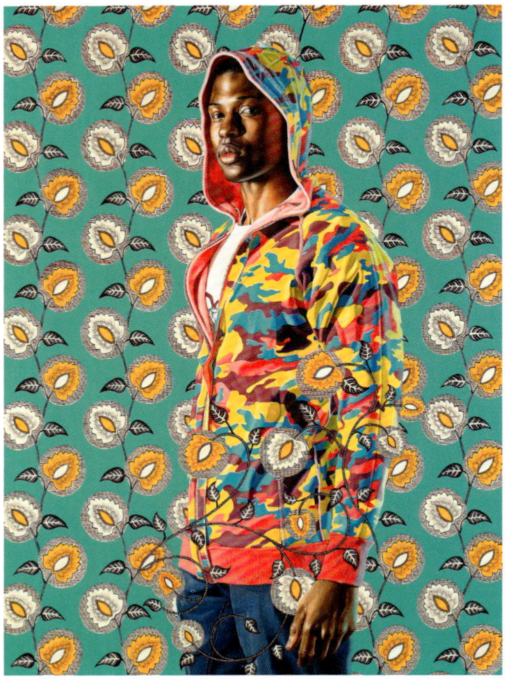

Fig. 4. Raymond Pettibon
*No Title (Support our Catholic)*, 1987
Pen and ink on paper
23 x 15 ½ in. (58.4 x 39.4 cm)

Fig. 5. Kehinde Wiley
*Rubin Singleton*, 2008
Oil on canvas
96 x 72 in. (243.8 x 182.9 cm)

in Water Mill, New York, and curated by Avis Berman, this exhibition garnered considerable national critical recognition, including a feature review in the *New York Times* by Roberta Smith. Smith launched her review by highlighting the long-held prejudicial appraisal of Glackens and by pointing out that this exhibition redeemed his reputation, noting, "Once derided as a slavish admirer of Renoir, the painter and illustrator William Glackens is among the most intriguing and underestimated participants in the first wave of 20th-century American modernism."[27] Smith singled out Glackens's painting *Artist's Daughter in Chinese Costume*, 1918 (pl. 48), as a "demure portrait that is nonetheless a riot of the textured reds of rug, drapes, and upholstery." She conceded that Glackens was capable of innovation, noting that this full-length portrait of his daughter "is perhaps less derivative of Renoir than it is slightly ahead of late Bonnard."[28]

As a critic of contemporary art, Smith brought a fresh perspective to her Glackens review. The rise of an artist's reputation often is triggered by a more comprehensive look into the work, especially if it dispels long-held assumptions. Such was the case with the Glackens survey, which Smith commended for fleshing out the artist's career beyond his debt to Renoir. These changes of heart can also be the result of a paradigm shift. For instance, during the period in which Smith wrote her Glackens review, she expressed a similar admiration for contemporary artist Kehinde Wiley's paintings of African-American men and women, which, like Glackens's *Artist's Daughter in Chinese Costume*, are portraits resplendent with decoration.[29] After more than a century dominated by abstract painting and conceptual art, Wiley and other contemporary painters redirected the critical viewer's consideration of expressive portraiture in general and also widened the appeal for work of the past that did not conform to the modernist canon.

Smith made several observations in her Glackens review that reflect her own evolving positions on contemporary art. She was impressed by how Glackens "assiduously kept his gift for caricature out of his paintings," while also noting how his "unfailing eye for body language," honed as an illustrator, "is partly what distinguishes his paintings, giving many of his images the accurate immediacy of snapshots despite their heightened color and tactile brush work."[30] Smith's deprecation of Glackens's amazing talent for caricature is a holdover from academic formalism. Until recently, labeling an artist as an "illustrator" was a condescending estimation that relegated an artist's work to the so-called low end of the art hierarchy. Art historian Robert Rosenblum helped pave the way for the repositioning of illustrative art when he boldly championed Norman Rockwell in the late 1990s and was instrumental in the presentation of a controversial traveling exhibition at the Guggenheim, where he was curator of twentieth-century art. The timing of Rosenblum's and the retrospective's re-evaluation of Rockwell was synchronous with developments in contemporary art.[31] One could credit the cartoonish sketches Raymond Pettibon began making in the 1970s (fig. 4) for expanding the viewer's penchant for and receptiveness to the illustrative and narrative work of artists who emerged in the 1990s, including William Cordova, Nicole Eisenman, Trenton Doyle Hancock, William Kentridge, Matthew Ritchie, and Jim Shaw, to name a few. The conventional art hierarchy and resistance to illustration, however, still held sway well into the twenty-first century, as suggested by Roberta Smith's 2008 review of Kehinde Wiley's solo exhibition at the Studio Museum in Harlem, writing: "Conceptual rationale behind Mr. Wiley's paintings has tended to overpower their visual personae, which helps reduce them to illustrations. Like Norman Rockwell's paintings they look better in reproduction than in reality."[32] Smith responded positively to his new paintings in this review: "A lot of these problems are receding in the Studio Museum because Mr. Wiley is doing what all painters have to do: developing a surface of his own. To do so he is starting where most figurative painters have started, at least since the invention of oil paint: with the rendering of human skin. He is beginning to paint skin in ways you can't stop looking at [fig. 5]."[33]

This sentiment resonates in Smith's observation of Glackens's *In the Luxembourg* (fig. 6), which she described as "a creamy little vision of people in the Luxembourg Gardens," and identified it as Glackens's declaration of "his love for what is sometimes called 'pure painting.'" Ironically, this painterliness is one of the very characteristics Glackens absorbed from his study of Renoir, which aided his transformation from exceptional illustrator to modern painter.

Although Glackens was an admirer of Renoir's painting, he was no slavish follower. In her essay for this catalogue, Barbara Buhler Lynes explores Glackens's affinities with Renoir's work as well as the distinctions that set him apart. Glackens's close study of Renoir was in keeping with standard training for artists well into the twentieth century. Artists crafted their own style of painting by gleaning the lessons of the art of the past. Glackens purportedly

Fig. 6. William J. Glackens
*In the Luxembourg*, c. 1896
Oil on canvas
14 ⅞ x 17 ¼ in. (37.8 x 43.8 cm)
NSU Art Museum Fort Lauderdale; Bequest of Ira D. Glackens, 91.40.66

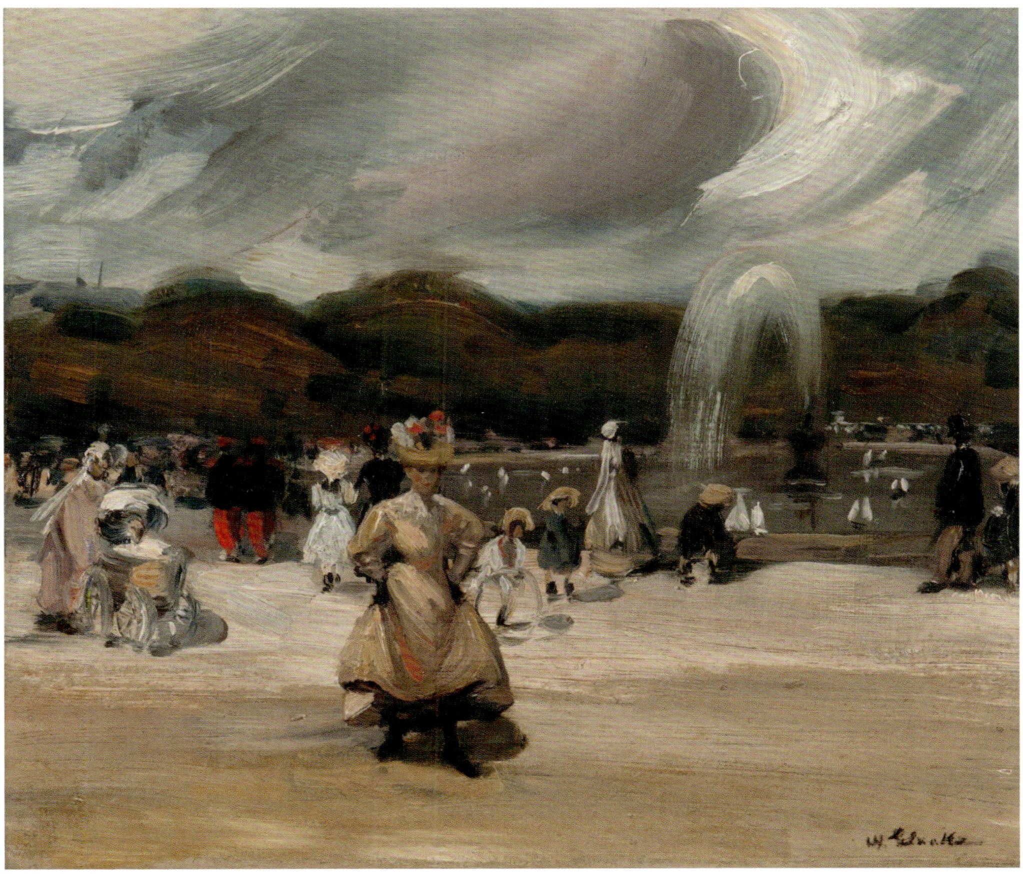

replied to direct inquiry on his apparent association with Renoir: "Can you think of a better man to follow than Renoir?"[34] My own inquiry into this exhibition's subject was piqued by art historian Martha Lucy's observation that Glackens was more interested in late Renoir works than paintings from his Impressionist period.[35] This perspective meant that, rather than appropriating the old-fashioned Impressionist mode of painting, Glackens, following Picasso's and Matisse's lead, was looking at Renoir as the way forward. His admiration for Renoir's work aided him in his ambition to forge a distinctly American form of modernism. This perspective made sense for an artist who was especially instrumental in promoting the interest in modern art in America. Having been trained at the Pennsylvania Academy of Art, he became a key player in the American painters known as the "The Eight," after they exhibited together in New York in 1908.[36] Glackens also obtained first-hand exposure to art in Paris which he first visited in 1895, lived from June 1895 to October 1896, and subsequently visited frequently. His daring semi-reclining nude, *Girl with Apple*, 1909–10 (fig. 26), which debuted at the *Exhibition of Independent Artists* (1910), was a "breakout work, not only for his own career," writes Teresa Carbone," but for progressive American art and culture as well," in that he advanced the modern realistic representation of a living woman, in the spirit of Manet's *Olympia*, 1863.[37] As previously mentioned, Glackens was an influence on the inception of Barnes's collection in 1912, and in 1913, he played an important role as the chairman of the Committee of Domestic Exhibits for the *International Exhibition of Modern Art,* known as the Armory Show (February 17 to March 15, 1913, New York) which introduced European and American vanguard art in America. Glackens was a natural choice for this position as his colleagues judged him to be open to the most advanced American painting, and Walt Kuhn, one of the show's main organizers, admired him for his determination "to keep the American stuff way up."[38]

Glackens helped organize other exhibitions of contemporary American artists and in 1917 was a founder and the first elected president of the Society of Independent Artists in New York when fellow board member Marcel Duchamp submitted his readymade *Fountain* (a mass-produced porcelain urinal) under the name of R. Mutt (fig. 7). Although the Society declared that any artist who paid the initiation fee could enter works for display in this jury-less exhibition and that no work would be rejected, *Fountain* was refused on the basis that the board considered it "obscene," thereby triggering the resignation of Duchamp and collector Walter Arensberg from the board and causing a headline-making scandal before the show's premiere in April 1917. *Fountain*'s centennial last year was the focus of an exhibition organized by NSU Art Museum Fort Lauderdale (May 14 – September 3, 2017), and the exhibition and catalogue highlighted Glackens's role in this key episode in modern art history. Although Glackens was rumored to have destroyed the offending work, evidence suggests that he may have conspired with Duchamp to shroud the disappearance of *Fountain* in mystery.[39] Glackens and his family left New York to live in France in 1925. For an artist who was so deeply associated with American progressive art, his move marked a significant rupture in his participation in the nation's rapidly evolving art scene. The New York art world to which he returned in 1932 had bifurcated into those seeking a nativist art and those who had taken up the charge of the Surrealists and abstract artists of the international avant-garde. Not long after Glackens's death many leading European artists, gallerists and critics began their exile in New York and other parts of the Americas as they escaped tyranny and war in Europe. Their presence was an important catalyst for American artists, who forged a distinctive new avant-garde art movement, Abstract Expressionism, which ultimately eclipsed Glackens and his peers' early contribution to American modernism.

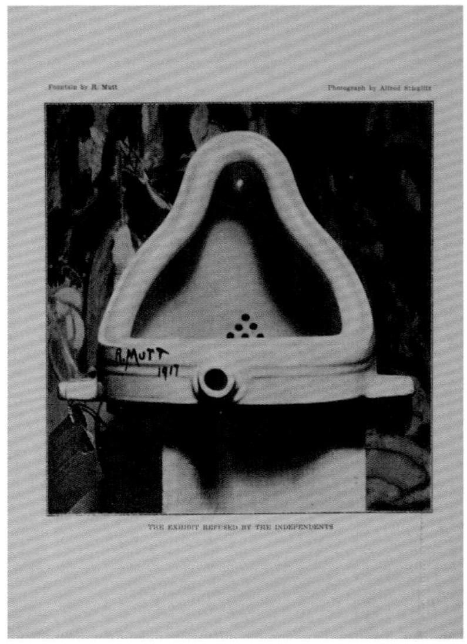


Fig. 7. Alfred Stieglitz
*Fountain*, 1917
Photograph of *Fountain* by Marcel Duchamp (1887–1968)
Printed in *The Blind Man*, no. 2 (May 1917)
11 x 8 1/16 in. (27.9 x 20.5 cm)
The Metropolitan Museum of Art, New York, Thomas J. Watson Library (Purchased with income from the Jacob S. Rogers Fund)

1. Roger Fry was a British critic recognized by art historian Kenneth Clark as "incomparably the greatest influence on taste since Ruskin . . . In so far as taste can be changed by one man, it was changed by Roger Fry." Ian Chilvers, "Roger Fry," in *Oxford Dictionary of Art and Artists* (Oxford, 1990), 251.
2. Barbara Ehrlich White, *Renoir: An Intimate Biography* (New York: Thames & Hudson, 2017), Kindle version, loc. 3140 of 12591.
3. Ibid., loc. 3140 of 12591.
4. Ibid., loc. 5520 of 12591.
5. Judith F. Dolkart, "William Glackens: 'Intensely Sincere and Intensely Brave,'" in *William Glackens*, ed. Avis Berman, exhibition catalogue (New York and Philadelphia: Skira Rizzoli Publications, Inc., and The Barnes Foundation, 2014), 128.
6. Ibid.
7. See Willem de Kooning, "The Renaissance and Order," talk delivered at Studio 35, 8th Street, New York, autumn 1949, in Thomas B. Hess, *Willem de Kooning* (New York: The Museum of Modern Art, 1968), 141–43. Reprinted from *Trans/formation* 1 no. 2 (1951), 85–87. Even clothed, Renoir's figures tended to fill the canvas, providing expansive areas for the artist to pursue his love of painting. In 1956, de Kooning's wife Elaine de Kooning, a painter and art critic, wrote admiringly of Renoir in a review of an exhibition of 32 of his paintings at the Sterling and Francine Clark Art Institute, Williamstown, MA:"His method is seduction and one must be in his presence to be seduced. Appreciating Renoir is primarily a physical experience – and an overwhelming one. And being physically confronted with him is always a surprise." Elaine de Kooning, "Renoir: As If By Magic," in *The Spirit of Abstract Expressionism: Selected Writings*, essay by Rose Slivka, preface by Marjorie Luyckx (New York: Braziller, 1994), 151–54.
8. It has been suggested that the work is an homage to Rubens's painting *Helena Fourment with Her Eldest Son, Frans*, 1635, in the Alte Pinakothek, Munich – see Claudia Einecke and Roger Benjamin, *Renoir in the 20th Century*, exhibition catalogue (Ostfildern: Hatje Cantz, 2010), 284 – but the depiction with the one exposed breast and rigid hierarchal arrangement of mother and child is specific to the numerous examples of the Nursing Madonna in Medieval art. The motif remained popular through the seventeenth century, as seen in Bartolomé Esteban Murillo, *Madonna Nursing the Christ Child*, c. 1670 (Gallerie Nazionali Barberini Corsini, Rome).
9. Michael C. Fitzgerald, *Making Modernism: Picasso and the Creation of the Market for Twentieth-Century Art* (Berkeley, Los Angeles, London: University of California Press, 1995; paperback edition, 1996), 130.
10. *Renoir*, Museum of Fine Arts, Boston, October 9, 1985 – January 5, 1986 (co-organized with the Arts Council of Great Britain and Réunion des Musées Nationaux; presented in London at the Hayward Gallery, January 30 – April 21, 1985, and Grand Palais, Paris, May 14 – September 2, 1985); *Renoir Landscapes: 1865–1883* (The National Gallery, London, February 21 – May 20, 2007; The National Gallery of Canada, Ottawa, June 8 – September 9, 2007; Philadelphia Museum of Art, October 4, 2007 – January 4, 2008); *Renoir in the 20th Century* (Galeries Nationales, Grand Palais, Paris, September 23, 2009 – January 4, 2010; Los Angeles County Museum of Art, February 14 – May 9, 2010; Philadelphia Museum of Art, June 17 – September 6, 2010); *Renoir, Impressionism and Full-Length Painting*, The Frick Collection, New York, February 7 – May 13, 2012.
11. Kristen Capps, "Why Absolutely Everyone Hates Renoir," *The Atlantic* (October 13, 2015), https://www.theatlantic.com/entertainment/archive/2015/10/why-everyone-hates-renoir/410335/.
12. Richard B. Woodward, "'Renoir: Father and Son: Painting and Cinema' Review: Creative Currents," in *Wall Street Journal* (May 5, 2018), https://www.wsj.com/articles/renoir-father-and-son-painting-and-cinema-review-creative-currents-1525518000.
13. Richard Artschwager, for instance, revealed to me in 2003, that, despite the impersonal appearance of his early paintings of the 1960s and 1970s that he based on found photographs, empathy always played an important role in his selection of subjects: see Bonnie Clearwater, *Richard Artschwager, Painting Then and Now* (North Miami: Museum of Contemporary Art, 2003), 4. As early as 1970, Frank Stella disputed the description of his early paintings as lacking emotion. Although his black-stripe paintings of 1959–60 were lean and repetitive, he considered them in the tradition of Mark Rothko's Color-Field painting, noting that no one called Rothko's paintings cold and unfeeling: Frank Stella Interview with William Rubin, Museum of Modern Art, New York, 1970, YouTube: https://www.youtube.com/watch?v=cN_rRCfRdmQ.
14. Clement Greenberg, "American-Type Painting," in Clement Greenberg, *Art and Culture: Critical Essays* (Boston: Beacon, 1961; Beacon Paperback, 1965), 208-229; first published in *Partisan Review*, 1955. For a study of the phenomenal rise of Monet's reputation in the U.S., see Michael Leja, "The Monet Revival and New York School Abstraction," in *Monet in the 20th Century* (New Haven: Yale University Press, 1998), 98-108.
15. Donald Kuspit, "A Note on Late Renoir," *Artnet.com*, 2010.
16. Clement Greenberg, "Renoir," in *Art and Culture*, 46. Essay first published in 1950.
17. Ibid., 48.
18. Ibid.
19. Ibid., 49.
20. Ibid.
21. Ibid.
22. Ibid., 48.
23. Kuspit, "A Note on Late Renoir."
24. See Barbara Ehrlich White, *Renoir: An Intimate Biography*, the Phillips Collection's *Renoir and Friends* (October 7, 2017 – January 7, 2018), which explored its celebrated Renoir, *Luncheon of the Boating Party*, 1880–81 (fig. 14), and *Renoir: Father and Son / Painting and Cinema*, The Barnes Foundation, Philadelphia, May 6 – September 3, 2018.
25. Jason Farago, "Art Review: Like Impressionist, Like Filmmaker," *New York Times*, June 1, 2018, C13, C18. Although art historians and critics have been reassessing the late work of Renoir for decades (including a symposium that was published in *Art in America*) old prejudices persist and each generation seems to discover the merits of these works anew. See "Renoir: A Symposium," *Art in America* (March 1986), 102–25.
26. Anne E. Dawson, *Pierre-Auguste Renoir and Modern Painting* (San Diego: San Diego Museum of Art, 2002), 41.
27. Roberta Smith, "The Beauty of the Everyday," *New York Times*, August 15, 2014, C 21.
28. Ibid.
29. Roberta Smith, "Hot Conceptualist Finds the Secret of Skin," *New York Times*, September 4, 2008, B21, B24.
30. Ibid.
31. *Norman Rockwell: Pictures for the American People*, exhibition catalogue (Atlanta and Stockbridge: High Museum of Art and Norman Rockwell Museum, 1999). Traveled to seven American Museums including the Solomon R. Guggenheim Museum, New York, November 3, 2002 – March 3, 2003.
32. Smith, "Hot Conceptualist Finds the Secret of Skin."
33. Ibid.
34. Vincent J. de Gregorio, "The Life and Art of William J. Glackens," Ph.D. dissertation (Ann Arbor: University Microfilms, 1955), 270. Gregorio cited an interview with Forbes Watson on this issue that took place on November 8, 1954.
35. Martha Lucy, "Glackens, French Art, and the Language of Modernism," in *William Glackens*, exhibition catalogue (New York: Skira Rizzoli Publications, Inc., and The Barnes Foundation 2014), 204.
36. "The Eight" were Arthur B. Davies, William Glackens, Robert Henri, Ernest Lawson, George Luks, Maurice Prendergast, Everett Shinn, and John Sloan.
37. Teresa A. Carbone, "All About Eve? William Glackens's Audacious *Girl with Apple*," in *The World of William Glackens*, vol. 2 (New York: the Sansom Foundation, Inc., 2017), 83–122.
38. Walt Kuhn, quoted in Dolkart, 131. The Armory Show traveled to the Art Institute of Chicago, March 24 – April 16, 1913. A smaller edition traveled to the Copley Society of Art, Boston, April 28 – May 19, 1913. (Due to space restraints, the American works were not shown.)
39. See Bonnie Clearwater, "The Mysterious Case of Richard Mutt," in *Some Aesthetic Decisions: A Centennial Celebration of Marcel Duchamp's "Fountain,"* exhibition catalogue (Milan: Skira, 2017), 17–18.

1910

# From Daring to de rigueur: American Collectors of Renoir

*Avis Berman*

"I am convinced I cannot get too many Renoirs," the Philadelphia collector Albert C. Barnes announced in 1913,[1] and he backed this assertion by amassing the largest collection of the work of Pierre-Auguste Renoir in existence. Between 1912 and 1942, Barnes bought 181 Renoirs;[2] 178 of them are paintings, and their rich color and seductive surfaces are suffused throughout the galleries of the Barnes Foundation, the eponymous institution he chartered in 1922. No one surpassed Barnes in volume or voracity in the quest to possess Renoirs, but he was not alone nor the first to be consumed by that same passion. The most adventurous of the pioneering Americans who collected the great French Impressionist's work had dared to espouse it 40 years before Barnes. From the formative decade of the 1880s, when Renoir was first exhibited in this country to a mixed reception, to the late 1930s, when his name was established as an essential acquisition for museums, moguls, and movie stars, Renoir's acceptance in the United States was slower than would be supposed. What twenty-first century viewers see as genius – the creation of a lush world of iridescent color and flickering light – was once derided as a cacophony of bizarre color contrasts and terrifyingly bad taste. This essay examines the trajectory of the other Americans who shared Barnes's grand obsession.

Renoir's work was initially shown in the United States in September 1883 in Boston, as part of a group exhibition organized to celebrate the hundredth anniversary of the Treaty of Paris.[3] Paul Durand-Ruel (fig. 8), the Parisian dealer who had championed the Impressionists for more than a decade, sent 80 paintings to the show. Three of them were by Renoir, including the lambent *A Box at the Theater (At the Concert)*, 1880 (fig. 9), but, set among formulaic Salon canvases and decorative wares, the entire group was "badly hung and indifferently received."[4] Nevertheless, Durand-Ruel intended to succeed in America, because in 1885 the dealer was nearly bankrupt from buying so many paintings by Renoir and Claude Monet. In desperation, he accepted an invitation to participate in a large international exhibition held at the American Art Association in New York during the spring of 1886. Durand-Ruel arrived with 264 paintings, including 38 by Renoir; the exhibition opened in the Association's galleries on Madison Square on April 10 and an expanded version moved to the National Academy of Design on May 25.[5] The newpapers' response was positive, if puzzled, and Durand-Ruel sold $18,000 worth of pictures.[6] Buoyed by sales and critical plaudits, he wrote to Henri Fantin-Latour, "Do not think that Americans are savages. On the contrary they are less ignorant, less close-minded than our French collectors."[7] The dealer organized another Impressionist exhibition a year later and in 1888 he opened a gallery in Manhattan, managed by his sons. From then on, modern French paintings were always available in New York.

Well before Renoir and the other Impressionists were ever exhibited in the United States, two American women were their most powerful promoters. Their proselytizing spread

Fig. 8. Pierre-Auguste Renoir
*Portrait of Paul Durand-Ruel*, 1910
Oil on canvas
25 ⅗ x 21 ¼ in. (65 x 54 cm)
Photo Archives Durand-Ruel

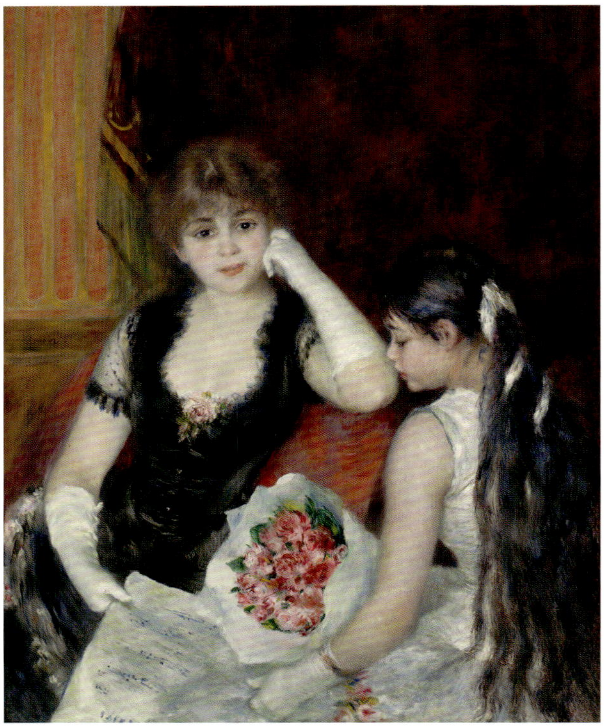

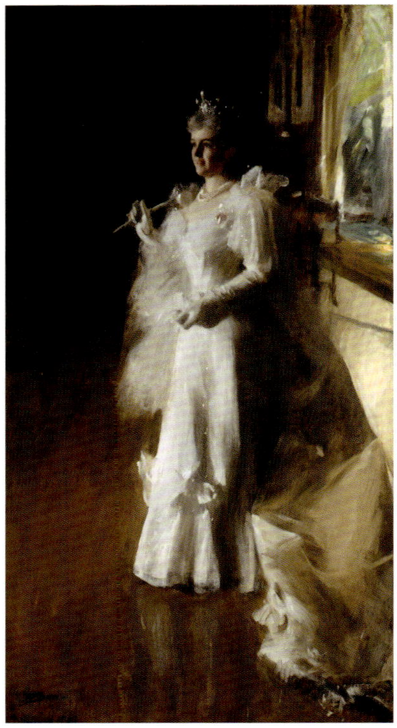

Fig. 9. Pierre-Auguste Renoir
*A Box at the Theater (At the Concert)* [*Une loge à l'opéra (dit Dans la loge)*], 1880
Oil on canvas
39 ⅛ x 31 ¾ in. (99.4 x 80.7 cm)
Sterling and Francine Clark Art Institute, Williamstown, MA; Acquired by Sterling and Francine Clark, 1928, 1955.594

Fig. 10. Anders Leonard Zorn
*Mrs. Potter Palmer*, 1893
Oil on canvas
101 ⅝ x 55 ⅝ in.
(258 x 141.2 cm)
Art Institute of Chicago, Potter Palmer Collection, 1922.450

the news of the French avant-garde on these shores, although their converts were limited to those wealthy few who could see the artists' work in Paris. Philadelphia-born Mary Cassatt, the only American artist to be included in the Impressionist exhibitions, had recognized the caliber of the group from her arrival in Paris in 1874. In 1875 she persuaded her friend, the 19-year-old Louisine Elder, to purchase a pastel by Edgar Degas and a Monet painting, making the young woman the first American patron of Impressionism. She also convinced her older brother, Alexander J. Cassatt, an executive with the Pennsylvania Railroad, to obtain work by her fellow Impressionists. He first bought works that she selected by Degas, Monet, and Camille Pissarro in 1881. Acting on his own while in Paris in March 1883, the elder Cassatt acquired a picture of a head of a young girl by Renoir from Durand-Ruel; he seems to have been the artist's first American buyer. Frank Thompson, one of Alexander Cassatt's colleagues, followed suit, and bought paintings by Monet, Renoir, Pissarro, Degas, Alfred Sisley, and Mary Cassatt in 1884.[8]

The second woman who influenced Impressionist collecting in America was also a native Philadelphian. After the Civil War, Sara Tyson Hallowell forged a unique career as a freelance curator and art agent based in Chicago, yet she spent most of her time in transit between the United States and France, arranging exhibitions and finding works of art for collectors and public institutions. She presumably met Mary Cassatt in Paris, and in 1889 she and later Cassatt encouraged Hallowell's most important clients – the real estate developer Potter Palmer and his wife, Bertha Honoré Palmer – to consider adding Impressionist canvases to their already considerable collection of Barbizon and American paintings. In 1889, when the Palmers were in Paris, Hallowell introduced them to Paul Durand-Ruel, and they made their first Impressionist acquisitions: a Degas pastel and Renoir's painting, *Madame Renoir in the Garden*, 1884 (Private Collection).

After Durand-Ruel's shows in New York, several bold collectors joined Alexander Cassatt and Frank Thompson as Renoir buyers. Catholina Lambert, an immigrant who became a prosperous silk manufacturer in Paterson, New Jersey, would buy at least four Renoirs, including *Still Life with Flowers and Prickly Pears*, c. 1885 (Metropolitan Museum of Art), which he acquired in 1888. The Bostonian Alexander Cochrane bought a Venetian scene – *Grand Canal, Venice*, 1881 (Museum of Fine Arts, Boston) in July 1889, and on February 9, 1892, George Vanderbilt II, the creator of the Biltmore estate, bought a landscape and two head-and-shoulder portraits. (The latter two canvases remain in the collection of Biltmore House in North Carolina.) Yet none of these collectors were imbued with the verve and drive of Bertha Palmer (fig. 10), who was determined to possess the most exciting art collection in the country. In fulfilling that quest, she became the first insatiable collector of Renoir. Already the queen of Chicago society, Palmer wanted only avant-garde art for her sprawling picture gallery, which was upholstered in red velvet from floor to ceiling. She believed in the Impressionists and was determined to make them chic as a corollary to her certainty that collecting was a pursuit befitting her social position. However, unlike most socially motivated buyers, she never clung to the conventional: she preferred the sensational effect to a hallowed tradition, precisely because she knew that whatever she did would be emulated and approved.

The bulk of the Palmers' collection was formed in 1891–92, when the couple traveled to Paris to publicize the 1893 World's Columbian Exposition in Chicago. After purchasing two superb canvases – *Near the Lake*, 1879–80 and *Lunch at the Restaurant Fournaise (The Rowers' Lunch)*, 1875 (both Art Institute of Chicago) from Durand-Ruel New York in March and April 1892 – the Palmers went on to France in May. With Sara Hallowell advising them, they bought 40 works from Durand-Ruel, in Paris, including 11 paintings by Renoir.[9] The jewel of the Paris canvases was *Acrobats at the Cirque Fernando (Francisca and Angelina Wartenberg)*, 1879 (fig. 11). This painting, which had been shown in the 1886 Impressionist exhibition in New York and cost $1,750, is a study of two sisters who performed as trapeze artists. The oranges at their feet were thrown by the audience in appreciation of their performance. *Acrobats at the Cirque Fernando* was Palmer's favorite painting, and it traveled with her to her various residences. The *Acrobats*, along with *Near the Lake*, *Lunch at the Restaurant Fournaise*, and *Seascape*, 1879, were the Renoirs included in the 52 Impressionist paintings from the Palmer collection donated to the Art Institute of Chicago in 1922. Through this gift, the Art Institute became the first American museum to possess a rich representation in Impressionism. Moreover, its example was transformative, encouraging other Chicagoans to add to the museum's French holdings with gifts and bequests of their own. Even in death, Bertha Palmer used her social leverage to get others to fall in line.

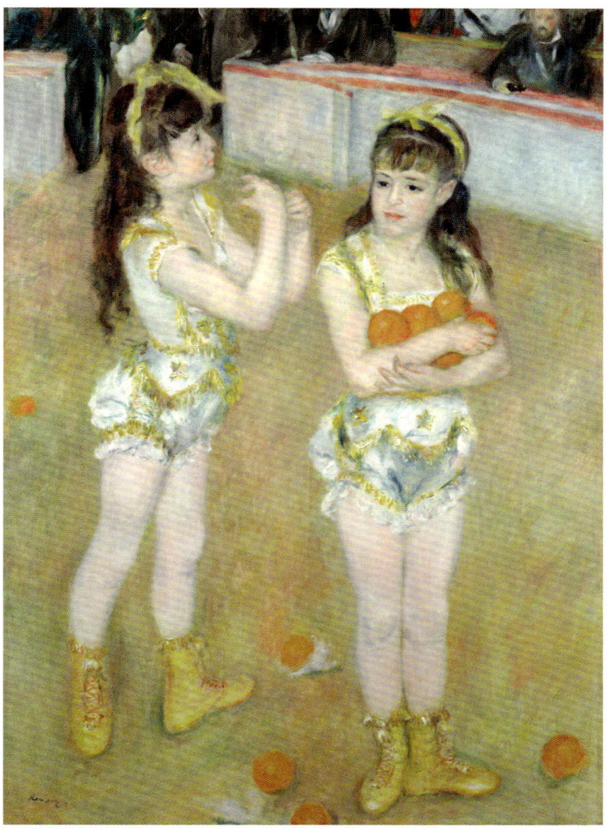

Fig. 11. Pierre-Auguste Renoir
*Acrobats at the Cirque Fernando (Francisca and Angelina Wartenberg)*
[*Acrobates (Saltimbanques ou Dans le cirque)*], 1879
Oil on canvas
51 ½ x 39 ¹⁄₁₆ in. (131.2 x 99.2 cm)
Art Institute of Chicago, Potter Palmer Collection, 1922.440

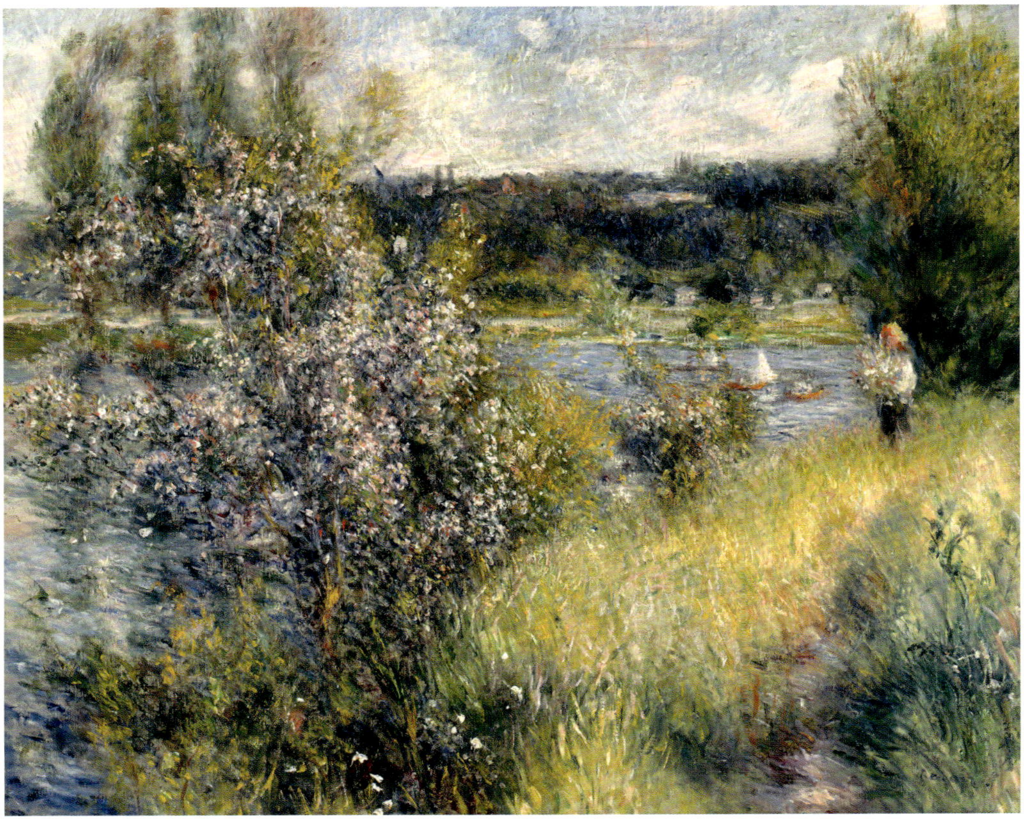

Fig. 12. Pierre-Auguste Renoir
*The Seine at Chatou* [*La Seine à Chatou*], 1881
Oil on canvas
28 ⅞ x 36 ⅜ in. (73.3 x 92.4 cm)
Museum of Fine Arts, Boston; Gift of Arthur Brewster Emmons, 19.771

Despite the Palmers' patronage, the 1890s belonged to Monet, and Renoir's American market lagged in comparison. Not only was Monet considered the leader of the new movement, but Impressionism was primarily classified as a kind of landscape painting, and Renoir was first and foremost a painter of figures. In response to an 1893 show of "the extreme open-air impressionists of France" at Durand-Ruel New York, a *New York Times* review was not atypical. The writer praised a Monet landscape, but sniffed that "Renoir's figure pieces are somewhat hard to digest; his idea of the form feminine is dumpy and commonplace and the faces of the models are triumphs of dull vulgarity."[10] Furthermore, Renoir's chief benefactors did not live in New York. Chicago and Boston were far more supportive, although Boston was a city known for its idolatry of Monet.

This cultural anomaly – the abdication of New York primacy in collecting modern art – is directly traceable to Louisine Elder, the trail-blazing Impressionist partisan of the 1870s. In 1883, she married Henry O. Havemeyer, a sugar tycoon. He preferred the Old Masters to the modern, and it was not until 1895 that she was able to win him over to her more vanguard tastes. Thus the Havemeyers as a couple, who were Durand-Ruel's most important American clients and eventually his pre-eminent Impressionist collectors, were not in the first wave of Impressionist stalwarts. Moreover, Louisine Havemeyer did not like Renoir's work. She experimented early, buying a pastel of a seated girl reading in 1889, but she returned it to Durand-Ruel in 1908. She somehow acquired a Renoir drawing of a fashionably dressed young woman that was in her collection at her death. In March 1899, Louisine Havemeyer bought her one Renoir painting: *By the Seashore*, 1883 (Metropolitan Museum of Art) from Durand-Ruel New York. (It came from Catholina Lambert, who had acquired it in April 1892.) She kept the picture in the couple's collection, but she was never comfortable with it, and was said to have regretted the purchase.[11]

As the American city where Impressionism was first shown, Boston had a head start on the new art. The critic William Howe Downes wrote in 1888 that in Boston circles "it is not altogether impossible to find extremists who already avow openly their admiration for those mad outlaws, the Impressionists!"[12] But Boston collectors traditionally skewed toward landscape painting, so they overwhelmingly chose to own Monets, to the exclusion of his peers. With audience reservations about Renoir in Monet-mad Boston, it fell to Arthur Brewster Emmons, a mining engineer with a Harvard law degree and the scion of old Boston and Newport families, to diverge from the rule. He was the first collector with Boston roots to acquire Renoir avidly. Perhaps that connection affected his choices, because he preferred landscapes to genre scenes or portraits. In 1906, on a Renoir tear, he bought three from Durand-Ruel: *The Seine at Chatou*, 1881 (fig. 12); *View of the Sea Coast near Wargemont in Normandy*, 1880 (Metropolitan Museum of Art); and *In the Meadow*, 1888–1892 (Metropolitan Museum of Art). *In the Meadow* had been a Palmer picture, as was *The Bay of Naples*, 1881 (Metropolitan Museum of Art), a lively seascape that he bought in 1911. (Palmer frequently traded in her pictures to take profits and upgrade her holdings.) During 1911, Emmons also acquired *Hills around the Bay of Moulin Huet, Guernsey*, 1883 (Metropolitan Museum of Art). In less than a decade, Emmons's faith in Renoir was justified. In a 1920 auction of 27 canvases from his Impressionist collection, two Renoirs fetched the especially high prices of $27,000 and $28,000, reflecting the climb in the market after the artist's death in 1919.[13] Emmons gave *The Seine at Chatou* to the Museum of Fine Arts, Boston, in 1919, and his widow later bequeathed three Renoirs to the Metropolitan Museum of Art.

Plungers into Renoir-buying like Emmons remained relatively rare during the first decade of the twentieth century, and momentum in Renoir collecting shifted from a small cadre of prescient private collectors to the public sphere. Impressionist canvases were still too crude, radical, and recent to be *purchased* by most museums: the Art Institute of Chicago had none until the Palmer gift in 1922. The Museum of Fine Arts, Boston, purchased a Degas in 1903, arguably the first American museum to *buy* an Impressionist painting; its first Monet arrived in 1906, as a gift. (The MFA did not have a Renoir until 1919, when Alexander Cochrane bequeathed *Grand Canal, Venice*, 1881, purchased 40 years earlier.) Very likely, the Metropolitan Museum of Art was the second museum in America to buy an Impressionist painting and it was certainly the first to buy a Renoir.

Fortune favored the Metropolitan. An impressive figural composition, *Madame Charpentier and Her Children*, 1878 (see fig. 1, p. 10), became available for the first time. Georges Charpentier, the publisher of Gustave Flaubert, Émile Zola, and Guy de Maupassant, and his wife, Marguerite, were loyal friends and patrons of Renoir, drumming up commissions and purchases when he most needed them. The painting depicts Marguerite Charpentier, two of her children, and their dog in a lavish dining room decorated in the fashionable Japanese style. This formal setting is a foil for the amplitude of Renoir's painterly means – warm color harmonies, densely applied impasto, and confident, spontaneous execution. Marguerite Charpentier died in 1904, and her husband in 1905, and their children were auctioning their collection in April of 1907.

At that time, the art historian and critic Roger Fry was the curator of European paintings for the Metropolitan Museum of Art, and the mythology surrounding the acquisition of the painting credits Fry, who is justly celebrated for his understanding of modern art, for finding this pearl at a great price and overcoming the balky trustees to get it.[14] Doubtless some trustees recoiled from the picture, but the records show that the acquisition process was not originated by Fry. On March 11, 1907, Joseph Durand-Ruel, of Durand-Ruel New York, wrote to William Church Osborn, the museum's president, to alert him of the imminent sale.[15] Osborn passed on the letter to Sir Caspar Purdon Clarke, then director of the museum. Clarke recognized the caliber of the canvas, and sent a photograph to Fry, who was then in London. On April 3, Fry wrote to Clarke, "As to the Renoir of which you sent me a photograph. I expect it is the kind of Renoir we ought to get."[16] Even allowing for British understatement, Fry was restrained in his approval, presumably because he had not inspected the picture in person. Once he was able to examine it, his opinion soared. Fry cabled Edward Robinson, the museum's assistant director: "Examined Charpentier Renoir magnificent museum masterpiece attractive purchase . . . would be great coup . . . recommend bid $20,000 but hope attain much less auction Thursday instruct quickly."[17]

Fry was told that he could buy the painting, but not to exceed $20,000; Paul Durand-Ruel bid for Fry and the museum, and got the picture for $19,680. Durand-Ruel waived his commission, but Fry observed that "it would of course be quite natural that he should like to see Renoir recognized by our Museum."[18]

The magnitude of the purchase rippled seismically through international circles: the museum proclaimed where it stood for those unsure of the artist, for, as Fry noted in an article about *Madame Charpentier*, Renoir had not been given his full due.[19] Once more, a Durand-Ruel had banked on American enlightenment, and once more he had won. The *New York Herald* declared, "When a definite place in the galleries of the museum shall have been assigned to the Renoir portrait group it will be one of the most interesting modern works of art acquired for the permanent collection of pictures, and the price paid for it . . . will be adjudged none too high."[20] Naturally the more progressive elements of the American art world, from artists and critics to dealers and collectors, made their pilgrimage to the museum, and Léonce Bénédite, the director of the Musée du Luxembourg, wrote an impassioned article for the *Burlington Magazine* on the acquisition, in which he applauded his American colleagues. He concluded with a magisterial paragraph that predicted the migration of additional works by Renoir and the rest of the French avant-garde across the Atlantic: "It is certainly to be regretted that the canvas which may be considered one of his [Renoir's] finest works should have left France, where its place awaited it by the side of the masterpieces of our national artists. But it will carry this message of light, youth, life and joy to the gallery of a great city where French art has already found a particularly generous and hospitable refuge. And we must congratulate the curators . . . wondering at the same time whether there may not be a moral in all this to be learnt by the French museums."[21]

A year later, the English translation of *Modern Art*, by the influential European critic Julius Meier-Graefe, was published in the United States. Meier-Graefe wrote a glowing chapter on Renoir and his peers, in which he enumerated the reasons for Renoir's superiority as an artist and characterized him as one of "the great heroes of painting."[22] His words carried weight, and his book swayed the choice of the Renoirs that Barnes sought and purchased.[23]

No one was as eager to capitalize on the incipient Renoir boom as Durand-Ruel New York. The gallery had never held a solo exhibition for Renoir in the 20 years it had been open.[24] All that changed with its organizing of the artist's first solo show in America, a retrospective that ran from November 11 to December 8, 1908. Although the gallery always had Renoirs on hand, this exhibition of 41 paintings and works on paper ranging from 1873 to 1907 offered a much more substantial view of the artist. Recognizing that the tide of critical popularity was swirling into a tidal wave, Durand-Ruel presented Renoir shows in 1912 and 1914, to profitable effect. Between 1911 and 1915, the Chicago businessman and connoisseur Martin Ryerson bought six Renoirs, and Robert J. and Hannah Marcy Edwards, Boston siblings who were heirs to a silk fortune, bought three between 1912 and 1915, all from Durand-Ruel New York.

In May 1912, the American critic and painter Walter Pach's laudatory essay on Renoir appeared in *Scribner's Magazine*, a publication that would have reached a much larger audience than Meier-Graefe's. When the article appeared, Pach, along with the artists Walt Kuhn and Arthur B. Davies, was deep in the process of planning the Armory Show, the sprawling international exhibition that dropped the bomb of European avant-garde art on an unsuspecting American public in February 1913. Henri Matisse, Pablo Picasso, Francis Picabia, and Marcel Duchamp were the stars – and thus most reviled artists – of the exhibition, but from the initial meeting of the Association's executive committee in December of 1911, Renoir was still modern enough to be included, and he was one of the seven French artists who were deemed mandatory for an accurate representation of the development of contemporary art.[25] One of the Armory Show's backers was Lillie P. Bliss, the daughter of

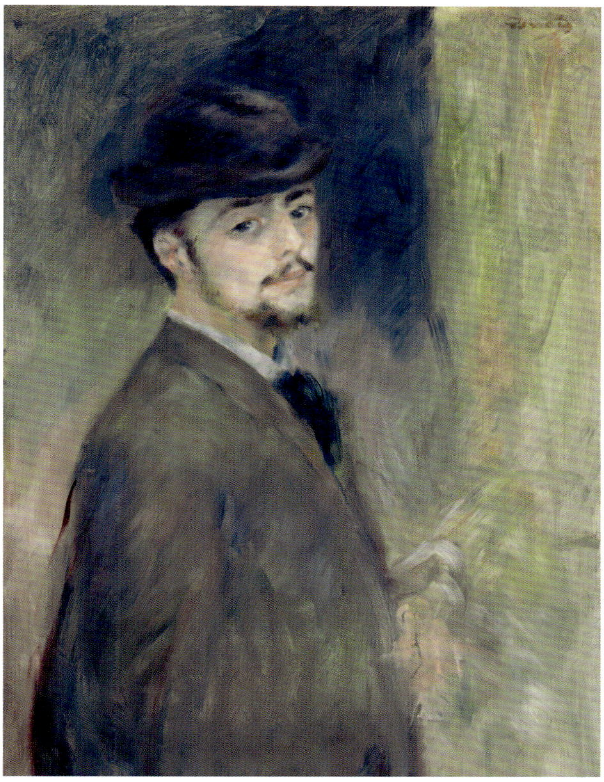

Fig. 13. Pierre-Auguste Renoir
*Self-Portrait [Autoportrait]*, 1876
Oil on canvas
28 7/8 x 22 9/16 in. (73.3 x 57.3 cm)
Harvard Art Museums/Fogg Museum; Bequest from the Collection of Maurice Wertheim, Class of 1906, 1951.61

a wealthy textile merchant. Bliss embraced vanguard art through her friendship with Davies. After meeting him in 1909, her collecting instincts were emboldened, and in 1913 she was a ready advocate of the new and vital. In January 1913, probably guided by Davies, she bought Renoir's *Fog on Guernsey*, 1883 (Cincinnati Museum of Art), and an oil and a pastel by Degas from Durand-Ruel New York. These three works were the first building blocks of her modern collection.[26] Bliss would go on to shape the dynamic of American culture by becoming a co-founder of the Museum of Modern Art.

Renoir was represented in the New York venue by five oils. *Algerian Girl*, 1881 (Museum of Fine Arts, Boston), was bought by Hannah Marcy Edwards some months after the painting had been returned to Durand-Ruel from the Armory Show's last stop in Boston. Its bright, fresh palette, quivering with the light of North Africa, must have affected artists who saw it as intensely as the more audacious color contrasts of Matisse. The Parisian dealer Ambroise Vollard sent lithographs by Renoir to the show; tellingly, three were bought by Bliss and six by John Quinn,[27] by then the country's foremost collector of vanguard American and European painting and sculpture.

The Armory Show had a profound effect on American taste, particularly that of art-conscious New Yorkers who visited it often. Between the Armory Show and the end of World War I, Renoir became exponentially more attractive to New York buyers. A vital and lesser-known Renoir enthusiast of this period was Josef Stransky, a Czechoslovakian composer engaged by the New York Philharmonic as the conductor to succeed Gustav Mahler after his death in 1911. Already a cultivated collector, Stransky arrived in New York with German and Austrian pictures, but perhaps the anti-German sentiment that gripped America during World War I impelled him to change his preferences. Starting in about 1916, he investigated Impressionism and Post-Impressionism, and he would purchase at least seven Renoirs. In January 1917, he bought *Woman with a Parasol and Small Child on a Sunlit Hillside*, 1874–76 (Museum of Fine Arts, Boston), believed to be a portrait of Camille Monet. Stransky gravitated toward personal pictures or those steeped in associations – he bought an 1876 self-portrait of Renoir (fig. 13), in which the young man can be seen with a large, ambitious canvas. Two other Stransky pictures were *Madame Édouard Bernier*, 1871 (Metropolitan Museum of Art) and *Captain Édouard*

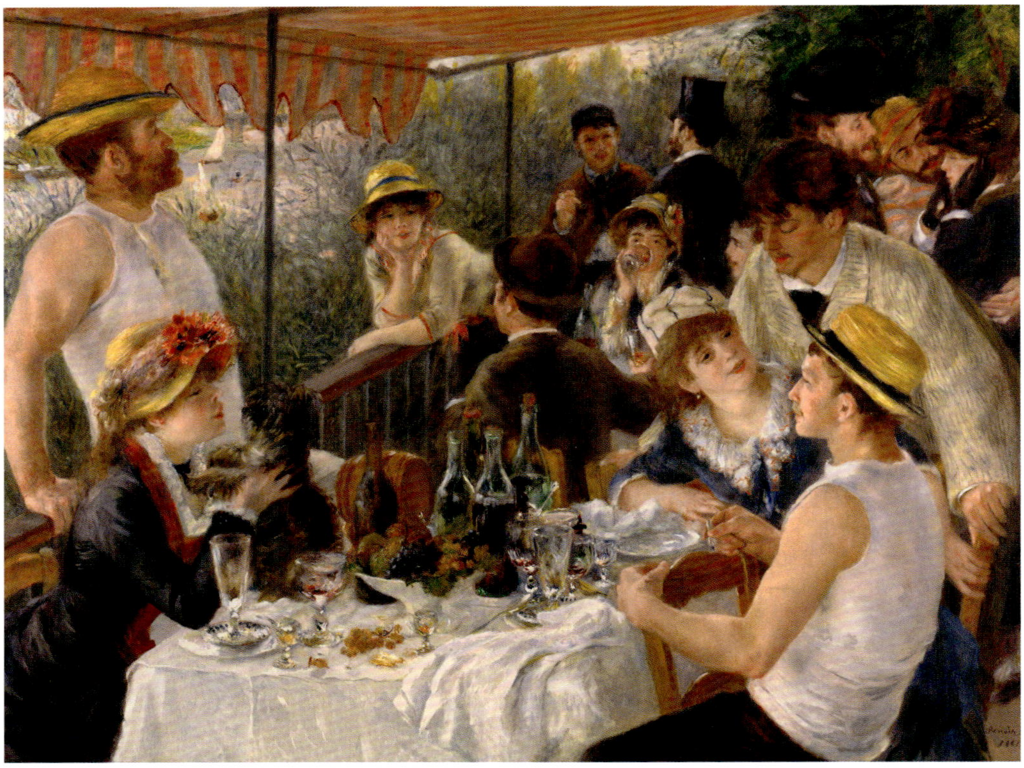

Fig. 14. Pierre-Auguste Renoir
*Luncheon of the Boating Party*
[*Le déjeuner des canotiers*],
1880–81
Oil on canvas
50 ⅜ x 68 ⅛ in. (128 x 173 cm)
Phillips Collection

*Bernier*, 1871 (Staatliche Kunstsammlungen, Dresden), portraits of the commander of Renoir's regiment during the Franco-Prussian War and his wife. Stransky was so enamored of art collecting and the art world that in 1923 he resigned his post at the Philharmonic to become an art dealer.

Stransky sold many of his paintings, including *Madame Édouard Bernier*, to Adolph Lewisohn, a mining magnate who had retired from business to devote himself to art, classical music, and philanthropy. Lewisohn had been collecting for decades, but he began to buy Impressionist paintings after World War I. He acquired a group of excellent Renoirs, all well-provenanced from discerning earlier collectors. Through Durand-Ruel, he was the buyer of those two costly Renoirs from the Emmons sale of 1920: *Oarsman at Chatou*, 1879 (National Gallery of Art, Washington, D.C.) and *In the Meadow*. By 1921 he owned *The Mussel Harvest*, 1879 (National Gallery of Art, Washington, D.C.). Lewisohn was emblematic of the next wave of Renoir collectors – those who opted for a nicely-charted path as opposed to traversing new ground. Renoir died in December 1919 and throughout 1920 his achievements were commemorated in American newspapers and periodicals. His prices rose, and Barnes, who owned 75 Renoirs by 1920,[28] had had an effect as a purchaser and advocate. It was no longer pioneering to espouse Renoir – he was now a sound if orthodox choice. This does not mean that splendid collections were not made, but their creators were tribunes and converts rather than missionaries.[29]

Indeed, the 1920s were the splashiest years in the annals of Renoir in America, when many of the best pictures were collected and deposited into public institutions. The Barnes Foundation was incorporated as an educational entity in 1922, and Barnes went forward with plans for a new building that would welcome a carefully culled public in 1925. But preceding Barnes by a year was Duncan Phillips, a banking and steel heir who opened the Phillips Memorial Gallery (now the Phillips Collection), "a museum of modern art and its sources,"[30] in Washington, D.C. From the start, the institution was a singular beacon in an aesthetically ossified city, but Phillips desired a more ambitious position for it. In 1923 Phillips and his collection leapt from provincial iconoclast to international attraction when he made the most memorable Renoir acquisition since the Metropolitan's buying of *Madame Charpentier and Her Children* 16 years before.

*Luncheon of the Boating Party*, 1880–81 (fig. 14), a grand scene of Parisians at leisure starring Renoir's friends and family, is a seamless mélange of landscape, still life, genre painting, and portraiture. Renoir integrates 14 figures, each of them in distinctive attitudes, poses, and dress: it is a sumptuous studio picture in the tradition of Titian and Gustave Courbet, but glittering with the illusion of plein-air spontaneity. The painting was in the personal collection of Paul Durand-Ruel. He installed it in his dining room and for decades had refused all offers to sell it. But Durand-Ruel père died in 1922, and when Joseph Durand-Ruel had Duncan and Marjorie Phillips to lunch at the family apartment in Paris in June 1923, they were mesmerized by the canvas and could not be dissuaded from possessing it, even at the then-unheard price of $125,000.[31] Their sincerity must have impressed Joseph Durand-Ruel, because he had stated publicly that he would not allow such a masterpiece to leave France unless it went to a museum; his anointment of the Phillips put the institution on the map. Phillips wrote excitedly to the museum's treasurer, "The Phillips Memorial Gallery is to be the possessor of *one of the greatest paintings in the world*. . . . It will do more good in arousing interest and support . . . than all the rest of our collection put together. Such a picture creates a sensation wherever it goes."[32] As the most important Renoir canvas in America, *Luncheon of the Boating Party* became an anchor and magnet of the Phillips Collection. The picture also had an impact on Phillips in defining the museum's canon of modernism. Buying the Renoir spurred him toward Post-Impressionism and his first purchases of Paul Cézanne and Vincent van Gogh.

Second only to Barnes in appetite and commitment as devotees of Renoir were Robert Sterling Clark (fig. 15) and his wife Francine Clary Clark (fig. 16), who bought 39 works between 1916 and 1951.[33] Sterling Clark, as he was known, was an heir to the Singer sewing machine fortune. After a career as a soldier and an explorer, he settled in Paris in 1910, buying a Second-Empire townhouse that he proceeded to decorate with Old Master paintings. In the same year, he also met Francine Clary, an actress in the Comédie Française, and they became lovers. Although he lived in Paris, it took a visit to New York in late 1916 to make Clark a Renoir owner. Catholina Lambert had suffered several years of business losses and had to sell his collection. The dealer Stevenson Scott successfully bid $16,200 for *Woman Crocheting*, c. 1875 (fig. 17), at Lambert's auction in February and charged Clark $20,000 for it in December. In 1919, Clark and Clary were married, and they moved to the United States in June 1920.[34] Sterling Clark could afford any work of art he wished, but he was mindful of price and value, and he noted that the cost of art had risen. There was more competition for Renoirs than in 1916, but they were a fraction of Old Master prices. Sterling

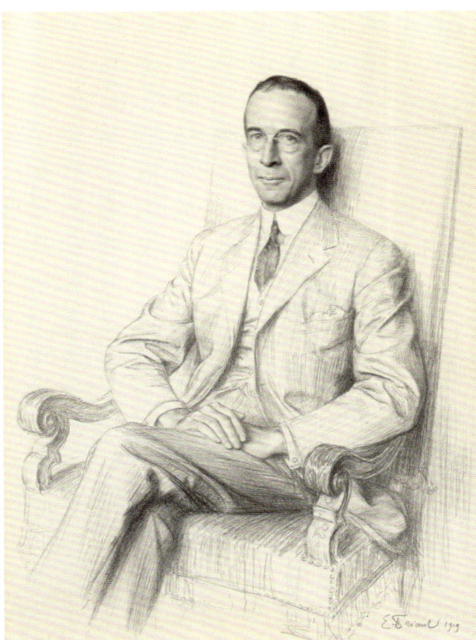

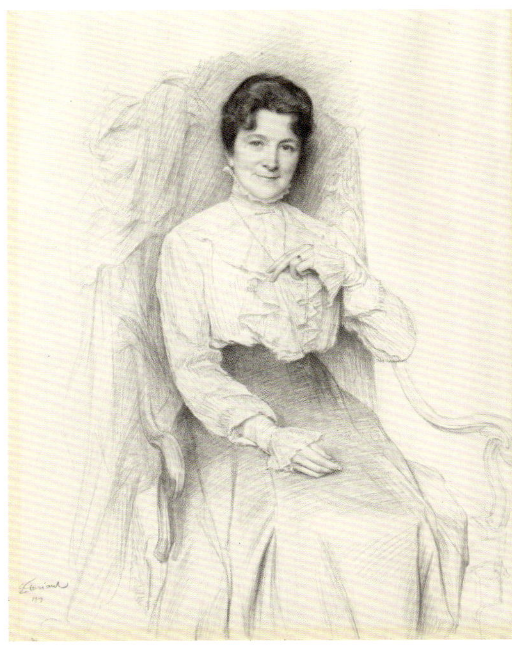

Fig. 15. Émile Friant
*Portrait of Robert Sterling Clark*, 1919
Graphite on paper
21 ¾ x 16 ½ in. (55.2 x 41.9 cm)
Sterling and Francine Clark Art Institute, Williamstown, MA;
Acquired by Sterling and Francine Clark before 1955, 1955.742

Fig. 16. Émile Friant
*Francine J. M. Clark*, 1919
Graphite on paper
21 ½ x 17 ⅛ in. (54.6 x 43.5 cm)
Sterling and Francine Clark Art Institute, Williamstown, MA;
Acquired by Sterling and Francine Clark before 1955, 1955.743

and Francine Clark were increasingly attracted to the Impressionists and other nineteenth-century artists, and Renoir was their favorite. Sterling Clark did the buying, but no purchase was final without his wife's approval; he trusted her judgment much more than that of any art historian or expert. In 1922, Sterling bought one Renoir in Paris from Durand-Ruel and another from the New York branch, which began a life-long relationship with the gallery. Of the 39 Renoirs the Clarks acquired, 28 were from Durand-Ruel.[35] Eventually Clark was given his own storeroom in Durand-Ruel's New York building.[36]

Clark visited 57th Street nearly every day to compare pictures and pick up gossip of the trade, so he wielded insider knowledge as well as memory and judgment when he negotiated. As Herbert Elfers, a director of Durand-Ruel New York, told another dealer, "[N]o one sold [Clark] pictures; [he] bought them."[37] Clark purchased seven Renoirs between 1922 and 1930, including *The Onions*, 1881; *Sleeping Girl with a Cat*, 1880; *Blonde Bather*, 1881; and *At the Concert*. The last two cost $80,000 and $100,000 respectively. When prices plummeted during the Depression, he bought six Renoirs in 1933 alone. Clark was exacting in his choices. His favorite period of Renoir was 1880–82, and he rarely ventured beyond any work painted in 1890. He believed that he had a better collection of Renoir than Barnes because the latter bought too many later and often poorly executed works, a benighted consequence of desiring examples from all phases of the artist's oeuvre.[38] Nor did Clark like Barnes's bombastic personality or penchant for publicity. Clark lent anonymously and only invited close friends to see what he had, but he nourished a vision of philanthropy and legacy. In the late 1940s, Sterling Clark plotted to establish a museum that would make the couple's entire collection available to the public. He lived to see the opening of the Francine and Sterling Clark Art Institute in Williamstown, Massachusetts, on May 17, 1955. It became – and remains – an intellectual and aesthetic ornament of the state and the region.[39]

Along with the Clarks, the other unstoppable collecting couple of the 1920s were Chester and Maud Dale. Chester Dale was a street-wise financier who had begun working on Wall Street at age 15 and taught himself how to trade and invest by watching what his bosses did. At 35, Dale was rich enough to retire from formal business, so he spent his time

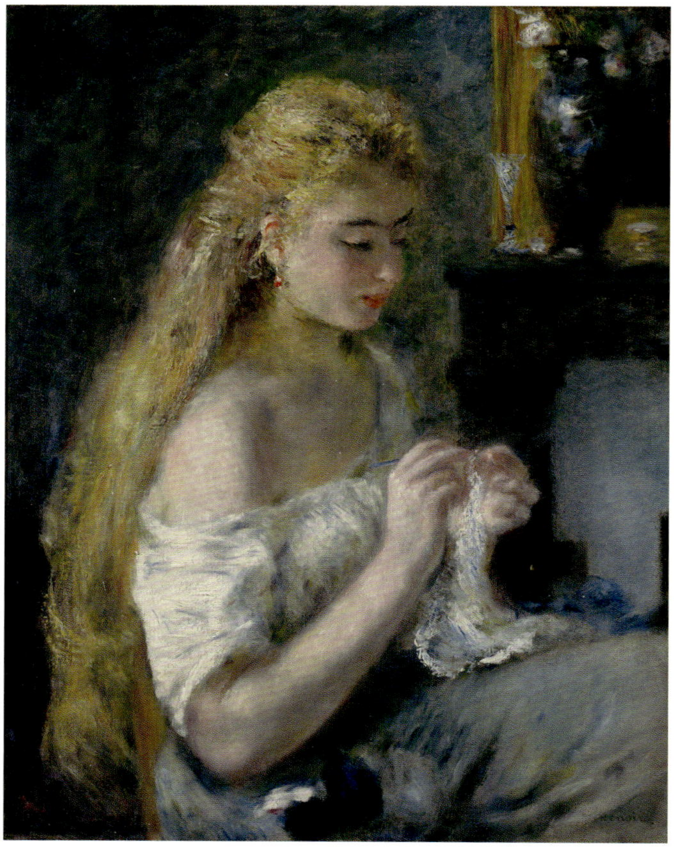

Fig. 17. Pierre-Auguste Renoir
*Woman Crocheting* [*Jeune femme cousant*], c. 1875
Oil on canvas
28 15/16 x 23 3/4 in. (73.5 x 60.3 cm)
Sterling and Francine Clark Art Institute, Williamstown, MA;
Acquired by Sterling Clark, 1916, 1955.603

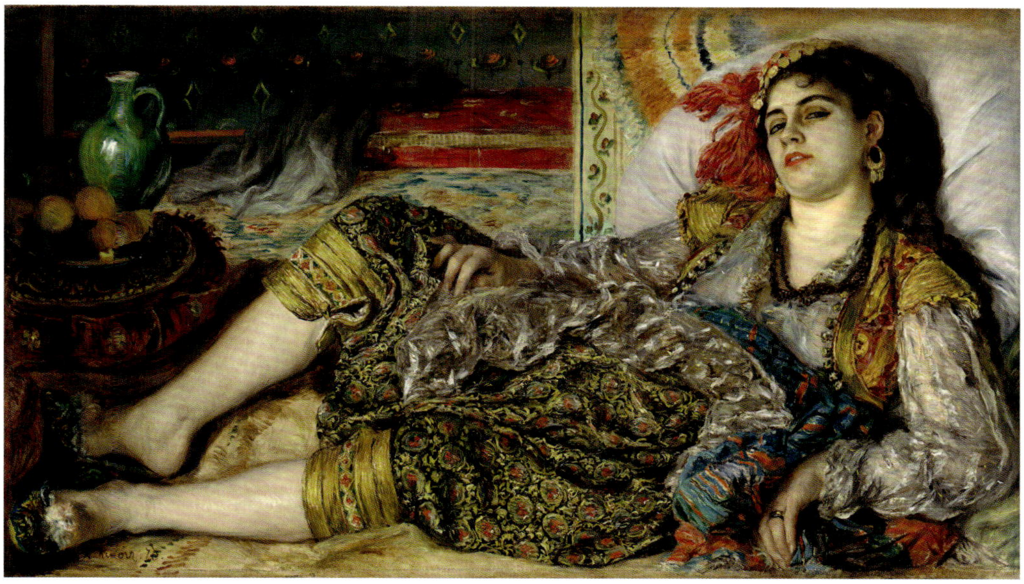

Fig. 18. Pierre-Auguste Renoir
*Odalisque* [*Odalisque ou une femme d'Alger*], 1870
Oil on canvas
27 ¼ x 48 ¼ in. (69.2 x 122.6 cm)
National Gallery of Art, Washington, D.C., Chester Dale Collection, 1963.10.207

watching over his own money and ferreting out works of art.[40] In 1911, he married the painter Maud Murray Thompson and it was she who steered him into art. Starting in 1918, the couple bought American paintings, but in December 1925 Dale intrepidly acquired Matisse's *The Plumed Hat*, 1919 (National Gallery of Art, Washington, D.C.). When Maud Dale realized that her husband had the makings of a serious collector in imagination as well as in purchasing power, she suggested that he systematically begin collecting French nineteenth-century artists and their antecedents.

Dale bought his first Renoir in 1926.[41] At one point he owned 12 Renoirs, but only nine originally owned by him are in the National Gallery of Art, where he left his collection after tantalizing the Metropolitan Museum of Art, the Philadelphia Museum of Art, and the Art Institute of Chicago with it for years. Dale threw himself into art with the same shrewdness he had brought to the stock market. He bought a majority share in the Galerie Georges Petit in Paris so the firm could not bid against him, and he generally exploited cash-hungry dealers during the Depression. In 1933 the shimmering and sexy *Odalisque*, 1870 (fig. 18) was his, and in 1931 he had purchased the Renoir canvas that remains among the most popular paintings in the National Gallery of Art: *A Girl with a Watering Can*, 1876.

Despite the gulf in social position between the patrician Clark and the rough-hewn Dale, the two were friendly competitors who enjoyed each other's company. They shared the same opinions about Renoir, both preferring paintings of the 1870s and 1880s to later works, although Dale, whose taste also encompassed Picasso, Matisse, Georges Braque, Amedeo Modigliani, and Chaïm Soutine, was far less conservative than Clark. The latter wrote to a friend of the pleasure he took in talking with Dale, exulting, "Two crazy old picture collectors admiring each others pictures and actually saying so."[42]

It is no surprise that Clark and Dale abhorred Renoir's late work. Every major American collector of Renoir thought the same, with the prominent exception of Barnes. Renoir had grown impatient with the dissolving forms of Impressionism, and he jettisoned them for a more classical approach, emphasizing structure, mass, and volume. In the twentieth century, his representations of contemporary life gave way to female nudes and bathers (pl. 32) in unspecified environments, which were not greeted with approval. Mary Cassatt famously visited Renoir and, when writing a friend in 1913, was aghast at his paintings of "enormously fat red women with very small heads."[43] Yet Barnes's enthusiasm was validated by both Picasso and Matisse, who venerated the nudes and collected them. But theirs was a lonely conviction, and most buyers were not persuaded, which is why so few late Renoirs were to be found in American collections formed in the first decades of the twentieth century.[44]

By the 1930s, Impressionism and Renoir were staples of East Coast and Midwest collections,[45] but they were less common in California. The first significant Impressionist collection in Los Angeles was assembled by the actor Edward G. Robinson.[46] Born Emanuel Goldenberg in Bucharest, Romania, Robinson arrived in New York at age ten and grew up on the Lower East Side, and he was always enchanted by art and the idea of collecting. As an aspiring stage actor, he made friends with New York artists and bought their work when he could afford it. His passion was so obvious that it endeared him to more seasoned collectors – when he was a young man, he received an invitation to visit the Lewisohn collection. "I feasted my eye," Robinson recalled, "and I think I trained it."[47] On his first trip West, Robinson stopped in Chicago and immersed himself in the collections of the Art Institute. After he became a star with *Little Caesar* in 1931, it dawned on him that he could earn enough money to buy the modern French art he craved. He inaugurated his collection in 1933 with two Renoirs.[48] One of them was a 1910 nude, so he had no misgivings about the late work. As the 1930s wore on, Robinson frequented galleries in New York, London, and Paris, and eventually owned five Renoirs. Joking that he made movies so he could keep buying the pictures that "collected him,"[49] Robinson fit easily into the freemasonry of collectors and connoisseurs in New York and Chicago, but in Hollywood he was *sui generis*. Robinson, as well as Lewisohn and Phillips, along with museums drawing from the Palmer, Havemeyer, and Ryerson collections, lent to a 1937 Renoir retrospective organized by the Metropolitan Museum of Art. It was constituted solely of works from American collections and was such a triumph that the critic Henry McBride, in an extensive article on the exhibition and its lenders, noted that "all official uncertainty in regard to the work of Renoir had been completely dissipated."[50]

Renoir's popularity did not diminish among American collectors of modern art until after World War II, when Abstract Expressionism displaced traditional figurative painting and Monet was hailed as one of the new movement's progenitors. Those who were unperturbed by such changes would have sided instead with the critic Leo Stein when he wrote that "Renoir lovers are insatiable. Collectors of his pictures have them by the scores and find that each accession adds not itself alone, but gives addition also to the life of all the others."[51]

1. Albert C. Barnes, letter to Leo Stein, March 30, 1913, Yale Collection of American Literature, Beinecke Rare Book and Manuscript Library, Yale University, New Haven, Ct., MSS 76.
2. Martha Lucy, "Grappling with Renoir's Modernism in the Collection of Dr. Barnes," in Martha Lucy and John House, *Renoir in the Barnes Foundation* (New Haven: Yale University Press, in association with The Barnes Foundation, 2012), 21.
3. Jennifer A. Thompson, "Durand-Ruel and America," in Sylvie Patry et al., *Inventing Impressionism: Paul Durand-Ruel and the Modern Art Market* (London: National Gallery of Art, 2015), 139.
4. Pierre Assouline, *Discovering Impressionism: The Life of Paul Durand-Ruel* (New York: Vendome Press, 2004), 200; Frances Weitzenhoffer, *The Havemeyers: Impressionism Comes to America* (New York: Harry N. Abrams, 1986), 35.
5. Gary Tinterow, "The Havemeyer Pictures," in Alice Cooney Frelinghuysen et al., *Splendid Legacy: The Havemeyer Collection* (New York: Metropolitan Museum of Art, 1993), 8.
6. Weitzenhoffer, 41.
7. Ibid., 41–42.
8. Thompson, 139.
9. Weitzenhoffer, 87. Weitzenhoffer also reported (263, n. 13), "Although the Palmers bought the bulk of their Impressionist collection from Durand-Ruel in 1892, they continued to purchase works by these artists, usually from the same firm." They bought one Renoir in 1893 and another in 1894.
10. Anonymous, "Art Notes," *New York Times*, January 23, 1893, 4. However, less than a year later, the *Times* had softened on Renoir, granting that he had "an enthusiasm as a colorist that only Delacroix had before him expressed" and was an "individualist of undeniable merits," *New York Times*, November 3, 1894, 98.
11. Weitzenhoffer, 117.
12. William Howe Downes, "Boston Painters and Paintings: VI," *Atlantic Monthly* 62, no. 374 (December 1888), 782.
13. See *Highly Valuable Paintings of Sterling Artistic Distinction Belonging to Private Collectors and to Several Estates* (New York: American Art Association, 1920), for details of the auction. A catalogue with marked prices is in the collection of the Frick Art Reference Library.
14. As recently as 2016, Charles Molesworth, in *The Capitalist and the Critic: J. P. Morgan, Roger Fry, and the Metropolitan Museum of Art* (Austin: University of Texas Press, 2016), erroneously asserts (128) that Fry "managed to sour some of his colleagues – especially the then director Robinson – when he bought a painting that did not meet the approval of the trustees. Fry had approached Robinson and secured permission to bid on a major painting by Pierre-Auguste Renoir." As the documents reveal, Durand-Ruel approached Caspar Purdon Clarke, the then director, about the auction. Robinson, who would become director in 1910, was assistant director, and took over handling the matter.
15. Joseph Durand-Ruel, letter to William Church Osborn, March 11, 1907, Purchases – Authorized – Paintings – Renoir, "La Famille

Charpentier," 1907–08, 1919 folder, Office of the Secretary Records, The Metropolitan Museum of Art Archives, New York (hereafter, P-A-P-R, MMAA). I thank Angela Salisbury of the MMAA for providing access to these files.
16. Roger Fry, letter to Sir Caspar Purdon Clarke, April 3, 1907, P-A-P-R, MMAA.
17. Fry, cable to Edward Robinson, April 9, 1907, P-A-P-R, MMAA.
18. Fry, letter to Robinson, April 12, 1907, P-A-P-R, MMAA.
19. Fry, "The Charpentier Family by Renoir," *The Metropolitan Museum of Art Bulletin* 2, no. 6 (June 1907), 102.
20. Untitled clipping, *New York Herald*, May 19, 1907, P-A-P-R, MMAA.
21. Léonce Bénédite, "*Madame Charpentier and Her Children*, by Auguste Renoir," *Burlington Magazine* 12, no. 57 (December 1907), 135.
22. Julius Meier-Graefe, *Modern Art: Being a Contribution to a New System of Aesthetics*, vol. 1, translated by Florence Simmonds and George W. Chrystal (New York: G. P. Putnam's Sons, 1908), 295. Meier-Graefe published the first biography of Renoir in 1911.
23. See Colin B. Bailey, "The Origins of the Barnes Collection, 1912–15," in *The World of William Glackens: The C. Richard Hilker Art Lectures*, vol. 1 (New York: D.A.P./Distributed Art Publishers, 2011), 54, 56, 58.
24. In 1892, Durand-Ruel in Paris mounted a tremendously successful Renoir exhibition. I have found no explanation as to why it took the New York branch so long to catch up.
25. Milton W. Brown, *The Story of the Armory Show*, 2nd ed. (New York: Abbeville Press, 1988), 85.
26. Rona Roob, "A Noble Legacy," *Art in America*, no. 11 (November 2003), 76. Bliss bequeathed *Fog on Guernsey* to the Museum of Modern Art, which de-accessioned it in 1943. See *Renoir 1841–1919: Artists in Guernsey* (Guernsey Museum and Art Gallery, 1988), 18. As early as 1934, writing in the Museum of Modern Art's catalogue *The Lillie P. Bliss Collection*, Alfred H. Barr, Jr., asserted that Cézanne was more important to the museum as a principal founder of "the contemporary tradition" than Renoir and Degas (7). The Cincinnati Museum of Art acquired the painting in 2004.
27. Brown, 310.
28. Lucy, 25.
29. Space does not permit discussions of the collecting history of John Taylor Spaulding (1870–1948), who bequeathed the Museum of Fine Arts 2,000 works of art, including six Renoirs, nor that of the Chicago collector Annie Swan Coburn (1856–1932). Like Spaulding, Coburn began collecting the Impressionists in the 1920s. She did not hesitate to pay top dollar, so she was offered remarkable Renoirs. Several are among the Art Institute of Chicago's great treasures, most notably *Two Sisters (On the Terrace)*, 1881. See Frederic A. Sharf, *Art of Collecting: The Spaulding Brothers and Their Legacy* (Boston: Museum of Fine Arts, 2007); and Stefan Germer, "Traditions and Trends: Taste Patterns in Chicago Collecting," in *The Old Guard and the Avant-Garde: Modernism in Chicago, 1910–1940*, ed. Sue Ann Prince (Chicago and London: University of Chicago Press, 1990), 186–88, for information on Spaulding and Coburn as collectors.
30. Quoted in David W. Scott, "The Evolution of a Critic: Changing Views in the Writings of Duncan Phillips," in *The Eye of Duncan Phillips: A Collection in the Making*, ed. Erika D. Passantino (New Haven and London: Phillips Collection, in association with Yale University Press, 1999), 12–13.
31. Sylvie Patry, Anne Robins, Christopher Riopelle, Joseph J. Rishel, and Jennifer A. Thompson, "Paul Durand-Ruel, an 'Unrepentant Risk-taker,' " in Patry et al., 28; Marjorie Phillips, *Duncan Phillips and His Collection* (Boston: Little, Brown and Co., 1970, 63.
32. Duncan Phillips, letter to Dwight Clark, July 10, 1923, in Grayson Harris Lane, "Pierre-Auguste Renoir (1841–1919)," in Passantino, 108.
33. James A. Ganz, "From Paris to Williamstown: Robert Sterling Clark's Life as a Collector," in Michael Conforti et al., *The Clarks Collect: Impressionist and Early Modern Paintings* (Williamstown, MA: Sterling and Francine Clark Art Institute, 2006), 81.
34. Ibid., 60.
35. Ibid., 81.
36. Steven Kern, "A Passion for Renoir," in Steven Kern et al., *A Passion for Renoir: Sterling and Francine Clark Collect, 1916–1951* (New York: Harry N. Abrams, in association with Sterling and Francine Clark Art Institute, 1996), 14.
37. Ibid., 16.
38. Ibid., 17.
39. Robert Sterling Clark's brother, Stephen Carlton Clark (1882–1960) was also an illustrious art collector, but his interests lie outside this inquiry. Although he did bequeath four Renoirs (bought in the 1930s, partly to pique his brother) to the Metropolitan Museum of Art, Stephen Clark was far more celebrated for his purchases of major works by Seurat, Cézanne, Matisse, and Edward Hopper, which he donated to the Metropolitan Museum, the Museum of Modern Art, Yale University Art Gallery, and the Addison Gallery of American Art.
40. Philip Kopper, *America's National Gallery of* Art (Princeton, N.J.: Princeton University Press, 2016), 70.
41. Kimberly A. Jones, "Cultivating the Chester Dale Collection," in Kimberly A. Jones and Maygene Daniels, *The Chester Dale Collection* (Washington, D.C.: National Gallery of Art, 2009), 4.
42. Robert Sterling Clark, letter to Paul Clemens, November 15, 1945, quoted in Ganz, 96.
43. Mary Cassatt, letter to Louisine Havemeyer, January 11, 1913, quoted in Sylvie Patry, "One must do the painting of one's time," in Claudia Einecke and Roger Benjamin, *Renoir in the 20th Century*, exhibition catalogue (Ostfildern: Hatje Cantz, 2010), 360.
44. In "Got a Few Million? Christie's May Have a Monet for You. Or Five," a recent story by Ted Loos (*New York Times*, April 17, 2018) on the red-hot Monet market, an Impressionist and Post-Impressionist collector named Scott M. Black opined, "With Renoir, you don't really want to buy one after 1890. It was downhill after then, let's be frank."
45. For example, the encyclopedic collectors Grenville Winthrop (1864–1943) and Robert Lehman (1891–1969) both took care to acquire multiple examples of works by Renoir as they proceeded. Winthrop left his collection to the Fogg Museum and Lehman to the Metropolitan Museum of Art.
46. Walter and Louise Arensberg, among the most radical collectors of twentieth-century avant-garde art, moved to Los Angeles from New York in 1921. To augment the couple's collection of work by Duchamp, Brancusi, Picasso, Braque, Picabia, Léger, Kandinsky, and Klee, Walter Arensberg bought *Bather* (1917–18; Philadelphia Museum of Art), a very late nude by Renoir, and hung it below Duchamp's *Nude Descending a Staircase (No. 3)*, 1916 (Philadelphia Museum of Art). Theirs was probably the first late Renoir to reach Los Angeles.
47. Edward G. Robinson, with Leonard Spigelgass, *All My Yesterdays: An Autobiography* (New York: Hawthorne Books, 1973), 296.
48. Ibid., 133.
49. "Statement by Edward G. Robinson," in "Paintings From Well-Known Edward G. Robinson Collection to Go on View at Museum," Museum of Modern Art press release (March 1953), 3. www.moma.org/documents/moma_press-release_325890.pdf.
50. Henry McBride, "The Renoirs in America: In Appreciation of the Metropolitan Museum of Art's Exhibition," *Art News* 35, no. 11 (May 1, 1937), 59. *Renoir: A Special Exhibition of His Paintings* was on view from May 18 – September 12, 1937.
51. Leo Stein, "Renoir and the Impressionists," *New Republic* (March 30, 1918), 260.

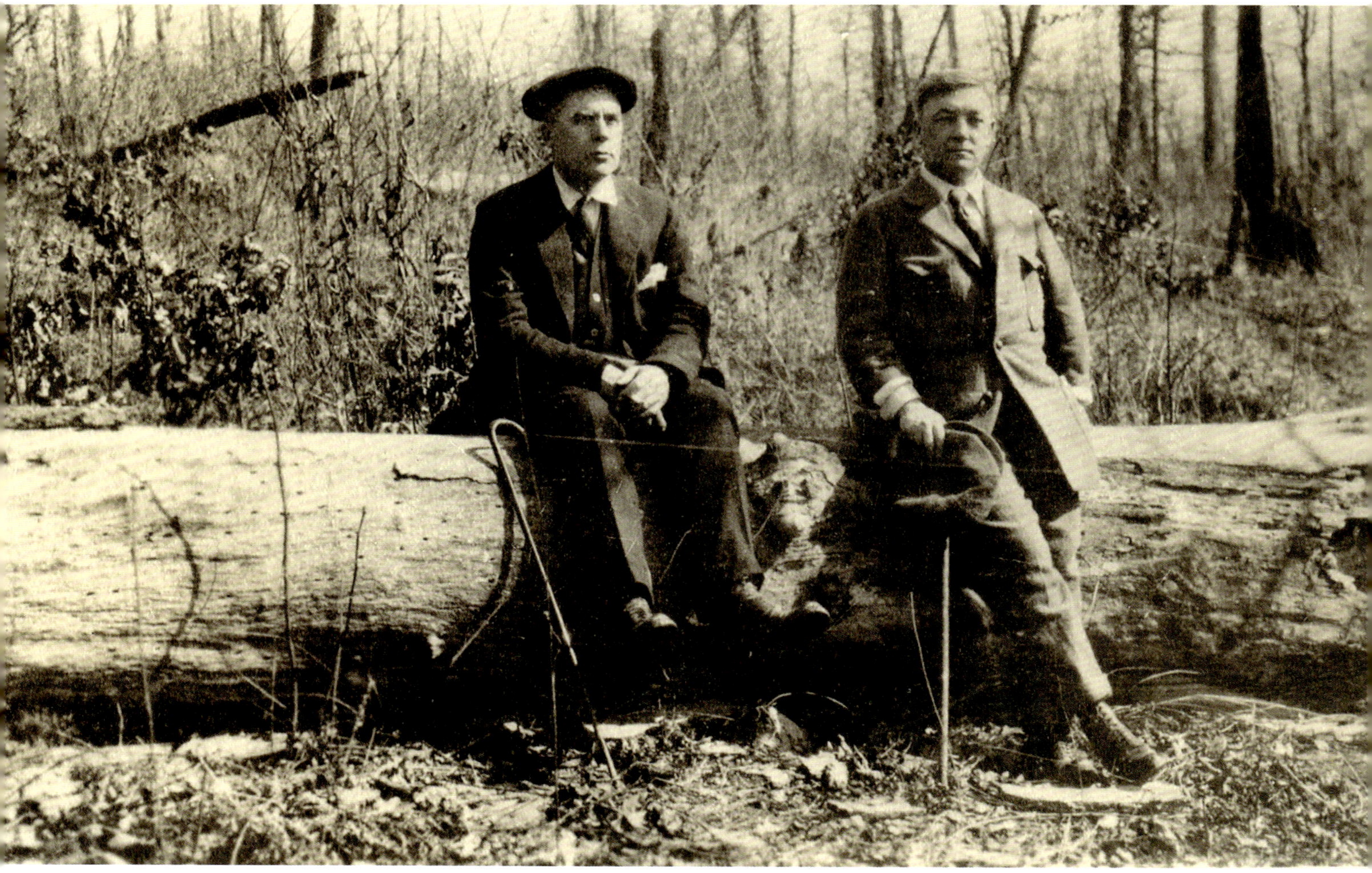

# William J. Glackens and the Renoirs of Albert C. Barnes

*Martha Lucy*

Between 1912 and 1951, the Philadelphia scientist and pharmaceutical mogul Albert C. Barnes amassed the world's largest collection of works by Pierre-Auguste Renoir. William J. Glackens's role in the genesis of this collection has frequently been discussed. Barnes himself acknowledged his influence in 1935, penning this inscription in Glackens's copy of a book he had written: "To Butts – who started my interest in Renoir."[1] It was Glackens, after all, who had encouraged Barnes's passion for modern art, guiding him through galleries and studio visits, and who purchased Barnes's first five canvases by Renoir during a buying trip to Paris in February 1912. Surely he could not have imagined that over the course of the next four decades Barnes would go on to acquire 176 more.

If Glackens's part in the development of Barnes's Renoir obsession is well documented, what is less discussed is how much the influence also flowed in the other direction. Barnes was central to Glackens's own thinking about Renoir after 1912. In Barnes, Glackens had found an interlocutor who was as devoted to Renoir as he was – an intellectual companion who had submitted himself to rigorous study of Renoir's work, eventually becoming one of the country's foremost critics. Even more important was the unimaginable visual resource that Barnes supplied: as the acquisitions poured in, Glackens found himself with a massive Renoir collection at his disposal that he could study first-hand. What, exactly, did he see during his visits with Barnes? How might we relate his experience there to his later production?

Barnes built his Renoir collection steadily over several decades, but the first few years immediately after his "awakening" were particularly explosive.[2] "I am convinced I cannot get too many Renoirs," he announced to Leo Stein in 1913 with characteristic self-assurance.[3] Barnes purchased Renoir voraciously, snapping up works at auction and traveling to New York and Paris to survey the stock at Vollard's, Bernheim, and the Galerie Durand-Ruel, often buying eight or ten works at a time. Barnes made his intentions clear to Paul Durand-Ruel in 1915: "[Please tell] Renoir that I think he is the greatest of modern painters . . . it is fair to say that I have spent in purchasing paintings by Renoir the sum of a million and a half francs, and it is my hope to make this collection one of the best in the world."[4] By 1918, just six years after that first purchase by Glackens, Barnes had acquired 65 Renoirs.

Significantly, it was a particular *kind* of Renoir that Barnes was after. While most of his contemporaries coveted the Impressionist works, Barnes was ultimately more interested in the paintings that Renoir produced much later in life – the timeless bathing groups and Arcadian landscapes that seemed to ache with nostalgia for a pre-industrial way of life. *Five Bathers*, for example, painted in 1918 (Barnes Foundation, BF902), is a flesh-filled dreamscape, a fantasy of humans in total harmony with nature. American critics and collectors were generally dismissive of the late period works (c. 1890–1919). The nudes

Fig. 19. *Albert C. Barnes and William J. Glackens*, c. 1920
Photograph
Photograph Collection, Barnes Foundation Archives, Philadelphia, PA. Reprinted with permission

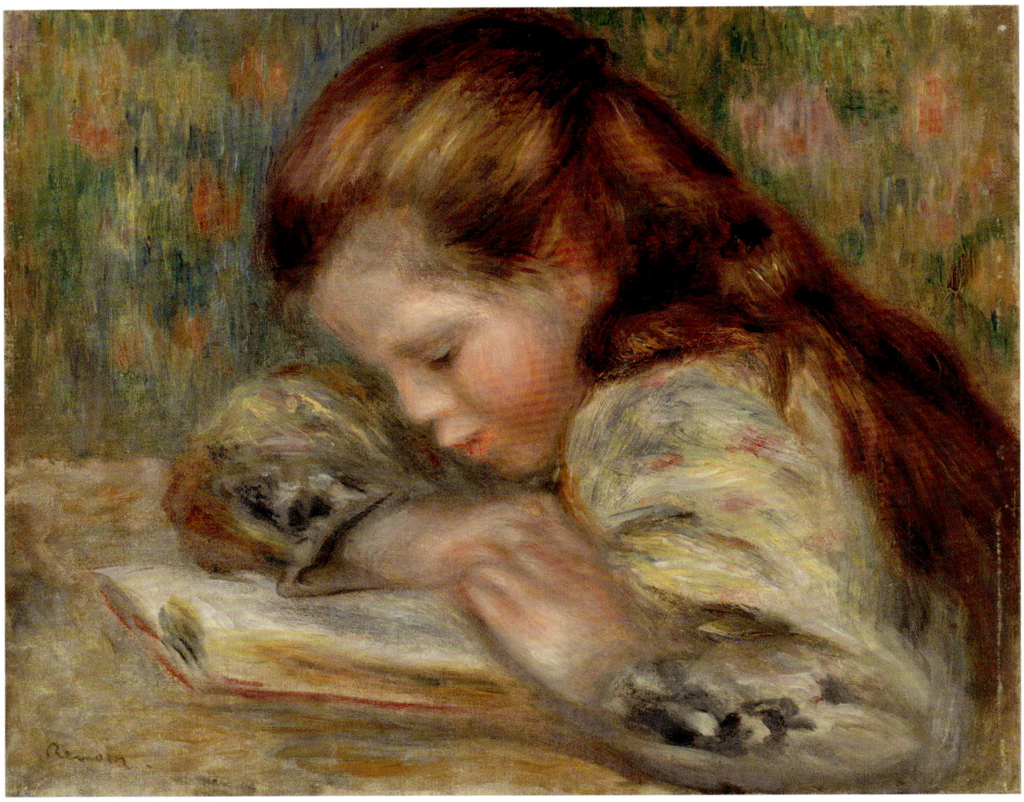

Fig. 20. Pierre-Auguste Renoir
*Child Reading* [*Enfant lisant*],
early 1890s
Oil on canvas
12 13/16 x 16 1/4 in. (32.6 x 41.3 cm)
The Barnes Foundation,
Philadelphia, PA, BF51

were particularly distressing, described over and over as "pneumatic" and excessively fleshy (see, for example, fig. 21). Roger Fry summarized the attitude in 1921: "A few critics and a good many dealers have circulated the report that in his last years Renoir never did anything comparable to those works of his prime."[5]

Yet Barnes remained convinced of the superiority of Renoir's later output. He continued his pursuit, getting a large batch from the Renoir sons after their father's death, and several from the Bignou Gallery during the 1930s. "Perhaps his best work is that which dates from the 90s up to the time of his death," he said in a 1924 letter. "My large canvas, 'Les Baigneuses,' . . . represents the summation of his powers."[6] Barnes made an extended argument in support of the late works in *The Art of Renoir*, the ambitious 1935 tome in which he set out to explain Renoir using an "objective" method rooted in the rigorous study of visual form.[7] Barnes analyzes hundreds of paintings in excruciating detail, explaining the design principles that gave them their structure and balance.

Glackens, of course, was always keen to see Barnes's new acquisitions, as were many of the young American modernists of his generation. In the 1910s and 1920s, Charles Demuth and Maurice Prendergast made frequent visits to Barnes's home in Merion, Pennsylvania, anxious to see what he had added to his collection. Demuth was riveted by the Cézannes. Charles Sheeler visited in 1914, as did Georgia O'Keeffe years later."[8] For a generation of artists that lacked easy access to the works of Pablo Picasso, Henri Matisse, and Paul Cézanne – MoMA did not yet exist – Barnes's collection was something of a revelation; indeed, Demuth referred to it as "one of the modern seven wonders" of the world.[9]

But it was Glackens who spent the most time with Barnes. The friendship between the two men – honest, heartfelt, and profound – was one of the few to survive Barnes's famously difficult personality. "I loved Butts as I ever loved but a half dozen people in my lifetime," he wrote to Glackens's wife Edith at the time of William's death (fig. 19).[10] Barnes and Glackens spent countless hours discussing Renoir, pouring over his paintings, exchanging ideas. Barnes prodded his friend for his insights into specific works – he trusted his eye more than anyone else's – and Glackens, in turn, digested Barnes's own copious writings on the

Fig. 21. Pierre-Auguste Renoir
*Seated Odalisque [Femme en chemise de tulle assise sur des coussins verts; Odalisque assise]*, 1918
Oil on canvas
20 ½ x 18 ½ in. (52 x 47 cm)
The Barnes Foundation, Philadelphia, PA, BF237

Fig. 22. Pierre-Auguste Renoir
*Writing Lesson [La Leçon d'écriture]*, c. 1905
Oil on canvas
21 7/16 x 25 13/16 in. (54.5 x 65.5 cm)
The Barnes Foundation, Philadelphia, PA, BF150

artist. "I like the Renoir [piece] very much indeed," Glackens wrote to Barnes in 1924, "and think you have made a very fine analysis of his work and what he stood for."[11] Glackens accompanied Barnes on his visits to Durand-Ruel's New York gallery, especially when there was a new Renoir exhibition to take in, and he traveled frequently to Philadelphia to see Barnes's new purchases. "Shall be delighted to see your latest acquisitions," Glackens wrote in 1913, and many times after that.[12] When Glackens wasn't able to visit in person, Barnes kept him updated about his new purchases by sending lists and sometimes photographs; one batch sent in 1923 included images of new Cézannes, a Matisse, and "eight other small Renoirs, all done in the late manner."[13]

In Glackens's own work, one can sometimes see a conscious engagement with specific acquisitions. His c. 1918 *Lenna Painting* (pl. 53), for example, is as much a tribute to Renoir's *Child Reading*, early 1890s (fig. 20) as it is a portrait of his daughter. Glackens would have known *Child Reading* well, having selected it himself from Durand-Ruel's stock in 1912; this was the picture he described, excitedly, in a letter to his wife written from abroad: "I got a fine little Renoir at Durand-Ruel, a little girl reading a book."[14] In addition to echoing the subject – a close-up of a young girl with loosely pulled-back hair absorbed in her task – Glackens chooses a composition that is nearly identical, down to the angle of the girl's shoulders, elbows, and head. The canvases are even the same size.

*Negress in Oriental Costume*, c. 1923 (pl. 60), seems closely related to Renoir's *Seated Odalisque*, 1918 (fig. 21) – one of the "eight small late Renoirs" Barnes had acquired that year.[15] There is, first of all, the obvious mimicking of subject matter: a model dressed up in exotic garb, surrounded by pillows and draperies. But notice also the colors used by Glackens: green and red are the principle tones, each setting off the other and bumping up against passages of white. In *Artist's Daughter in Chinese Costume*, 1918 (pl. 48), Glackens seems to be echoing the color combinations of Renoir's *Writing Lesson*, c. 1905 (fig. 22), which Barnes had acquired three years earlier. Deep reds suffuse both pictures, interacting with zones of blue. Glackens was the first to admit his debt to Renoir, especially when it came to color. "My Renoir influence is obvious," he wrote to Barnes in 1924.[16] In trying to emulate Renoir's use of color, Glackens seems to have been searching for another means of expressivity beyond the more narrative conventions – gesture, movement, and physiognomy – on which he, as a caricaturist, had long relied.

It is perhaps in his nudes that Glackens most reveals his debt to Barnes's Renoir collection. Renoir's late nudes – those fleshy, monumental figures arranged in classical poses

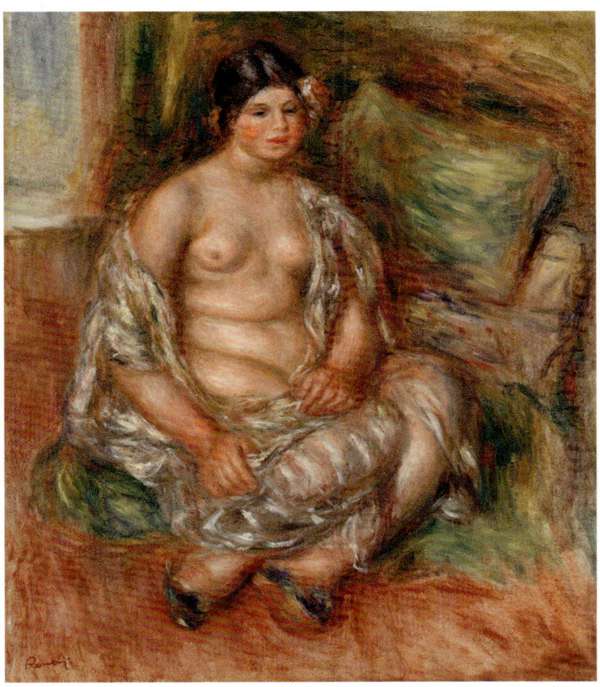

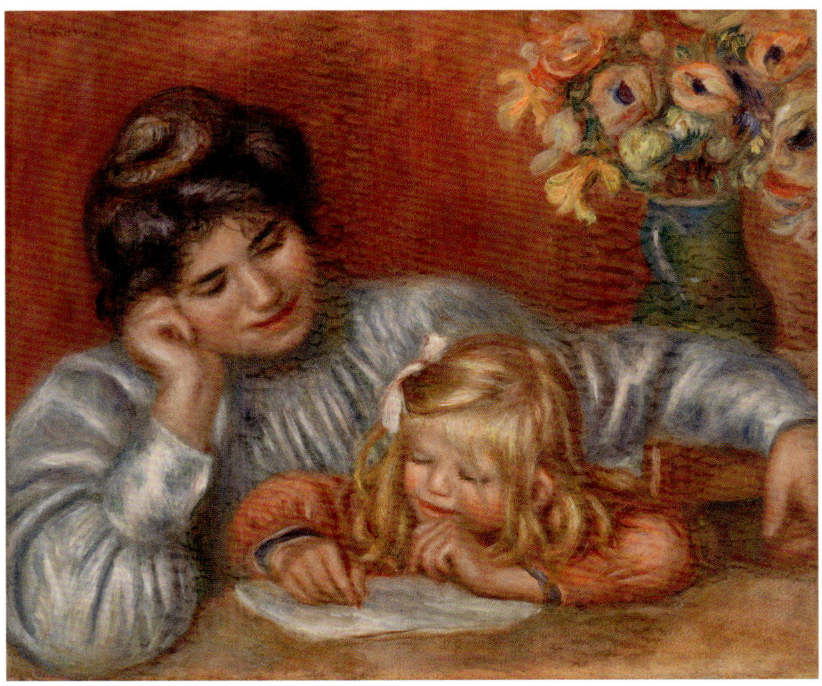

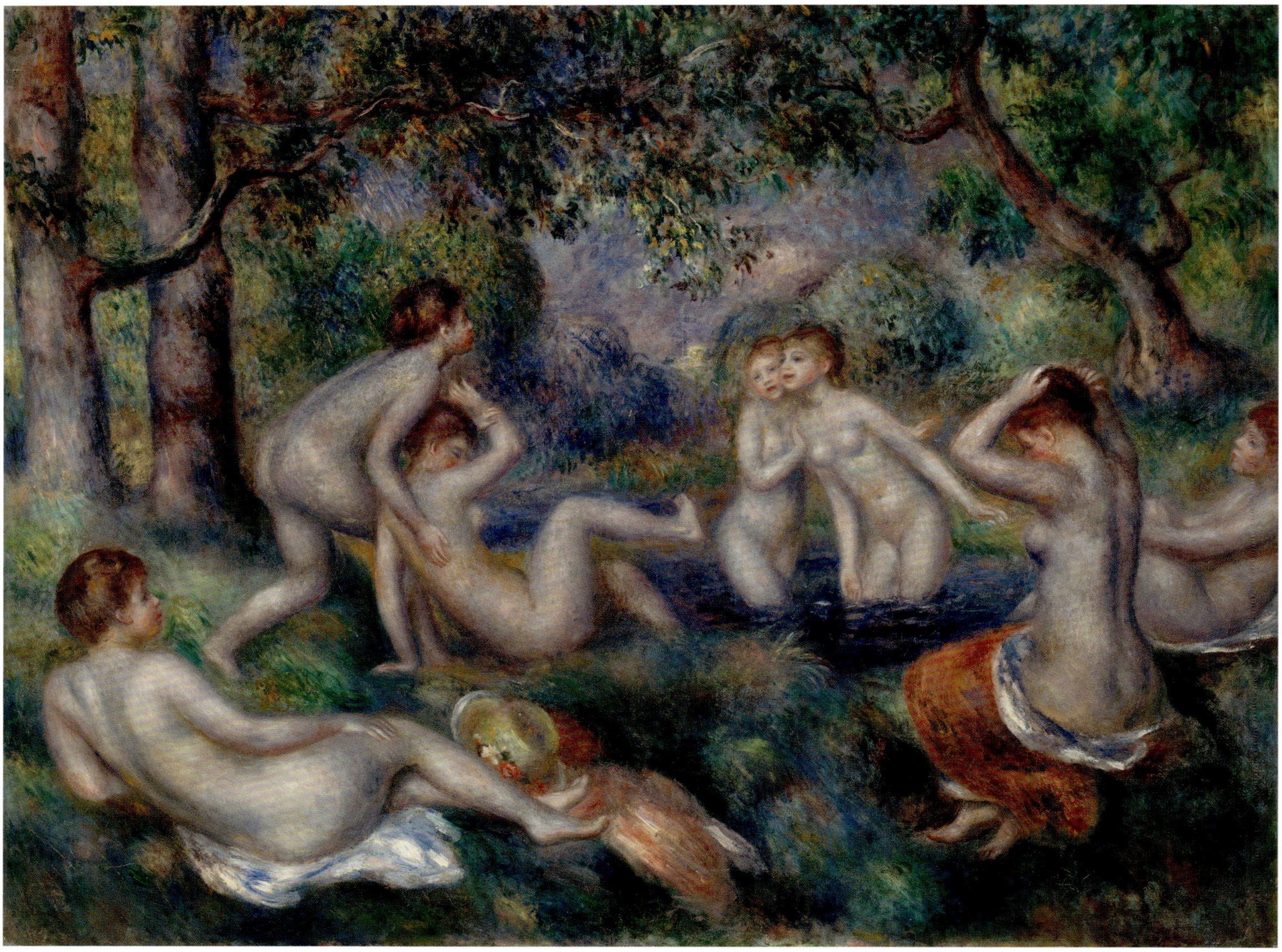

Fig. 23. Pierre-Auguste Renoir
*Bathers in the Forest* [*Baigneuses dans la forêt*], c. 1897
Oil on canvas
29 ⅛ x 39 ⅜ in. (74 x 100 cm)
The Barnes Foundation, Philadelphia, PA, BF901

and painted with the thinnest of glazes – were certainly well represented; Barnes had at least 28 by the time of his friend's death in 1938. Glackens's immersion in this universe of sensual bodies is evident in works like *Back of Nude*, c. 1930s (pl. 63), which we might compare to Renoir's *Bather in Three-Quarter View* (BF284) and *Seated Female Nude* (BF16), acquired in 1916 and 1918 respectively. Like Renoir, Glackens presents a self-absorbed figure close to the picture plane, seemingly unaware of the viewer's gaze; and like Renoir, flesh is rendered to appear velvety and soft – so soft that the body's edges blur into the background colors. *Bathers in the Forest*, c. 1897 (fig. 23), purchased from Bignou in 1932, might have had an even greater impact on *Back of Nude*. One of the most jarring aspects of Glackens's picture is the green strip running down the figure's back; indeed we find this device used repeatedly in *Bathers in the Forest*, especially in the bather in the right foreground, where a bluish-purple tint demarcates the spine to exaggerated effect. Glackens certainly knew this picture. It was a major acquisition – one that Barnes was especially proud of (fig. 24) – and we know Glackens was in Philadelphia when it entered the collection in 1932.[17]

In these late nudes, Renoir uses color (rather than light and shade) as a structural element to build convincingly solid forms. Glackens, by his own estimation, had difficulty applying this lesson. Perhaps this is what he meant when he lamented to Barnes, "I have found out that the pursuit of color is hard on drawing just as the pursuit of drawing is hard on color. Renoir survived but who else?"[18]

A popular theory was that in emulating Renoir, Glackens was simply attempting to paint pictures that would sell. The rumor, as Barnes explained it, was that after deliberately stoking

Barnes's Renoir craze, Glackens then developed his own Renoiresque style, knowing he would have a likely buyer. This is why, in a 1923 article about the Foundation, Barnes played down Glackens's role in forming his collection; reminding the public of the important 1912 buying trip would only rejuvenate that suspicion.[19] If churning out Renoir knock-offs for profit had really been Glackens's aim, he would have focused on Renoir's Impressionist period; those were the pictures most collectors desired, and we know that he was certainly capable of working in that style. And yet he was drawn to the strange, difficult, hard-to-categorize canvases from the late period – canvases that continue to confound historians of modern art.

It is important to remember, however, that despite their lukewarm reception among certain collectors, Renoir's late works were revered by members of the European avant-garde. Picasso, Matisse, and Braque all had Renoir's late paintings (or reproductions) hanging in their studios. According to Leo Stein, Picasso raved about Renoir's late works during the famous Saturday salons at the Stein atelier. He studied them at Paul Rosenberg's gallery, which was right next to his studio, and bought several for his own collection. One can see Picasso channeling Renoir in his canvases from the early 1920s, in which massive nudes, at once hulking and delicate, seem crammed into their space. Between 1917 and 1919, Matisse regularly visited Renoir in Cagnes-sur-Mer, surveying the older artist's newest canvases. Matisse spoke candidly of Renoir's influence, and in 1918 he wrote about his importance for modernist practice: "After the work of Cézanne whose tremendous influence is paramount among artists, Renoir's work saves us from the dryness of pure abstraction."[20]

For the European avant-garde of this period, Impressionism was of little interest. The approach was too slavishly representational, too concerned with recording external appearances. Renoir's late work, on the other hand, seemed to represent a pure engagement with form, a privileging of color, design, and compositional relationships over everything else. A canvas like *Five Bathers* is not an indexical representation of real bodies in real space; it is an arrangement of formal elements – of colors, lines and shapes deployed toward overall pictorial unity rather than toward a faithful description of the real-world objects they reference.

It is hardly surprising, then, that Glackens would have looked to Renoir at this point in his career. His artistic goals had changed: gritty images of contemporary life were no longer tenable as a modernist approach. "The early Americans were illustrative," he said in 1912. "It was France that showed them the error of their project."[21] Modernism instead resided in

Fig. 24. Pierre Matisse
*Albert C. Barnes with Renoir's "Bathers in the Forest [Baigneuses dans la forêt]"*, c. 1932
Photograph
Photograph Collection, Barnes Foundation Archives, Philadelphia, PA. Reprinted with permission

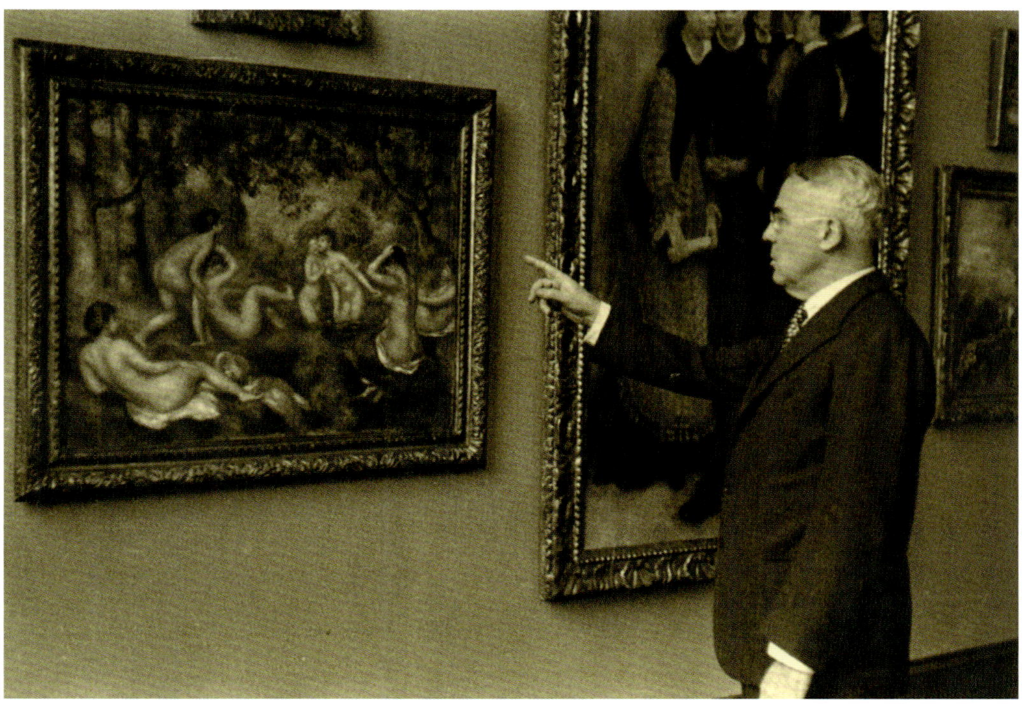

the forms themselves, in the idea of painting as a complete, self-enclosed system. In *Artist's Daughter in Chinese Costume* and *Negress in Oriental Costume*, and in the later nudes as well, Glackens has constructed his own self-enclosed system. These are fictive, made-up images, with dressed-up models posed against artificial backgrounds. For each picture, he has carefully selected and arranged its parts, authoring his own reality rather than recording the world as it is.

Glackens's debt to Renoir was much discussed during his lifetime. For many critics, Glackens's color was too close to Renoir's, his subjects too similar, leading to the conclusion that he had lost his way and become a mere imitator. Barnes was fiercely protective of his friend's reputation. On one occasion, after overhearing someone call Glackens's pictures "imitation Renoirs," Barnes reproached the stranger but regretted he "did not have the opportunity to tell the bastard what I thought of his appearance, his profession and his opinions."[22] When William Huntington Wright described Glackens as painting "with a Renoir technique," Barnes promised Edith that he was determined to "make Glack and Prend recognized for what they are . . . and if I don't succeed it will be my first failure in life."[23]

Barnes knew better than anyone what it was that Glackens saw in Renoir and what he hoped to achieve in his own painting. In a 1924 essay titled "The Art of William Glackens," he delivered a fiery defense of his friend, attempting to squash the "imitator" label once and for all. It is true, Barnes acknowledges, that Renoir and Glackens share a similar outlook on life: both painted from a place of sincerity and joy. Barnes also perceived in each of them a desire to get at the essence, or truth, of their subjects. But there were clear distinctions: "Those of us who have lived with the work of both men . . . never would mistake one for the other nor admit that Glackens is either an imitator of Renoir or less of an individual artist because he has expressed himself in color which we associate with Renoir's work."[24]

What Barnes does not discuss here, but which is crucial to disentangling Glackens's unique contribution, is his theory about artistic lineage. Renoir succeeded, Barnes reasoned, because he skillfully mined the art of the past, selecting only the best elements from the great traditions and deploying them to achieve a new form. In 1971, Barnes's longtime colleague Violette de Mazia applied this logic to Glackens. In an essay titled "The Case of Glackens vs. Renoir," de Mazia argued that to describe influence as a kind of plagiarism is to misunderstand the history of art.[25] Artists, like scientists, build on the work of their predecessors; indeed it is logical, even efficient, to proceed this way. Glackens did not *imitate* Renoir, but rather *learned* from him, selecting certain key elements and adapting them to his own individual experience. As Glackens himself put it in 1913, "Art, like humanity, every time has an ancestry."[26]

1. On Glackens's role in the Barnes Foundation and his friendship with Dr. Barnes, see Richard J. Wattenmaker, *American Paintings and Works on Paper in the Barnes Foundation* (Merion: The Barnes Foundation, in association with Yale University Press, 2010) and Judith F. Dolkart, "William Glackens: 'Intensely Sincere and Intensely Brave,'" in *William Glackens*, ed. Avis Berman, exhibition catalogue (New York and Philadelphia: Skira Rizzoli Publications, Inc., and The Barnes Foundation, 2014), 126–39.
2. For a chronology of Barnes's Renoir purchases, see Martha Lucy and John House, *Renoir in the Barnes Foundation* (New Haven: Yale University Press, in association with The Barnes Foundation, 2012), 340–67.
3. Albert C. Barnes to Leo Stein, 1913, Yale Collection of American Literature, Beinecke Rare Book and Manuscript Library, Yale University, New Haven, Ct.
4. Albert C. Barnes to Paul Durand-Ruel, January 25, 1915, Barnes Foundation Archives (hereafter, BFA).
5. Roger Fry, "The Last Works of Renoir," *Arts & Decoration* 14 (January 1921), 246–47.
6. Albert C. Barnes to Harold Van Doren, 1924, BFA.
7. For a discussion of Barnes's book and the critical reaction to it, see *Renoir in the Barnes Foundation*, 36–37.
8. Charles Sheeler to Alfred C. Barnes, November 12, 1914, BFA.
9. Charles Demuth to Alfred C. Barnes, undated (1921), BFA.
10. Alfred C. Barnes to Edith Glackens, June 3, 1938, quoted by Ira Glackens, *William Glackens and the Ashcan Group* (New York: Crown Press, 1957), 259.
11. This was in response to Albert C. Barnes's draft manuscript for his 1925 book, *The Art in Painting*. William J. Glackens to Albert C. Barnes, September 27, 1924, BFA.
12. William J. Glackens to Albert C. Barnes, undated (probably early 1913 based on his mention of the upcoming Armory show), BFA.
13. "Your list of newly acquired works sound most interesting." William J. Glackens to Albert C. Barnes, July 3, 1924. Barnes's letter with the enclosed photographs is from August 14, 1923, BFA.
14. Letter to Edith Glackens, Paris, February, 16, 1912. Cited in Ira Glackens, *William Glackens and the Eight: The artists who freed American art* (New York: Horizon Press, 1983), 158.
15. Barnes acquired this work from Galerie Barbazanges, Paris, on July 7, 1918.
16. William J. Glackens to Albert C. Barnes, 1924, undated, probably in the fall, BFA.
17. See Emily Wood's chronology in *William Glackens*, 2014.
18. See William J. Glackens to Alfred C. Barnes, 1924, BFA.
19. Of course Barnes was partly motivated by his desire for proper credit in building his own collection, and he admitted as much in a letter to Glackens's wife. "I would resent absolutely any statement that my collection is merely an echo of Butts – that collection as it now stands is the result of my own efforts." Albert C. Barnes to Edith Dimock Glackens, February 19, 1923, BFA.
20. See Matisse's essay on Renoir in *Modern French Painting*, exhibition catalogue (Kunstnerforbundet, Oslo, 1918), 290.
21. William Glackens, "The American Section: The National Art," *Arts & Decoration* 3, no. 5 (March 1913), 160. For more on Glackens's absorption of French art, see Martha Lucy, "Glackens, French Art, and the Language of Modernism," in *William Glackens*, 2014.
22. Albert C. Barnes to William J. Glackens, January 17, 1917, BFA.
23. Albert C. Barnes to Edith Glackens, February 21, 1916, BFA.
24. Draft manuscript, BFA, for an essay published in French in *Les Arts à Paris* 10 (1924).
25. Violette de Mazia, "The Case of Glackens vs. Renoir," *The Barnes Foundation Journal of the Art Department* 2, no. 2 (Autumn 1971), 24.
26. Glackens, "The American Section: The National Art," 159–64.

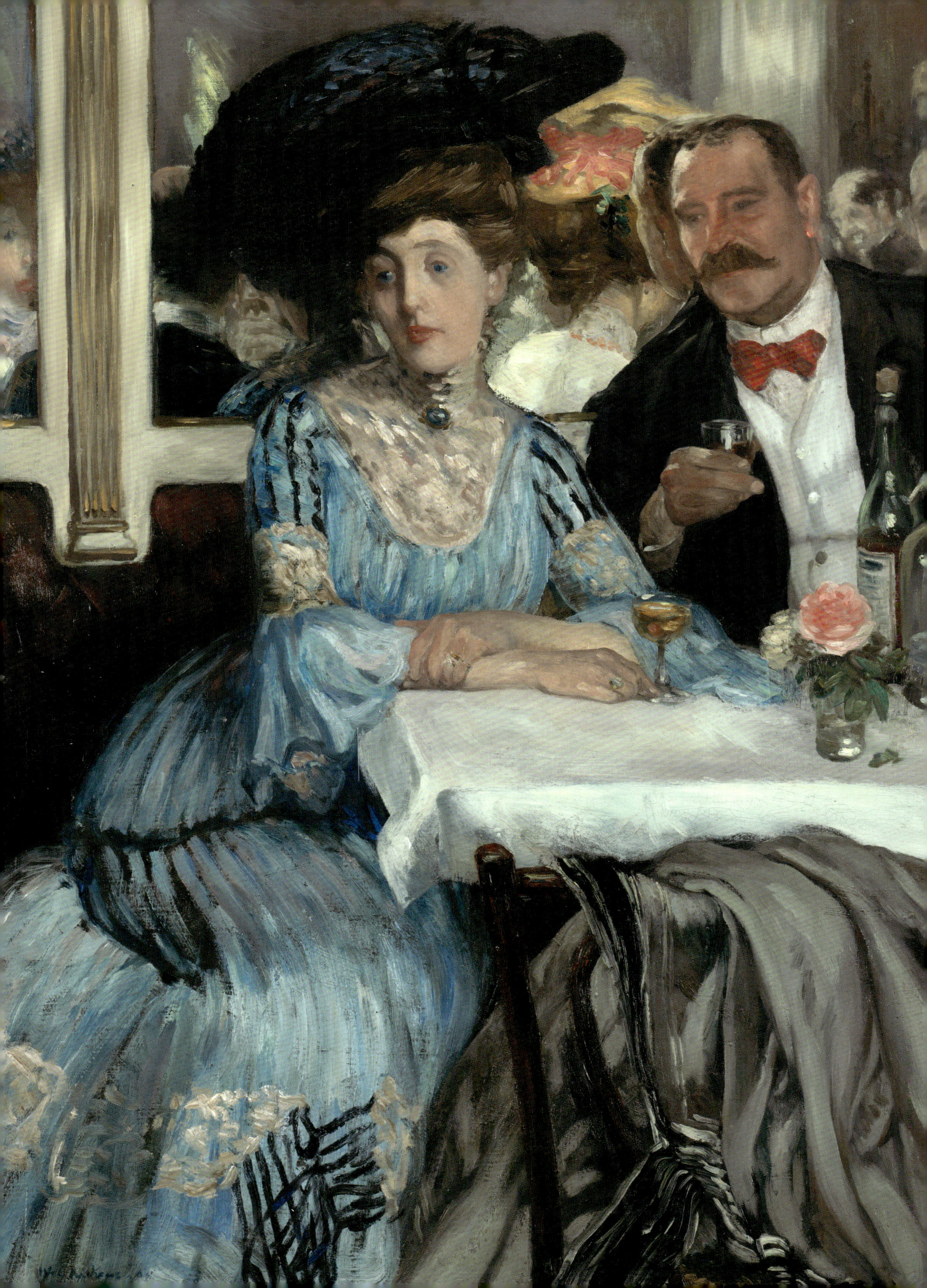

# William J. Glackens and Pierre-Auguste Renoir: Affinities and Distinctions

*Barbara Buhler Lynes*

In 1908, William J. Glackens and seven of his colleagues organized an exhibition of their own work at Macbeth Galleries, New York, to protest the conservatism of the National Academy of Design that had consistently rejected these artists' works from the Academy's annual exhibitions.[1] For Academy jurors, the subjects of these painters' works were too radical: scenes of ordinary daily life in the modern city, people of varying social and economic status, including immigrants, beggars, and figures from the demimonde. Yet, the exhibition caused a sensation, its artists were dubbed "The Eight" and identified as harbingers of a new and progressive American art. Since the 1890s, Glackens had been celebrated as one of America's most distinguished illustrators and was now seen as one of its leading, modern painters.[2]

In reviewing the 1908 exhibition, James J. Huneker referred to the "singular veracity" of Glackens's *At Mouquin's*, 1905 (fig. 25) and that it "slightly evoked" the work of Pierre-Auguste Renoir.[3] He drew stronger parallels between the works of the two artists when referring to Glackens's *Girl with Apple*, 1909–10 (fig. 26), on view at the 1910 Society of Independent Artists exhibition. He asserted that Glackens's "big nude is surprisingly brilliant," while being Renoiresque, "particularly in the color scheme."[4] From this point forward, critics so consistently related the sumptuous colors and feathery brushstrokes in Glackens's work to similar qualities in Renoir's art that he became known long before his death as "the American Renoir."[5]

Those writing subsequently about Glackens's work continued to associate it with Renoir's, some in a complimentary way by arguing for its individuality amidst its dependence on the work of the French artist, while others characterized it pejoratively as slavish imitation. Yet, none was specific about precisely what Glackens borrowed from Renoir, as Richard J.Wattenmaker noted in his 2010 book on American art in the Barnes Foundation: "There is never any analysis of what technically Glackens took from Renoir or what he saw."[6] And in her essay for the 2014 retrospective exhibition, *William Glackens*, co-organized by NSU Art Museum Fort Lauderdale, the Barnes Foundation, and the Parrish Art Museum, Martha Lucy pointed out: "Glackens's debt to Renoir needs to be better understood."[7] Indeed, Glackens's fascination with Renoir's art has been an ongoing topic in Glackens studies since 1908, but the meaning and significance of this important historical phenomenon as it relates to the artist's work have not been sorted out.

In what follows, I will consider Glackens's debt to Renoir from the perspective of the modern art Glackens is known to have seen in New York from 1908, the year the first exhibition of Renoir's work in America took place at the Durand-Ruel Galleries, to 1935, when he completed *The Soda Fountain* (pl. 67), his last monumental painting three years before his death. In assessing the changes that occur in Glackens's art in these decades, which the paintings and prints in the exhibition exemplify, I will relate them to the work

Fig. 25. William J. Glackens
*At Mouquin's*, 1905
Oil on canvas
48 ⅛ x 36 ¼ in. (122.4 x 92.1 cm)
Art Institute of Chicago, Friends of American Art Collection, 1925.295

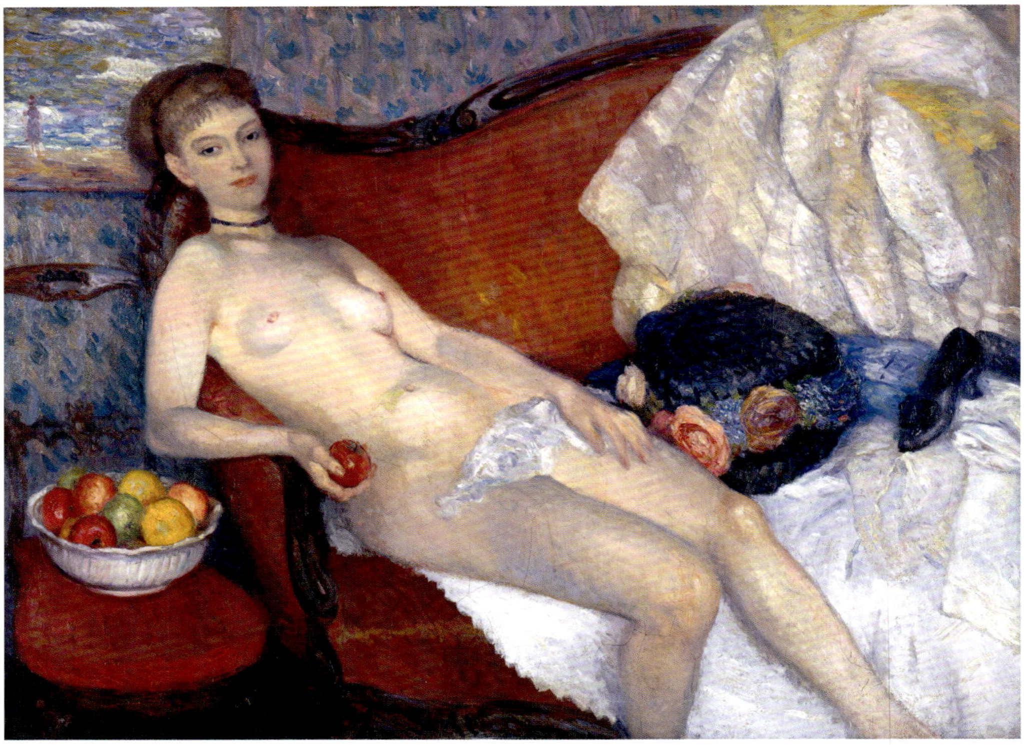

Fig. 26. William J. Glackens
*Girl with Apple*, 1909–10
Oil on canvas
39 7/16 x 56 3/16 in.
(100.2 x 142.7 cm)
Brooklyn Museum, Dick S. Ramsay Fund, 56.70

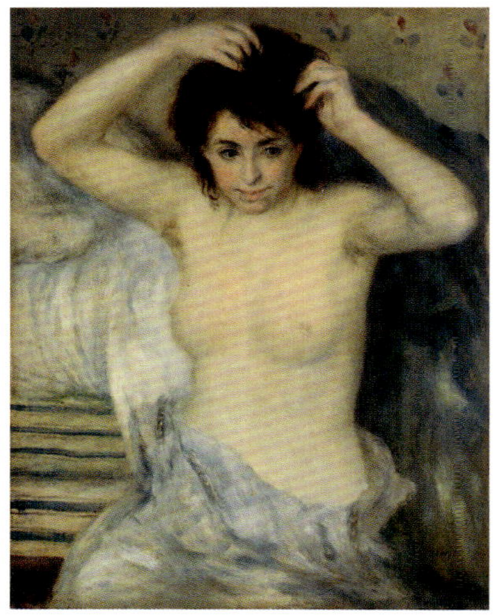

Fig. 27. Pierre-Auguste Renoir
*Before the Bath* [*Avant le bain*], c. 1875
Oil on canvas
32 5/16 x 26 3/16 in. (82 x 66.5 cm)
The Barnes Foundation, Philadelphia, PA, BF9

of other American and European artists Glackens saw in the 1913 *International Exhibition of Modern Art* (the Armory Show) and the modern art collection (to which he had carte blanche access) of his high-school friend, Albert C. Barnes, one of America's leading collectors during the first half of the twentieth century. I will also relate Glackens's work to the art of Charles and Maurice Prendergast and to Italian painting that Glackens saw first-hand in 1926. My discussion will establish that Glackens's *The Soda Fountain* is one of his most innovative and important works because it exemplifies a previously unrecognized development in his art and sheds light on Glackens's ambitions for the emergence of a national art in America.

The 1908 Durand-Ruel Renoir exhibition included 41 paintings dating from 1873–1907. Works in it, like *Before the Bath*, c. 1875 (fig. 27) had an immediate effect on Glackens's art, which can be seen in his *Nude Dressing Her Hair*, 1909 (pl. 37). Both are depictions of semi-nude women, gesturing similarly as they arrange their hair, and each calls attention to the figures' breasts, albeit more directly in the Renoir painting. Glackens's use of blue, his handling of drapery, which bunches around the woman's lower body, the positioning of the figure against a flat, flowered wallpaper, and the intimacy of the scene, parallel these qualities in Renoir's painting.

Each painting's structure pushes figures toward the viewer, a device that was not new to Glackens's work in 1909. He had used it in *Bal Bullier*, c. 1895 (fig. 28), *Seated Actress*, c. 1905 (Sansom Foundation), and *At Mouquin's*, when Glackens's art was influenced by that of Édouard Manet and Edgar Degas. But seeing how Renoir used this device in *Before the Bath*, as well as in other works in the 1908 Renoir exhibition, sharpened Glackens's understanding of this structural device, which he further refined in paintings of 1909 and 1910. In *Semi-Nude with Hat*, c. 1909 (pl. 38) and *Miss Olga D.*, 1910 (pl. 40), figures become quasi-sculptural forms seen against the flatness of either blue or blue and yellow-flowered wallpaper, their frontal poses perhaps recalling that of Renoir's nude in *Before the Bath*.

Colors become increasingly lush in these works, as do their decorative qualities. Bright pigments, rounded or curving shapes repeat, interact, and enliven surfaces. Glackens saw these qualities in many of Renoir's late works (c. 1890–1919) and explored them more extensively in the rhythmic juxtaposition of warm and cool colors and shapes of the monumental painting, *Girl with Apple*. His subject pays homage to the tradition of

Fig. 28. William J. Glackens
*Bal Bullier*, c. 1895
Oil on canvas
23 13/16 x 32 in. (60.5 x 81.3 cm)
Terra Foundation for American Art, Daniel J. Terra Collection, 1999.59

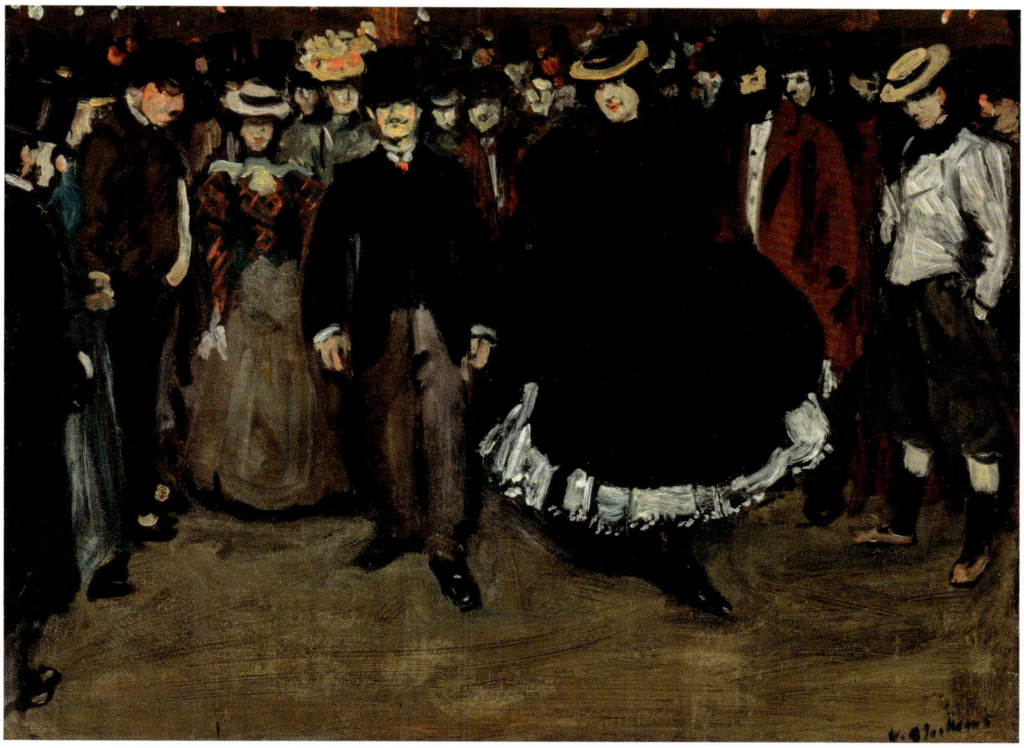

the reclining nude that dates from the sixteenth century with Titian's *Venus of Urbino*, 1538 (Uffizi Gallery), into which Manet breathed new life with *Olympia*, 1863 (Musée d'Orsay). The intensity of reds and red-oranges in Glackens's art from 1909–10 was inspired by the Renoir show he saw in 1908, with works such as *Algerian Girl*, 1881 (Museum of Fine Arts, Boston), *Young Mother*, 1881 (Barnes Foundation), or *Fruits of the Midi*, 1881 (Art Institute of Chicago). But they also recall Fauve color, which Glackens may have seen in an exhibition of Henri Matisse's work in New York that year at Alfred Stieglitz's famous 291 gallery.[8]

Glackens could have also come to know Fauve color through the work of his artist friends Alfred Maurer and Maurice Prendergast. The latter had seen Matisse's 1908 retrospective in Paris, made drawings of his *Le Luxe II*, 1907 (Art Institute of Chicago), and was deeply influenced by Matisse's work. Whatever the case, Glackens's *Cape Cod Pier*, 1908 (NSU Art Museum Fort Lauderdale), completed when he and Prendergast painted together at Cape Cod that year, has long been associated, together with Glackens's *Race Track*, 1908–09 (Barnes Collection), as marking a shift in his palette toward brighter, richer color. The artist's decision to eliminate black from his palette in *Cape Cod Pier* was reversed shortly thereafter, with *Semi-Nude with Hat*. Whether inspired by Renoir or the Fauves, Glackens's subsequent paintings display his developing commitment to lush colors, textures, and decorative patterns.

Glackens's awareness of modern French painting expanded exponentially in February 1912, when Barnes sent him to Paris to purchase art for his then fledgling collection. While there, Glackens visited Leo and Gertrude Stein's collection of avant-garde European art, which included works by Paul Cézanne, Paul Gauguin, Matisse, Pablo Picasso, and Renoir's late work. The five Renoirs Glackens acquired for Barnes were examples of Renoir's late art, choices perhaps inspired by those he saw in Stein's collection. What he purchased, as others have noted, sparked Barnes's passion for Renoir.[9] The lush colors and feathery brushwork of Renoir's *Child Reading*, early 1890s (see fig. 20), and dominance of red and orange in *Woman's Head with Red Hat*, 1890s (fig. 29), both of which Glackens purchased for Barnes, inspired his Renoiresque portraits of his daughter, *Lenna at One Year*, 1914 (pl. 41) and *Lenna Painting*, c. 1918 (pl. 53).

Glackens visited Barnes frequently in the 1910s, where Barnes showed him his latest acquisitions, which included additional purchases of late Renoirs and works by other

American and European modernists. Thus, Glackens was among a handful of American artists who could see and study this extensive collection of modern art, which was shaped by Barnes's passion for Renoir's late work, well before the Museum of Modern Art opened in 1929.[10] Red is an ongoing, sometimes dominant, and occasionally jarring component of the Renoirs Glackens acquired for Barnes. Mary Cassatt had noticed the prevalence of the color in Renoir's art when visiting her friend and disparaged it in a letter to another friend in 1913. She wrote, "[Renoir] is painting pictures or rather studies of huge red women with very small heads which are the most awful imaginable."[11]

A small cadre of important artists, collectors, and critics, however, held these and other components of Renoir's late style in high esteem: Barnes, Leo Stein, Clive Bell, Roger Fry, Walter Pach, Cézanne, Matisse, and Picasso. They admired Renoir's references to classical art that had emerged in his work after his 1881 trip to Italy and the richness of his color, especially red. Renoir synthesized both with the new, gestural, feathery application of paint that had been a mark of French Impressionist art and his own paintings since the mid-1860s. Cézanne, Matisse, and Picasso greatly admired this synthesis of the traditional and modern in Renoir's late work, seeing it as charting a new path for modern art, and it subsequently influenced the work of Matisse and Picasso, who, along with Cézanne, are now considered more important artists than Renoir.[12]

As Chair of the American Section of the Armory Show, Glackens most probably attended the exhibition daily during its three-week run and became increasingly aware of European modern art. The exhibition included works by Pierre Bonnard, Cézanne, Gustave Courbet, Marcel Duchamp, Degas, Gauguin, Matisse, Francis Picabia, Picasso, Renoir, and Vincent van Gogh, among many others. Glackens had purchased works by some of these artists for Barnes in 1912, and the exhibition included Renoir's *Algerian Girl*, which he had first seen in 1908 at Durand-Ruel's. But nothing prepared him or any of the thousands who attended the show for the extraordinary innovations in the European art on display, which demonstrated that American artists were far behind their European colleagues.[13]

This was disconcerting to Glackens, and he subsequently faulted American artists for not being innovative and failing to produce a national art. In a 1913 article in *Arts and Decoration* Glackens stated: "We have no innovators here [America] . . . Everything

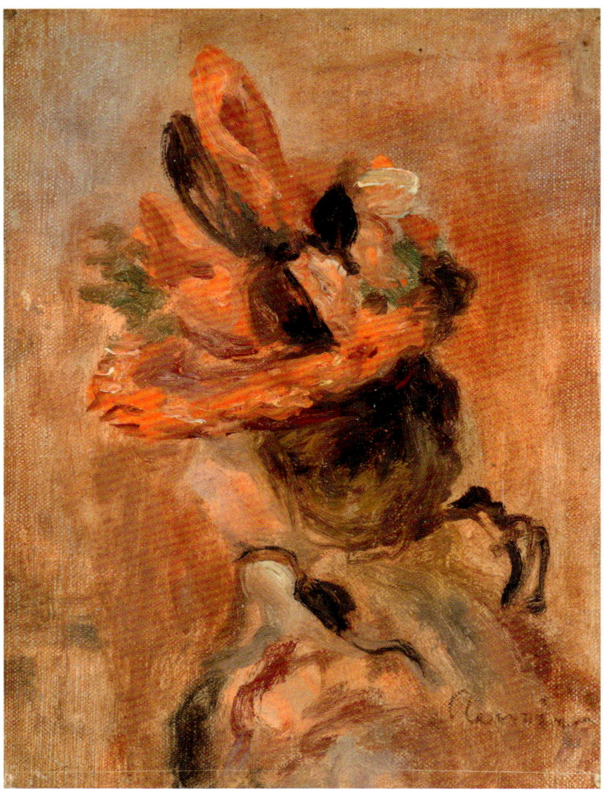

Fig. 29. Pierre-Auguste Renoir
*Woman's Head with Red Hat* [*Tête de femme avec un chapeau rouge*], 1890s
Oil on canvas
5 ⅞ x 4 ¾ in. (15 x 12 cm)
The Barnes Foundation, Philadelphia, PA, BF63

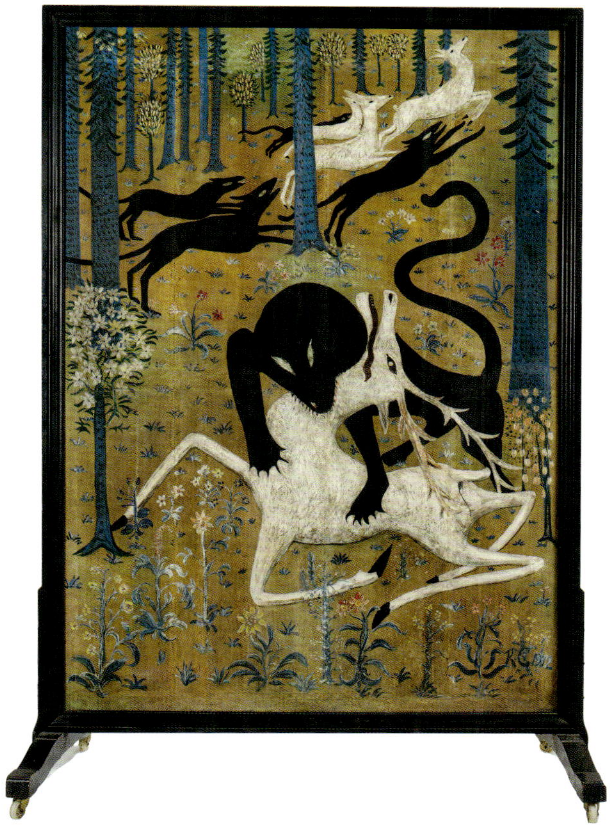

Fig. 30. Robert W. Chanler
*Leopard and Deer*, 1912
Gouache or tempera on canvas mounted on wood
76 ½ x 52 ½ in. (194.3 x 133.4 cm)
Rokeby Collection, Red Hook, NY

worthwhile in our art is due to the influence of French art. We have not yet arrived at a national art. The old idea that American art . . . is to become a fact by the reproduction of local subjects . . . has long since been put to the discard . . . Our own art is arid and bloodless. It is like nothing so much as dry bones. It shows that we are afraid to be impulsive, afraid to forget restraint, afraid above everything to appear ridiculous."[14]

Yet, he was hopeful. He wrote: "But there is a promise of a renaissance in American art. The signs of it are everywhere. This show coming at the psychological moment is going to do us an enormous amount of good."[15] And Glackens, as well as his artist colleague, Arthur B. Davies, suggested new directions for such innovation in their praise for the work of one American artist, Robert Winthrop Chanler. Glackens wrote: "With Mr. Davies, I believe that the exhibits of . . . Chanler are to be one of the most significant features of the American section. He is a young man of enormous vitality, of an enthusiasm that is rare in America, with individuality and a fine sense of the decorative." Similarly, art critic Frank Crowninshield characterized Chanler's work as innovative, explaining why: "Mr. Chanler owes little excepting quality to the artists before him. If the major part of his art has any ancestry it is to be found in Persian rugs, in Japanese prints, or in old missals. He is an Oriental."[16]

Chanler's large, decorative, painted screens, such as *Hopi Indian Snake Dance* (Location Unknown) and *Leopard and Deer*, 1912 (fig. 30), were on view near the exhibition's entrance. Many of the elongated, elegant forms in these works derived from the art of cultures other than European, and Chanler was not alone in this interest. It characterized work on display in the Armory Show by André Derain, Gauguin, the American artist Marsden Hartley, Matisse, and Renoir. Indeed, seeing these works may have been the catalyst for Glackens's decision to experiment with non-Western subject matter.

Between 1914 and 1918, Glackens produced *Indian Series*, which consists of 23 known works (oils, watercolors, and sketches) that depict Indian scenes and motifs. Nineteen are housed at NSU Art Museum Fort Lauderdale, such as *Indian Series (Flautist on Peacock)* (pl. 47).[17] Glackens paints a flautist, who stares at the viewer while seated cross-legged on a peacock, which stands on a bull flanked by dancing nude bathers. Another nude lies amidst water lilies, arms angled to echo the repeating v-shapes of the dancers' bent arms and legs.

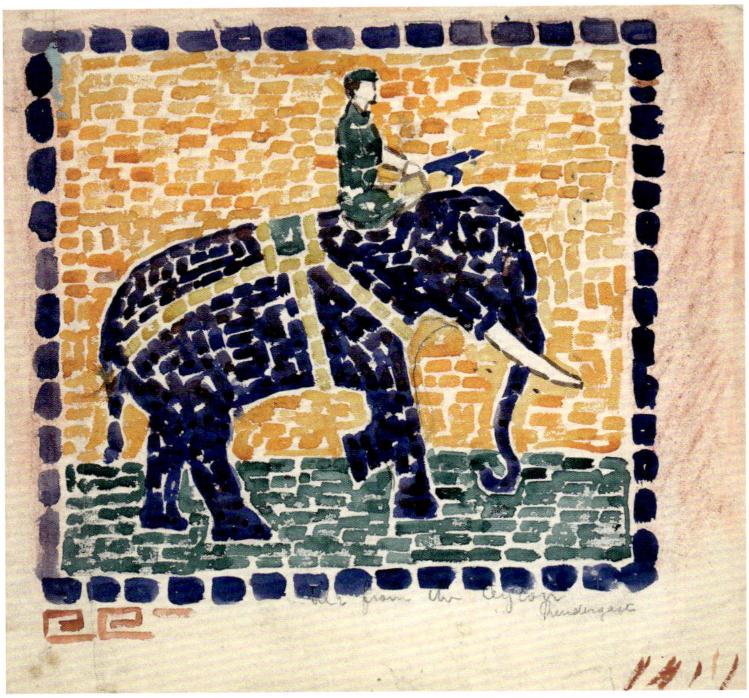

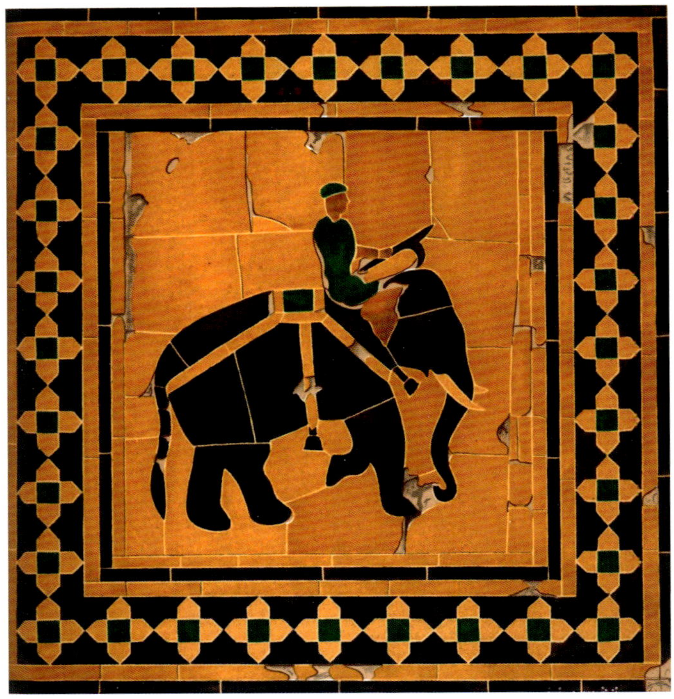

Fig. 31. Maurice Prendergast
*Elephant*, c. 1914
Watercolor and pencil on paper
10 1/16 x 11 1/8 in. (25.5 x 28.3 cm)
Williams College Museum of Art, Williamstown, MA; Gift of Mrs. Charles Prendergast (91.18.4)

Fig. 32. Tile from Lahore Fort, Lahore, Pakistan
Mughal Empire, 16th–17th centuries
Illustration from Vincent A. Smith, *A History of Fine Art in India and Ceylon: From the Earliest Times to the Present Day*, p. 447

Green and orange circular shapes decorate the upper section of the work, creating a pattern of interlocking forms that cut each other off. The flat ovals of green and purple mounds below this decorative band frame the series of circular shapes that halo the central figure. The geometry of these ovals and circles plays off against the sinuous lines of swaying vegetation, yellow snake-like forms, and nudes. The motifs of this highly decorative painting derive from the numerous photographs and illustrations of Indian art in a book by British art historian Vincent A. Smith, *A History of Fine Art in India and Ceylon* (Oxford Press, 1911).[18]

Glackens's turn to non-Western subject matter was prompted by his desire to move his art in a new direction and by his realization that the representation of "local subjects," which had characterized his art since the 1890s, would no longer be considered modern. Smith's book was also a source for Maurice Prendergast, as seen in his *Elephant*, c. 1914 (fig. 31), which imitates its source (fig. 32) directly, as do other Prendergast works of Indian subject matter.[19] Prendergast, his brother Charles, and Glackens had long been friends, but they became neighbors in 1914, when the brothers moved from Boston to New York and into the building where Glackens had a studio at 50 Washington Square South. They occupied the floor above Glackens and began interacting regularly; soon after, Glackens and Maurice worked from the Smith source, most probably side-by-side, each imitating exactly what they saw. For Maurice, Smith's book was a new source for arranging colors in flat patterns that had characterized his earlier work. But for Glackens, it provided motifs for breathing new life into his work, for being "impulsive" and doing something that could be considered "ridiculous."[20]

The close relationship between the three artists fueled Glackens's interest in the decorative, and Maurice may have shown Glackens the drawing he had made of Matisse's *Le Luxe II*, 1907. Prendergast's drawing and other works by Matisse in the Armory Show, which included *Le Luxe II*, may have prompted two Matisse-like paintings by Glackens that Barnes purchased, *Girl with Green Turban*, c. 1913, and *Woman in Red Blouse*, c. 1913–14 (both Barnes Foundation).[21]

The elongated, dancing nudes seen in contour in *Indian Series* (*Flautist on Peacock*) are a further refinement of dancers that Glackens saw in Smith's book and Matisse's art, and they differ dramatically from nudes in Glackens's earlier work, such as *Girl with Apple*, whose frontal, quasi-sculptural, sensual body is bathed in light. Seeing the work of both Prendergasts regularly beginning in 1914 also shaped Glackens's art in the years after the Armory Show.

Charles was a renowned frame maker, and Persian miniatures, Egyptian, Byzantine, and Medieval art had long been sources for the motifs of his carved, gilded frames. His work was in great demand by his artist contemporaries as well as Barnes, who regularly ordered Charles's frames for paintings in his collection. Glackens's increased awareness of motifs in Charles's work that were similar to those in Smith's book led to their collaboration on a wood panel whose motifs Glackens designed and were carved by Charles or both artists, *Indian Series (Wood Panel)*, c. 1914–18 (NSU Art Museum Fort Lauderdale). Through *Indian Series (Flautist on Peacock)*, Glackens realized the quality in his art that Crowninshield had most admired in Chanler's, "his sense of the decorative." Thus, Glackens and the Prendergasts were innovative in that they were the first American artists to introduce Indian art as a subject in their work.[22]

Two works from Glackens's *Indian Series* were listed in the catalogue for the artist's exhibition at the Montross Gallery in 1915. One was titled *Krishna and the Gobis* and the other *Hindu Legend,* and critics noted how they represented a change in Glackens's art.[23] The first may be *Indian Series (Flautist on Peacock)*. The second is probably *Hindu Legend*, the painting Barnes purchased from the show depicting a Brahmin. But Barnes titled it *Decoration* in letters he and Glackens exchanged, which is its current title (fig. 33). Although Barnes clearly admired the new direction Glackens's work had taken, neither he nor Glackens commented on Barnes's purchase of *Decoration*, why Barnes titled it that way, or what had stimulated Glackens's new subject matter. Yet, it marked a new direction in Barnes's thinking, as it was the first example of non-Western subject matter to enter his collection, which subsequently became famous not only for its modern American and European art, but also for objects by artists from Africa, Asia, and the American Southwest. It might be that Barnes's purchase of *Decoration* led to his subsequent fascination with the art of other cultures, just as Glackens's purchase of five Renoir late works in 1912 had sparked Barnes's passion for it.[24]

What Glackens learned from Indian art, Matisse, the Prendergasts, and Renoir paved the way for his splendid major painting, *Artist's Daughter in Chinese Costume*, 1918 (pl. 48). A red and yellow oval chair frames the petite seemingly weightless form of Glackens's five-year old daughter, Lenna, much as Glackens framed the central figure of *Indian Series (Flautist on Peacock)*. His daughter's costume nearly engulfs her, as she stands motionless as if on stage amidst the sumptuousness of heavy red, orange, and yellow curtains, the chair's red and

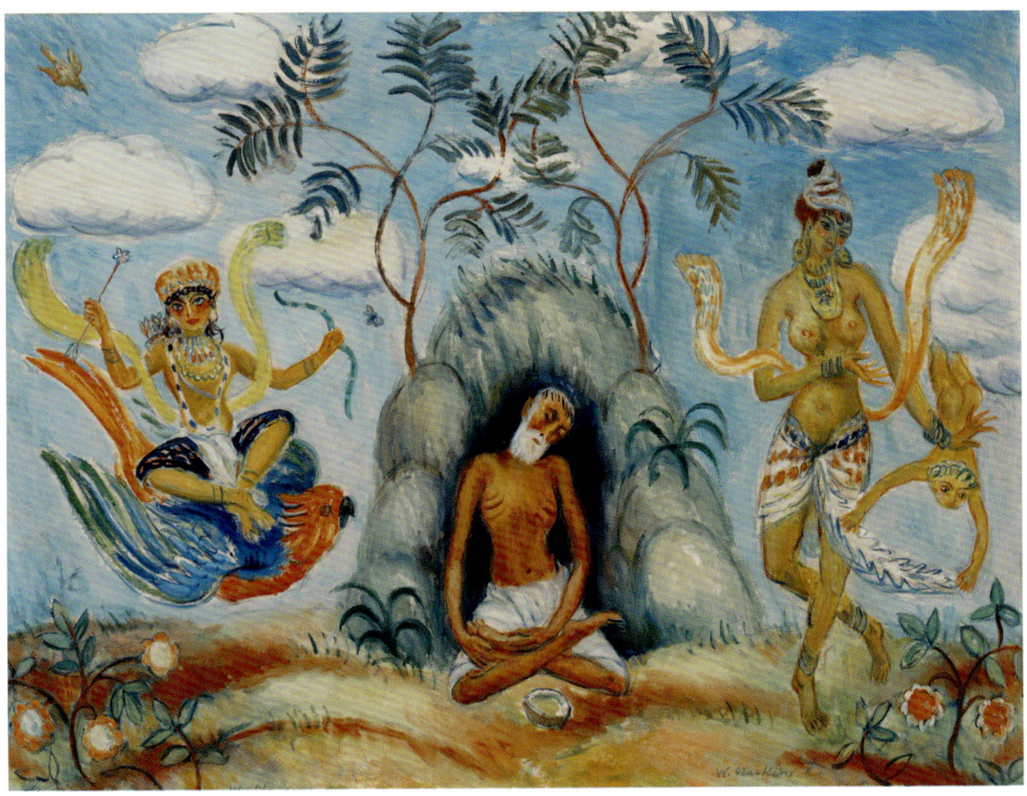

Fig. 33. William J. Glackens
*Decoration*, c. 1914
Oil and tempera on canvas
17 ½ x 23 in. (44.5 x 58.4 cm)
The Barnes Foundation, Philadelphia, PA, BF256

yellow patterned upholstery, and the abstract, geometric patterns of the Oriental rug at her feet. These warm colors reverberate with an intensity that energizes Glackens's painting and distinguishes it from any of his earlier work.

Glackens had been interested in red as a pigment since 1908, when he saw how Renoir used it in works in the Durand-Ruel Renoir exhibition, and red was a dominant color in four of the five Renoir paintings he purchased for Barnes in 1912. Glackens's awareness of this pigment dramatically increased when he saw how other artists used it in works in the Armory Show, such as Renoir's *Algerian Girl*, Hartley's *Still Life No. 1*, 1921 (Columbus Art Museum), Gauguin's *Still Life with Head-Shaped Vase*, 1899 (Tehran Museum of Contemporary Art), and Matisse's *The Red Studio*, 1912 (Museum of Modern Art, New York), *Joaquina*, 1910 (Národní galerie, Prague), and *Red Madras Headdress*, 1912 (Barnes Foundation). Red also played a major role in the Matisse exhibition at the Montross Gallery in 1915, which Glackens undoubtedly saw, in canvases such as *Cyclamen Pourpre*, 1912 (Private Collection), *Nude in the Woods*, 1906 (Brooklyn Museum), which had also been in the Armory Show, *The Studio under the Roof*, 1903 (Location Unknown), and *Goldfish*, 1906 (Pushkin Museum).[25]

Red is also important to Glackens's *Indian Series (Flautist on Peacock)*, as well as other paintings completed while he was working on the *Indian Series* (1914–18), such as *Julia's Sister*, c. 1915 (pl. 45) and *Girl in Red Dress Pinning on Hat*, c. 1915–16 (pl. 46). And he relied on this color to embolden works he completed after 1918, as in his early 1920s paintings of women of different ethnicities and races, such as *Andalusian Woman*, c. 1920s (pl. 58), *Negress in Oriental Costume*, c. 1923 (pl. 60), *Turkish Lady Seated*, c. 1920s (pl. 59), and his portrait of his daughter, *Lenna Dressed as Toy Soldier*, c. 1923 (pl. 57), which calls to mind Renoir's *The Young Soldier*, c. 1880 (pl. 1).

Yet, arguably nothing Glackens painted before or after *Artist's Daughter in Chinese Costume* realizes its lushness of red, implying he had come to think of the pigment as a mark of the modern and made it a subject of his painting, much as Matisse did in *The Red Studio*. The repeating decorative patterns in Glackens's painting lend it a new degree of abstraction. Indeed, *Artist's Daughter in Chinese Costume*'s richness, its weightless, nearly two-dimensional Lenna, and her Chinese costume convey the sense of the "Oriental" that Crowninshield had admired in Chanler's work.

Parallels between this work and Renoir's are unmistakable. The red-oranges of *Artist's Daughter in Chinese Costume* are similar to those in Renoir's portrait of his son, in *Claude Renoir in Clown Costume*, 1909 (Musée de l'Orangerie), and the fact that both artists made their family subjects in their work marked another affinity between them. This is evident in the seven Glackens portraits and eight by Renoir in this exhibition. Indeed, Renoir made lithographs from drawings of his family and friends that were sold as portfolios, entering American museums as early as 1925. *Paul Cézanne*, c. 1902, *Claude Renoir, Head Lowered*, c. 1904, and *Auguste Rodin*, c. 1910 (pls. 17, 18, 29), and five other works from the portfolio are in the exhibition (pls. 8, 14, 21, 23, 30). There is also a bronze relief from a marble sculpture, *Head of Coco*, 1908 (pl. 27), one of two sculptures Renoir made before he began working with an assistant.

Barnes greatly admired both artists' work. He purchased his first Glackens in 1912 and owned 71 examples of his art at the time of his death; during the same period, he acquired 181 Renoirs. It disturbed Barnes that Glackens was perceived as copying Renoir. He defended his friend against this charge, as he explains in a 1917 letter to Glackens when describing his reaction to a conversation overheard while attending an exhibition. He wrote: "I interrupted a conversation between her (Miss Thompson), Mrs. Gwynne and Mr. Stevenson, who I understand is a portrait painter, and whom I heard remark to Miss Thompson that your pictures are imitation Renoirs. I did not have the opportunity to tell the bastard what I thought of his appearance, his profession and his opinions."[26]

Glackens readily admitted his debt to Renoir in a letter to Barnes in 1924: "My Renoir influence is obvious, so I shan't mention it except that I have found out that the pursuit of color is hard on drawing just as the pursuit of drawing is hard on color. Renoir survived but who else!"[27] But when questioned by a critic about the influence of Renoir on his work, a seemingly embarassed Glackens shrugged it off, supposedly stating: "Can you think of a better man to follow than Renoir?," knowing full well that the sources of his work were far more extensive than his debt to Renoir and thus not imitations of the French master's art.[28]

Barnes commented on his friend's attitude about being faulted as an imitator of Renoir's art in a 1921 letter to Leo Stein, where he expressed his admiration for Glackens's work and his faith in its potential: "Glackens is going along on his own hook totally impervious to the thoughts and criticism of anybody else; the result is that he is doing some stuff that is really his own and that I think will live forever."[29] And he voiced similar praise for Glackens in a more elaborate appreciation written after Glackens won the Temple Gold Medal for *The Temple Gold Nude*, c. 1918 (Private Collection) exhibited that year at the Pennsylvania Academy of the Fine Arts.[30]

Barnes addressed Glackens's debt to Renoir, while staunchly defending the individuality and the distinctiveness of his work: " [Glackens's work] is the faithful expression of a personality which is itself rare . . . It is [the] very personal qualities of Glackens that any writer who would do justice to his work must be able to recognize, analyze and describe . . . that they are faithful expressions of his own reactions to life. . . . For color, the skillful, joyous use of brilliant, strong moving color, the only man of this generation who can be said to be his equal was Renoir. His psychology is so near that of Renoir, he saw the world in so nearly the same terms, that he has been much influenced by Renoir, especially in the use of color . . . but those of us who have lived with the work of both men long enough to know the characteristics of each, never would mistake one for the other nor admit that Glackens is either an imitator of Renoir or less of an individual artist because he has expressed himself in color."[31]

Glackens received the prestigious Temple Gold Medal the year before he moved with his family to France, where they lived with occasional returns to the United States from 1925 until 1932, an interlude in America later marked by the onset of the Great Depression. When Glackens arrived in France, the popularity of Renoir's art had soared in light of his recent death. Interestingly, Glackens soon completed a family portrait, *Breakfast Porch*, 1925 (pl. 61), in which he began to turn his art away from elements that could be associated with Renoir's. Although the bright colors of *Breakfast Porch* relate to Renoir's palette, Glackens's painting is overtly Matisse-like in its structure, as in Matisse's *The Music Lesson*, 1917 (Barnes Foundation). Barnes bought the Matisse in 1923, and Glackens could have seen and been inspired by the painting before moving to France. The dark rectangular shape behind Glackens's wife that separates pinkish-purple curtains flanked by shutters, establishes an opening in the back of the painting paralleling that in Matisse's painting. The open curtains behind Lenna in *Artist's Daughter in Chinese Costume* form a similar space, which is further developed in *Negress in Oriental Costume*. But in the *Breakfast Porch*, it becomes a series of interlocking geometric shapes as in Matisse's painting. Moreover, Glackens's figures are Matisse-like in their flatness and detachment from one another.[32]

Paintings Glackens subsequently completed in France, such as *The Promenade*, 1927 (pl. 62), *Back of Nude*, c. 1930s (pl. 63), *Bowlers, La Ciotat*, 1930 (pl. 64), and *St. Jean*, 1930 (pl. 65), represent a further departure from Renoir's work, which can be related to Glackens's first trip to Italy, where he and his family spent a month in 1926. They visited Assisi, Florence, Naples, Orvieto, Padua, Perugia, Pompeii, Siena, Rome, and Venice.[33] Glackens's figures in these paintings become increasingly solid and volumetric, characteristics that were hinted at in canvases he created shortly before he moved to France, as in *Lenna with Rabbit Hound*, c. 1922 (pl. 56). This component of *The Promenade* and *Back of Nude* can be related to the similarly solid, volumetric forms in Renoir's late work, such as *Seamstress at Window*, c. 1908–10 (pl. 25), *Portrait of Mme. Thurneyssen and Her*

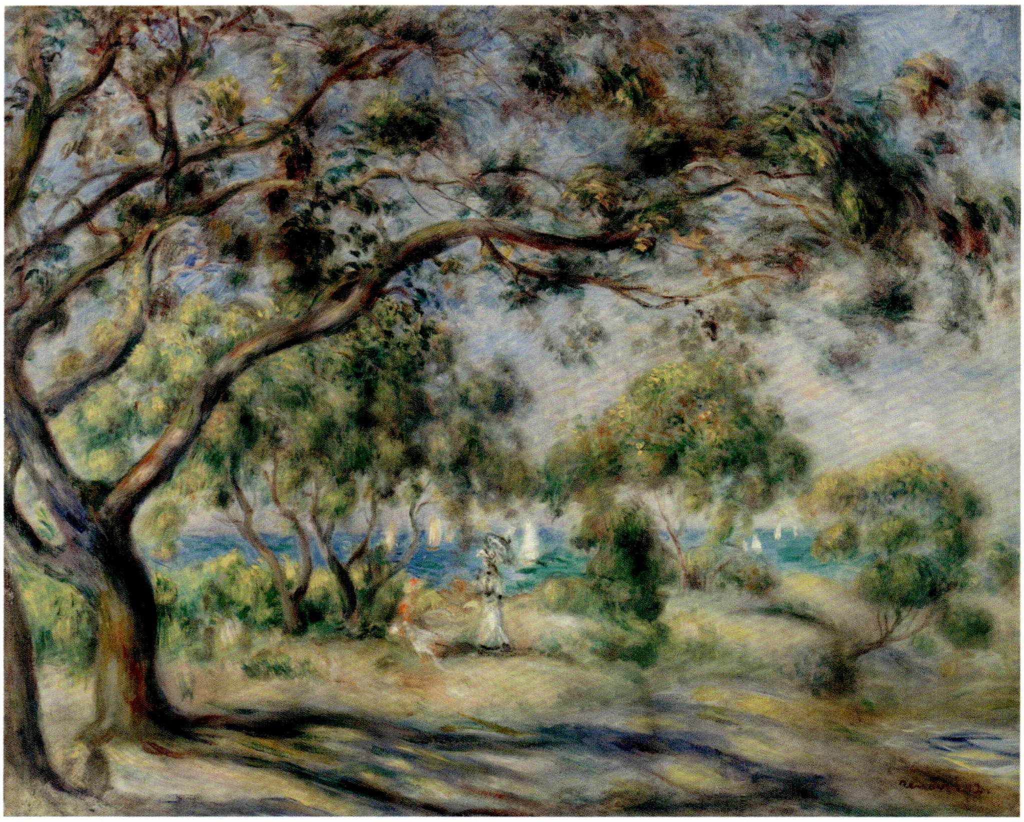

Fig. 34. Pierre-Auguste Renoir
*Woods at la Chaise [Bois de la Chaise (Noirmoutier)]*, 1892
Oil on canvas
25 13/16 x 31 7/8 in. (65.5 x 81 cm)
The Barnes Foundation,
Philadelphia, PA, BF163

*Daughter*, 1910 (pl. 26), *Woman at the Corner Stove* 1912 (pl. 31), and *Mlle. Estable*, 1912 (pl. 33). But they can also be related to paintings Glackens saw in Italian churches and museums, many of which present the Virgin as a frontal, iconic, volumetric, and monumental form, such as Giotto's *Ognissanti Madonna*, 1306 (Uffizi Gallery, originally in the church of San Salvatore di Ognissanti). Such works may have inspired the frontal Lenna, whose expressionless face and body loom before us in *The Promenade*. Certainly, Glackens had seen examples of Italian oil and panel painting in various museums in America and Europe. But seeing Italian art in situ made a great impression on Glackens's thinking about his work, just as it had Renoir's during his visit to Italy many decades earlier.

In Rome, Glackens became interested in classical sculpture, as in his *Sketch of Venus of Cnidus*, 1926 (NSU Art Museum Fort Lauderdale). And in Venice, he admired the work of Giovanni Bellini, Giorgione, Tintoretto, and Titian, especially their handing of nudes, which he emulates in *Back of Nude*. Glackens positions his model, who arranges her hair, in a non-descript, slightly illusional space, which relates it to the nebulous environments of Renoir's late paintings. But Glackens rejects the distortions of figures in Renoir's late work: heavy, ponderous, out-of-proportion women, as in *Bather*, 1912 (pl. 32) and *Bare-Breasted Sleeping Woman*, 1919 (pl. 35).

Another new compositional element in Glackens's work following his trip to Italy was his use of linear perspective. In *The Promenade*, for example, trees and architectural forms flanking the centralized, frontally positioned figure decrease in size as they appear further away. In earlier landscape paintings, Glackens nearly always blocked views into deep space with architectural and landscape forms, as in *Pier at Blue Point*, 1914 (pl. 43). Glackens depicts deep space regularly in beach or shore scenes, as in *The Little Pier*, 1914 (pl. 42), *Summer*, 1914 (pl. 44), *Beach Scene, New London*, 1918 (pl. 49) and *Boat Landing at Gloucester*, c. 1918 (pl. 50).[34]

Glackens further develops receding space in *Bowlers, La Ciotat*, especially on the right side of the composition, and such recession is a feature of Glackens's *St. Jean*, where a triangular wedge of land defines the far distance. This compositional device also informs Renoir's *Woods at la Chaise (Noirmoutier)*, 1892 (fig. 34) that Barnes purchased in 1914.

Glackens's interest in linear perspective could have also been stimulated by the work of Italian artists, whose masterful handling of it dissolves pictorial surfaces into illusions of infinitely receding space, as in the work of Giorgione and Titian.

The geometric shapes and colors of *St. Jean* recall paintings of the Southern French landscape by Cézanne and Renoir, as in the Renoirs in this exhibition: *Moulin Huet Bay, Guernsey*, c. 1883 (pl. 2), *Tamaris, France*, c. 1885 (pl. 3), and *Springtime in Essoyes*, c. 1900 (pl. 16). These characteristics, however, are also what the area's landscape and architectural forms look like. Yet, the pastel colors of Glackens's *St. Jean* are another new component of his art that first emerged in his *Bowlers, La Ciotat* – a change in his palette. This development may have been inspired by his first-hand awareness of Italian fresco paintings, such as those by Giotto in the Arena Chapel, Padua, the seeing of which, according to Glackens's son, Ira, had been his father's reason for going to Italy.[35]

Glackens continues to use this pastel-like palette in *The Soda Fountain*, completed three years after his return to the United States, and its juxtaposition of broad areas of orange and yellow seem to derive specifically from Giotto's narrative scenes, where orange and red are seen next to one another in *The Visitation*, *Judas's Betrayal*, *The Last Supper*, as well as *The Arrest of Christ (Kiss of Judas)*, among other vignettes. The increased solidity and volume of the women in *The Soda Fountain* also characterize figures in Giotto's frescoes, who appear in nearly bas-relief against flat backgrounds. The heightened geometric structure of Glackens's *The Soda Fountain* can also be related to that of Giotto's narrative scenes as well as to that in works by other Italian artists, such as Masaccio and the High Renaissance masters.

While Glackens's *The Soda Fountain* suggests his assimilation of Italian sources, in it he also looks back to his own work by re-introducing the quality that had first distinguished him in the last decades of the nineteenth century as one of America's most important illustrators – that is, his ability to capture the momentary, the here and now with gesture. One of the women in *The Soda Fountain* rests her gloved hand on her hip, thus calling attention to the curves of her sensual body, while the other woman in the painting absent-mindedly wipes the corner of her full, red lips with the pointed tip of a white napkin. Gesture had been absent from Glackens's monumental paintings since the 1910s. His renewed interest in it may have been inspired by its prominence in Giotto's Arena Chapel frescoes. However, Glackens does not use gesture to unite, as Giotto does with figures who embrace and look at one another. Rather, Glackens's figures seem unaware of one another despite their proximity, thus suggesting the anonymity and isolation of modern city life.

Glackens's painting of people enjoying themselves in moments of leisure is a "local subject," like those that had first distinguished him as a modern painter in the early 1900s, and it recalls his celebrated *At Mouquin's*. Glackens had rejected "local subjects" in 1913, but by 1935, he reversed his thinking by choosing a subject that resonates as particularly American – a soda fountain. Although the soda fountain machine was invented in Europe, soda fountain shops flourished primarily in America. Did he consider the synthesis in *The Soda Fountain* of its American subject, of new Italian sources, and references to his own earlier art, the realization of art free of "the French"? Did he feel that the synthesis of the new and old in *The Soda Fountain* paralleled that in Renoir's late painting that Glackens understood as charting a new direction in modern art? Did he feel he had realized a new national art that he had long anticipated emerging in America despite his painting's reference to *At Mouquin's*, which in turn recalls Manet's *A Bar at the Folies Bergère* and binds Glackens's painting to "the French"? Did he depict well-fed, seemingly sated figures in an American environment in hope that America would emerge from the devastations of the Depression? Or, could Glackens have painted *The Soda Fountain* as "an 'up-to-date' *At Mouquin's* to prove himself against newer figures on the contemporary art scene," as William H. Gerdts proposed in 1996?[36]

Glackens's intentions in *The Soda Fountain* may never be known, but it is clear that his thinking in 1935 could have paralleled Gerdts's suggestion. Glackens had long been in the limelight as a leading American modernist, and after the Armory Show, had consciously turned his art in what he thought was a new and modern direction. He had been out of the country except for occasional visits from 1925–32, and he may have wanted to reassert himself among his colleagues. Yet, Glackens had no reason to prove himself, as he had been known for almost 30 years as a prominent American artist, had won many prizes for his work, and his paintings had been exhibited nationally and internationally. Major American museums had recently made his work part of their collections, and beginning in 1924, what would become one of America's showcases for American art, Kraushaar Galleries, began representing his work.[37] Moreover, the "local subject" of *The Soda Fountain* and its figures share qualities with paintings of the 1930s by many of his contemporaries, who were also seeking a national art.[38]

Had Glackens wanted to "prove himself" among his contemporaries after his return from France, he would have had to move his art in a completely new direction. While *The Soda Fountain*'s interlocking geometric shapes and central pyramid-like structure lend this representational work an uncanny degree of modernist abstraction, it would not have occurred to Glackens to abandon the representational. It would be another decade before Jackson Pollock and the New York School of painters, later known as Abstract Expressionists, achieved a national art that could prevail on the international stage. But Glackens must have been very satisfied with *The Soda Fountain* because it meshed old and new, and because in its synthesis of color and line he had resolved the struggle he had mentioned when writing to Barnes in 1924. Moreover, late in his career, and especially in this painting, he had realized his own, distinctive style. Although Renoir's influence still echoes in this masterpiece, it melds with the many other sources Glackens absorbed through a lifetime of studying and learning from great artists of the past as well as his contemporaries. Indeed, as Barnes had predicted, Glackens had gone along on "his own" to realize a painting that would "live forever," powered perhaps because, unlike what Barnes had proposed to Leo Stein, Glackens was not "impervious to the thoughts and criticism" of those who had labeled him "the American Renoir."

1. The other artists were Arthur B. Davies, Robert Henri, Ernest Lawson, George Luks, Maurice Prendergast, Everett Shinn, and John Sloan.
2. Glackens decided to chart his way as a painter in the mid-1890s after attaining success as an illustrator.
3. See James G. Huneker, "Eight Painters," *New York Sun*, February 10, 1908, 6.
4. See James G. Huneker, "Around the Galleries," *New York Sun*, April 7, 1910, 6.
5. See Anne E. Dawson, *Pierre-Auguste Renoir and Modern Painting* (San Diego: San Diego Museum of Art, 2002), 41.
6. See Richard J. Wattenmaker, *American Paintings and Works on Paper in the Barnes Foundation* (Merion: The Barnes Foundation, in association with Yale University Press, 2012), 107. For a discussion of how works by Glackens and Renoir are similar or different in terms of "illustration . . . decoration and the expression of broad human qualities," see Violette de Mazia, "The Case of Glackens vs. Renoir," *The Barnes Foundation Journal of the Art Department* 2, no. 2 (Autumn 1971), 3–30.
7. See Martha Lucy, "Glackens, French Art, and the Language of Modernism," in *William Glackens*, ed. Avis Berman (New York and Philadelphia: Skira Rizzoli Publications, Inc., and The Barnes Foundation, 2014), 198–206.
8. "Drawings, Lithographs, Watercolors, Etchings: Henri Matisse," 291 Fifth Avenue Gallery of the Photo-Secession, New York, December 1–30, 1908.
9. Martha Lucy, "Grappling with Renoir's Modernism in the Collection of Dr. Barnes," and "Collecting Renoir: A Chronology: 1912–1942," in *Renoir in the Barnes Foundation* (New Haven: Yale University Press, in association with The Barnes Foundation, 2012), 21–45 and 346–53.
10. Glackens could also see examples of modern European art in A. E. Gallatin's Gallery of Living Art, now the Grey Art Gallery, New York University, which opened in 1927.
11. See Nicholas Wadley and Michael Hoog, *Renoir un peintre, une vie, une œuvre*, ed. Nicholas Wadley, preface Michael Hoog (Paris: Belfond, 1989), 257–58.
12. See John House, "Renoir: Between Modernist and Tradition," and Lucy in *Renoir in the Barnes Foundation*, 1–20 and 21–46; Laurence Madeline, "Picasso 1917 to 1924: A 'Renoirian Crisis,'" and Roger Benjamin, "Why did Matisse Love Late Renoir," in Claudia Einecke and Roger Benjamin, *Renoir in the 20th Century* (Ostfildern: Hatje Cantz, 2010), 122–35 and 136–45; and Claudine Grammont, "Matisse in the Laboratory of Dr. Barnes: How and Why Barnes Collected Matisse," in *Matisse in the Barnes Foundation*, ed. Yve-Alain Bois (Merion and London: The Barnes Foundation and Thames & Hudson, 2015), vol. 1, 28–41. For a discussion of the role others played in shaping Barnes's taste, see Colin B. Bailey, "The Origins of the Barnes Collection, 1912–15," *Burlington Magazine* 150, no. 1265 (August 2008), 534–43, and Wattenmaker, 65–70.
13. For the most recent discussions of the Armory Show and its works, see Marilyn Kushner, Kimberly Orcutt, Casey Blake et al., *The Armory Show at 100: Modernism and Revolution* (New York: Giles, 2015), and http://armory.nyhistory.org/about/ blogsit.
14. See William Glackens, "The American Section: The National Art, An Interview with the Chairman of the Domestic Committee, William J. Glackens," in the special exhibition issue, edited by Guy Pène du Bois, *Arts & Decoration* 3, no. 5 (March 1913), 159–64.
15. Ibid., 162.
16. Frank Crowninshield is quoted in "America's Most Imaginative Decorator," in *Current Opinion* 57 (July–December 1914), 427. For a recent consideration of Chanler's art, see Gina Wouters, *Robert Winthrop Chanler: Discovering the Fantastic* (New York: The Monacelli Press, 2016), 17.
17. When this painting entered the museum's collection in 2001, it was titled *Budda and the Maidens* and, along with other works in the *Indian Series*, was gifted to the museum by the Sansom Foundation. These works remained relatively unknown in Glackens's work until they were shown in the exhibition I organized, *William Glackens: A Modernist in the Making*, NSU Art Museum Fort Lauderdale, September 4, 2015 – January 14, 2018.
18. Wattenmaker associated the Glackens in the Barnes Foundation, *Decoration*, 1915 with the Smith book by reproducing one of the drawings Glackens made from it, but he did not mention the other drawings and paintings derived from this source.
19. See Nancy Mowll Mathews, "Maurice Prendergast and the Influence of European Modernism," in Nancy Mowll Mathews and Gwendolyn Owens, *Maurice Brazil Prendergast, Charles Prendergast, A Catalogue Raisonné* (Williamstown: Williams College Museum of Art and Munich: Prestel, 1990), 35–46. *Elephant* is dated c. 1912–15 (cat. 1162), but it most probably was completed c. 1914 and is dated as such here. Others in the catalogue that derive from Smith's book that are dated c. 1910–12, such as cats. 1130, 1132, 1134, also most probably date from c. 1914.
20. See Charles Prendergast to John Quinn, June 24, 1914 and November, 1914, John Quinn Papers, New York Public Library.
21. The date of Barnes's purchase of the first work is unknown, but he purchased the second in 1915. See Wattenmaker, 87, 90.
22. Indian motifs had been explored by Marsden Hartley in his painting *Portrait of Berlin*, 1913 (Yale Collection of American Literature, Beinecke Rare Book and Manuscript Library, Yale University, New Haven, Ct.), which includes a depiction of the Buddha sculpture he purchased in Berlin, but it is a motif rather than the subject of the work.
23. See "Moderns at the Montross Gallery," *Arts & Decoration* 5, no. 7 (May 1915), 286.
24. Other artists whose works in the exhibition treated Native American subjects were Marsden Hartley, Charles Rumsey, Myra Musselmann Carr, Edith Yandell, and Nessa Cohen Sunrise.
25. *Henri Matisse Exhibition*, Montross Gallery, New York, January 26 – February 27, 1915.
26. Albert C. Barnes to William J. Glackens, January 17, 1917, Albert C. Barnes Correspondence, Barnes Foundation Archives, Philadelphia, PA. Reprinted with permission, subsequently referred to as BFA.
27. See William J. Glackens to Albert C. Barnes, 1924, BFA.
28. See Vincent J. de Gregorio, "The Life and Art of William J. Glackens," Ph.D. dissertation (Ann Arbor: University Microfilms, 1955), 270.
29. Albert C. Barnes to Leo Stein, January 18, 1921, BFA.
30. This prestigious award was made from 1883 to 1968. For information on the date of the painting, see Richard J. Wattenmaker, "The Art of William Glackens," Ph.D. Dissertation (Ann Arbor: University Microfilms, 1972), 309, n. 2.
31. Albert C. Barnes, "The Art of William Glackens," BFA.
32. See *Matisse in the Barnes Foundation*, 172–73. In Glackens's *Finnish Woman*, 1920 (pl. 54), *Hallie Knitting in Red Hat*, c. 1920 (pl. 55), and *The Temple Gold Nude*, paintings line the walls, which may have been a nod to Matisse's *The Red Studio*.
33. See Ira Glackens, *William Glackens and the Eight: The artists who freed American art* (New York: Horizon Press, 1983), 203–04.
34. An exception is *Flying Kites, Montmartre*, 1906 (Museum of Fine Arts, Boston).
35. Ira Glackens, 204.
36. See William H. Gerdts, *William Glackens* (Fort Lauderdale, New York: NSU Art Museum and Abbeville Press, 1996), 73.
37. The Metropolitan Museum of Art purchased Glackens's *Central Park, Winter*, c. 1905, in 1921; Art Institute of Chicago, *At Mouquin's*, 1905, in 1925; Duncan Phillips, *Bathers at Bellport*, 1912, in 1929; the Detroit Institute of Art, *The Promenade*, 1927, in 1930; the Whitney Museum of American Art *Fête de Souquet*, 1933, in 1933 (later deaccessioned).
38. Syntheses between the old and new also occur in the work of, among others, Thomas Hart Benton, Reginald Marsh, and Charles Sheeler, whether from the art of Michelangelo or American Shaker furniture. I want to thank my colleague, Bonnie Clearwater, for her valuable suggestions on this point. See also the discussion of *The Soda Fountain* by Carol Troyen, "From the Stage to the Parlor: Glackens's Images of Women," in Berman, *William Glackens*, 112.

# Works

## Pierre-Auguste Renoir

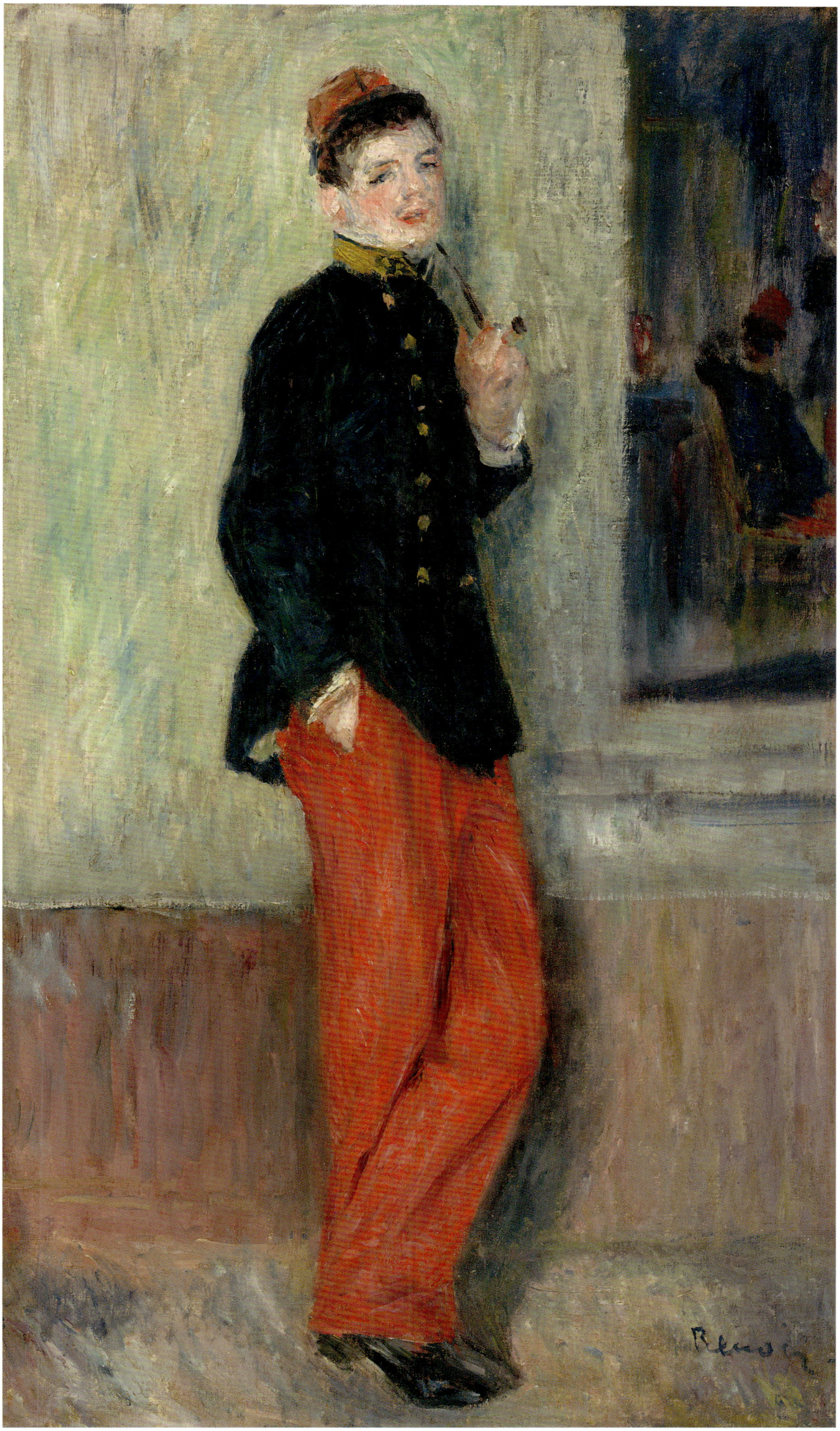

*Previous page*
1. Pierre-Auguste Renoir
*The Young Soldier* [*Le jeune militaire*], c. 1880
Oil on canvas
21 5/8 x 13 in. (54.93 x 33.02 cm)

2. Pierre-Auguste Renoir
*Moulin Huet Bay, Guernsey* [*La Baie du Moulin Huet, Guernesey*], c. 1883
Oil on canvas
11 1/2 x 21 1/4 in. (29.2 x 54 cm)

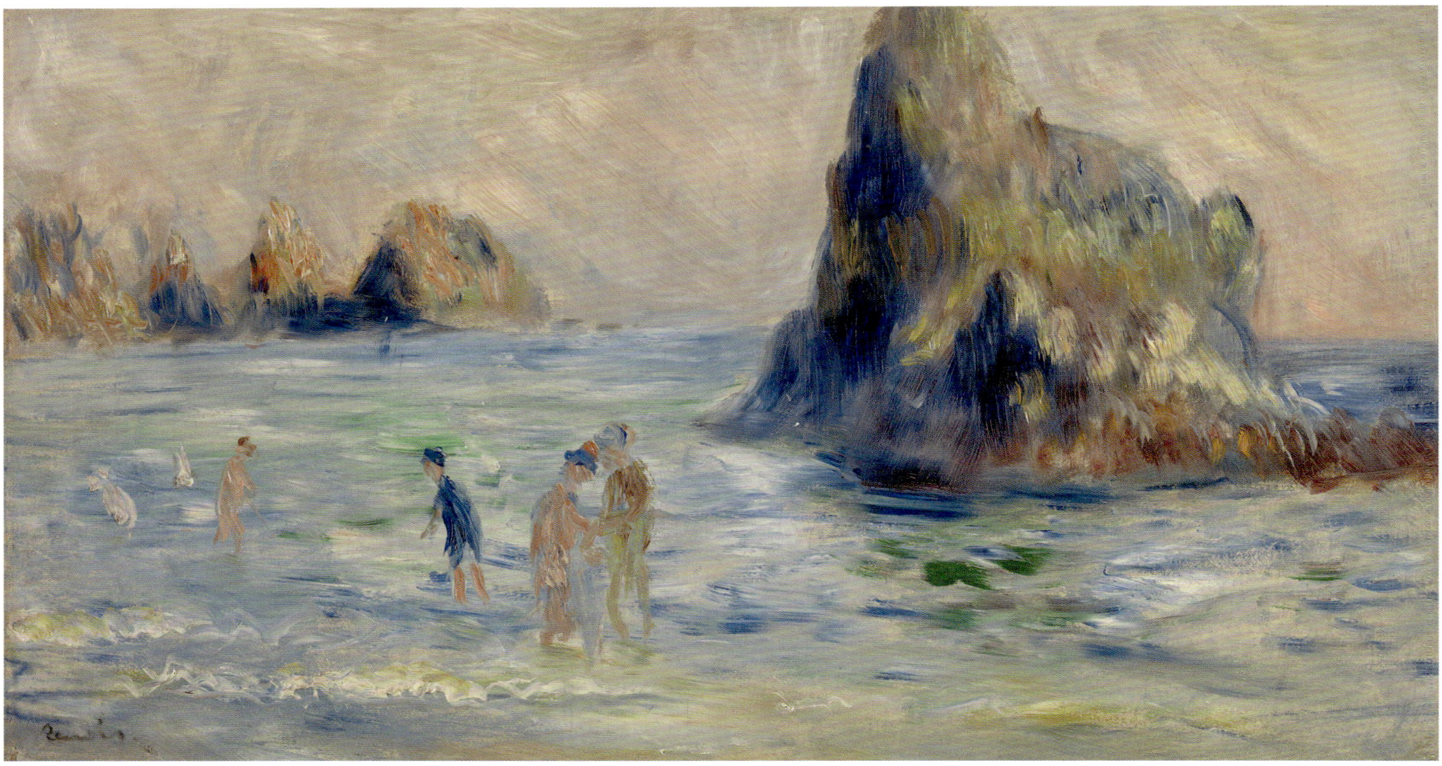

3. Pierre-Auguste Rencir
*Tamaris, France*, c. 1885
Oil on canvas
18 x 21 ⅝ in. (45.72 x 54.93 cm)

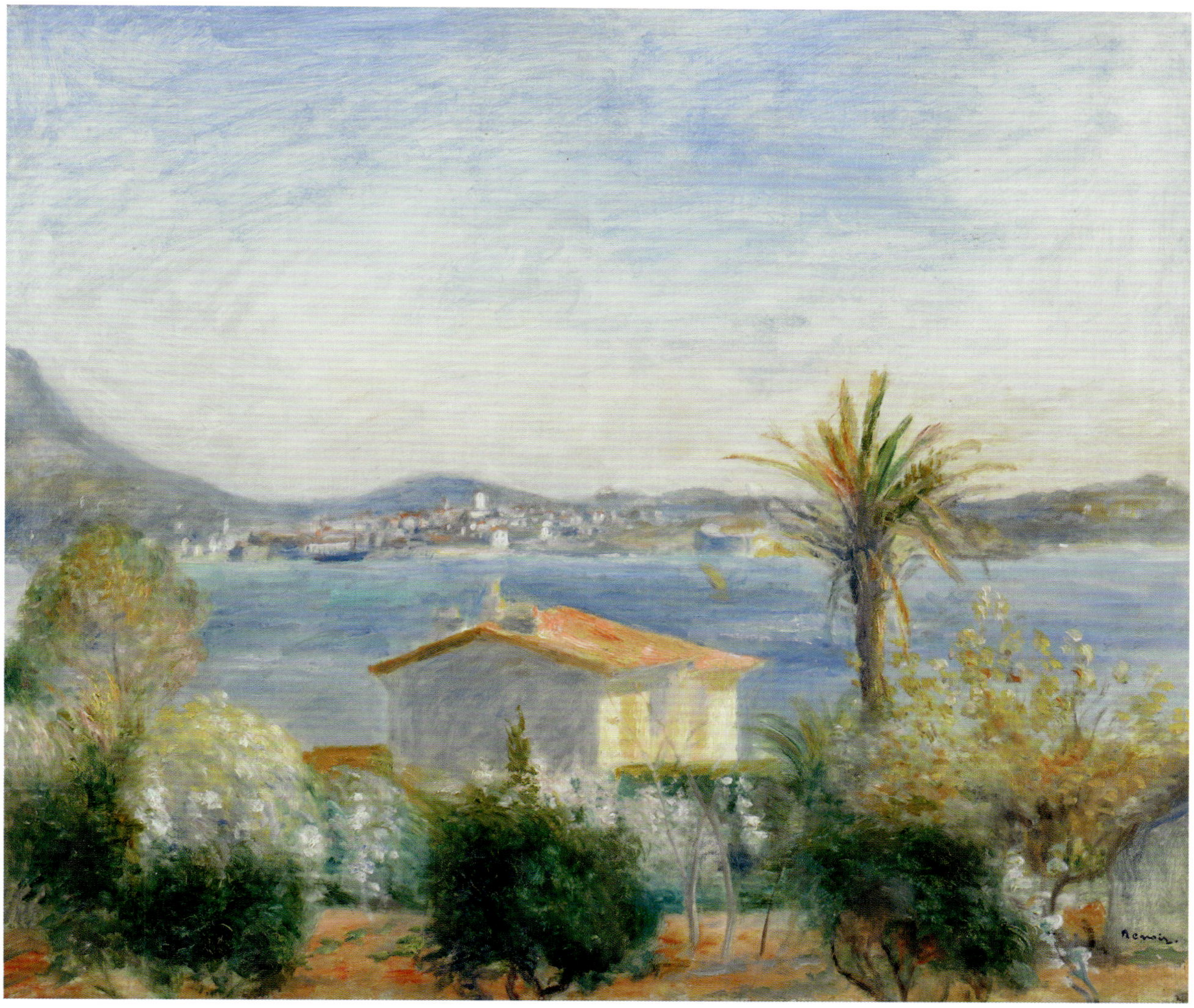

4. Pierre-Auguste Renoir
*Young Girls Styling Themselves*
[*Jeunes filles se coiffant*], c. 1885–90
Pastel on paper
31 1/8 x 24 3/8 in. (79 x 62 cm)

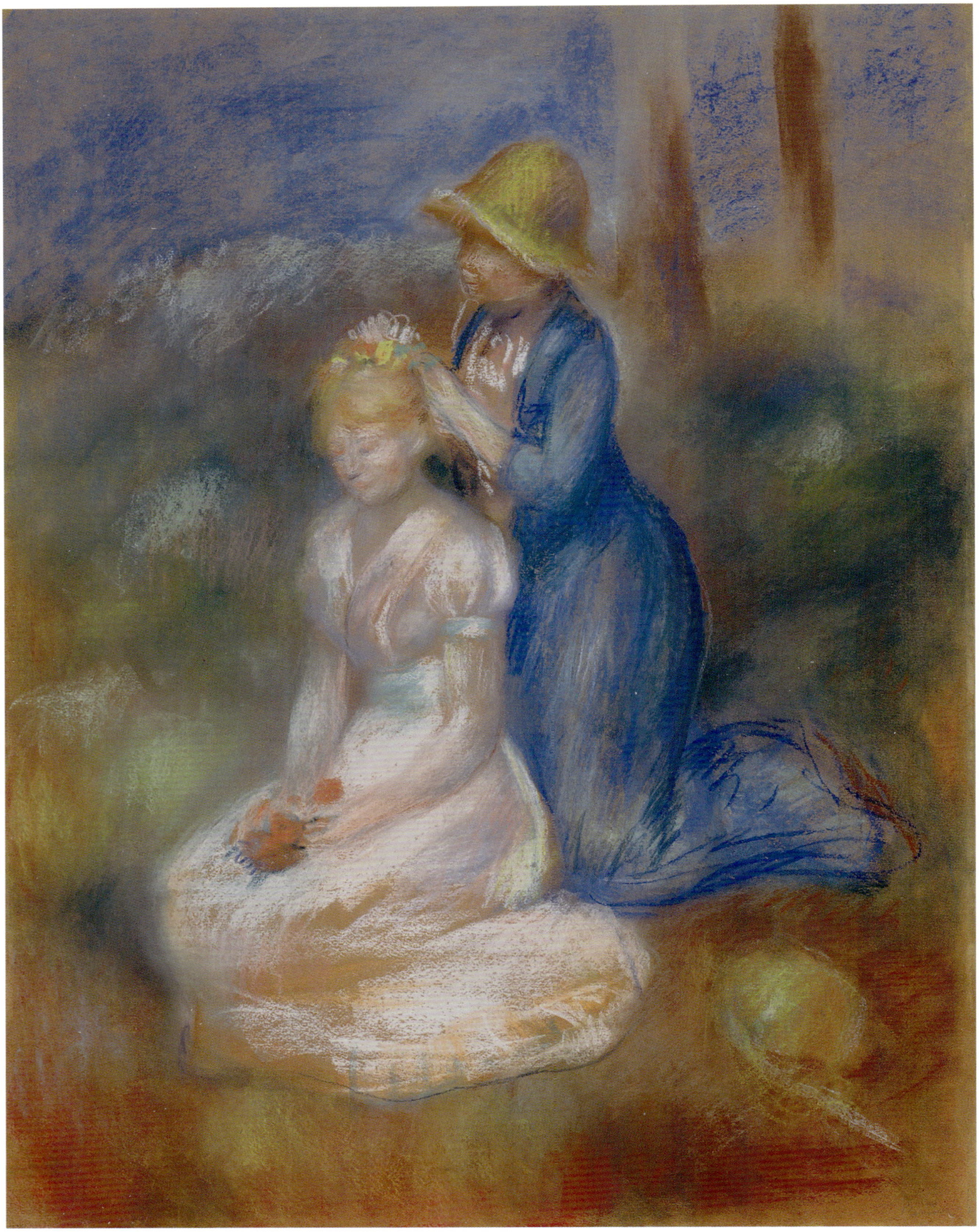

5. Pierre-Auguste Renoir
*Nude in a Chair* [*Nu au fauteuil*],
c. 1885–90
Pastel on paper
24 3/16 x 20 1/4 in. (61.5 x 51.5 cm)

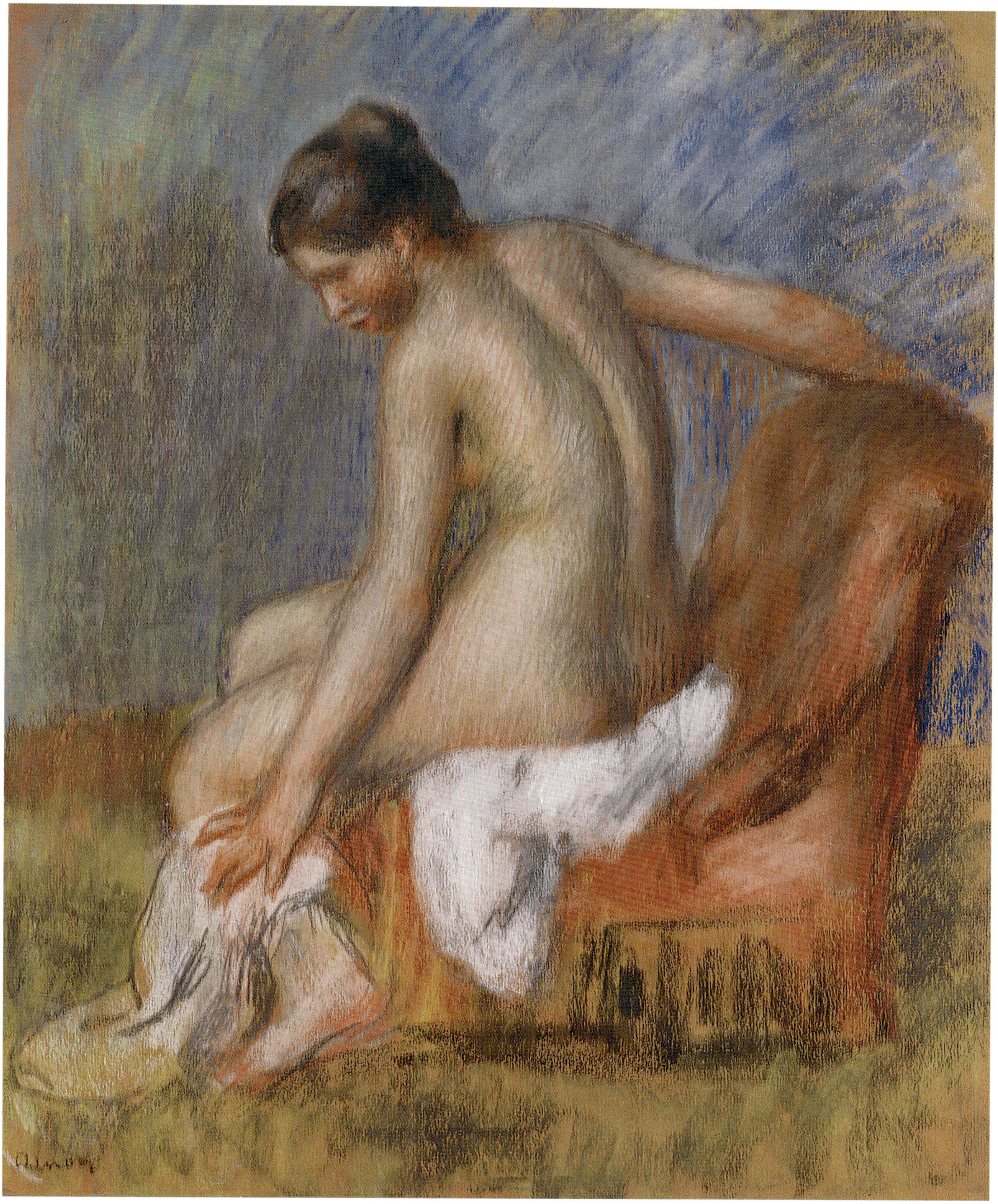

6. Pierre-Auguste Renoir
*Portrait of Pierre Renoir*
[*Portrait de Pierre Renoir*], 1890
Oil on canvas
12 7/8 x 9 3/4 in. (32 x 25 cm)

7. Pierre-Auguste Renoir
*Portrait of Edmond Renoir*
[*Edmond Renoir, neveu du peintre*],
1888
Oil on canvas
14 x 10 3/4 in. (35.56 x 27.3 cm)

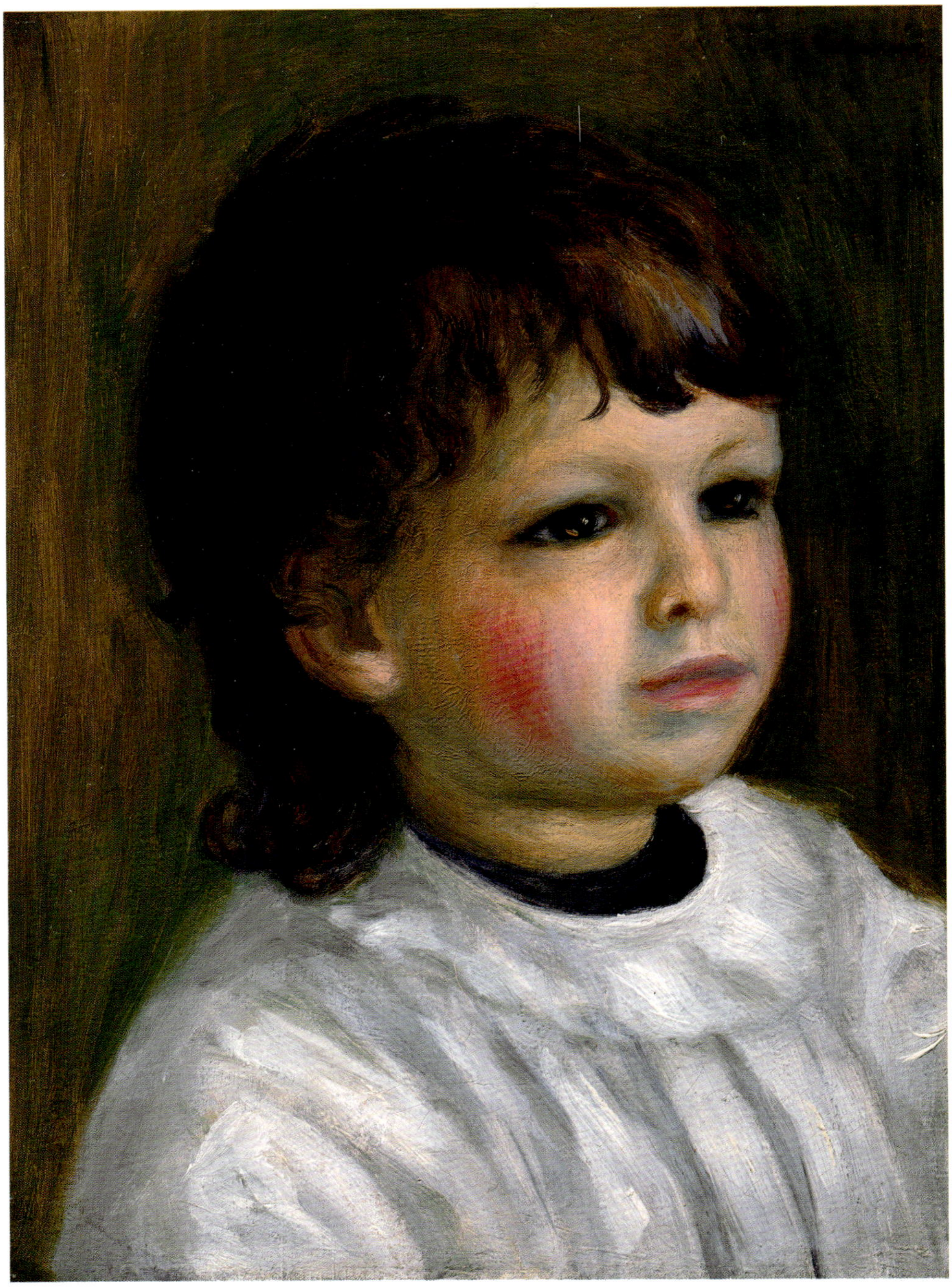

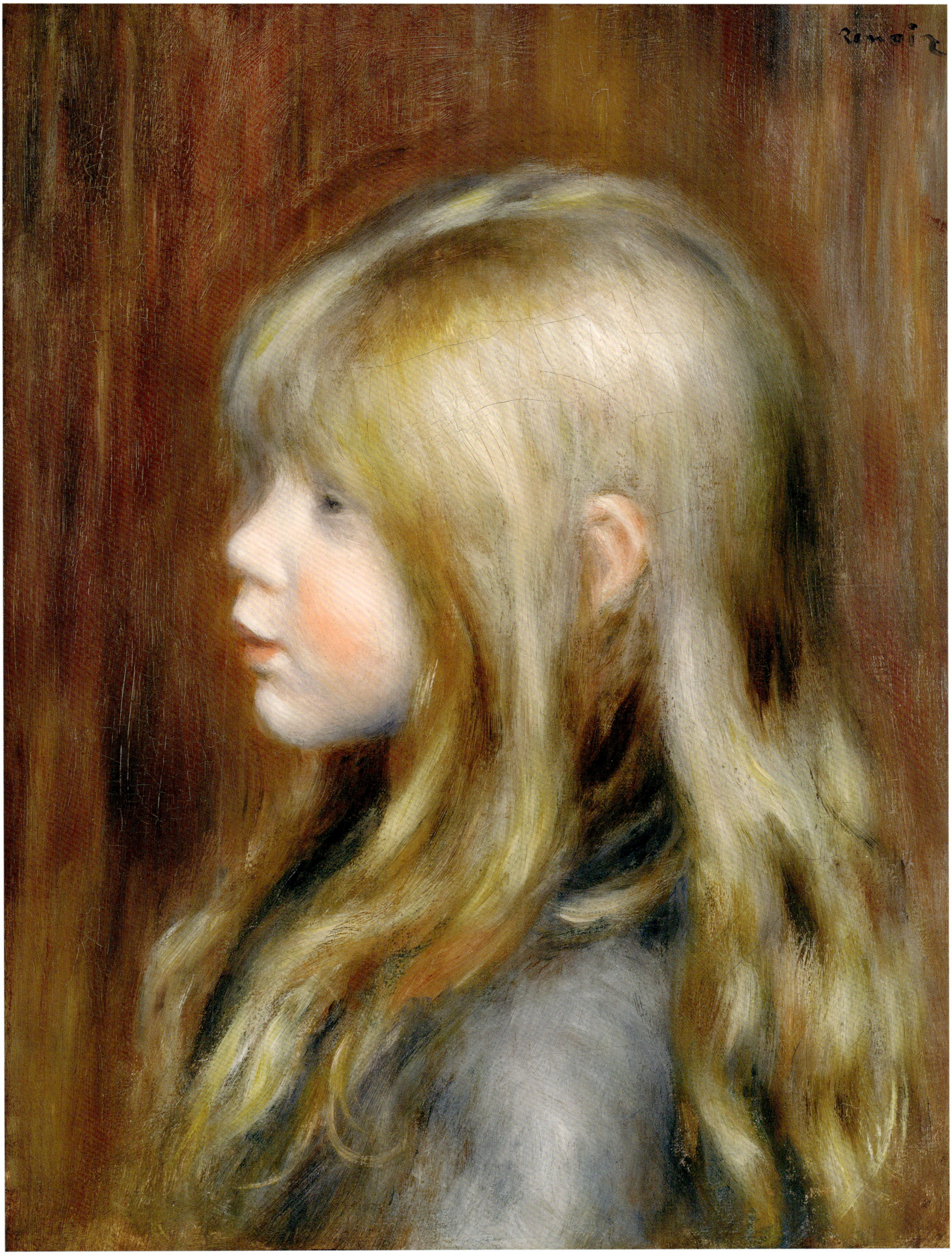
Renoir

8. Pierre-Auguste Renoir
*Dancing in the Country*
[*La danse à la campagne*], c. 1890
Etching
8 11/16 x 5 7/16 in. (22 x 13.8 cm)

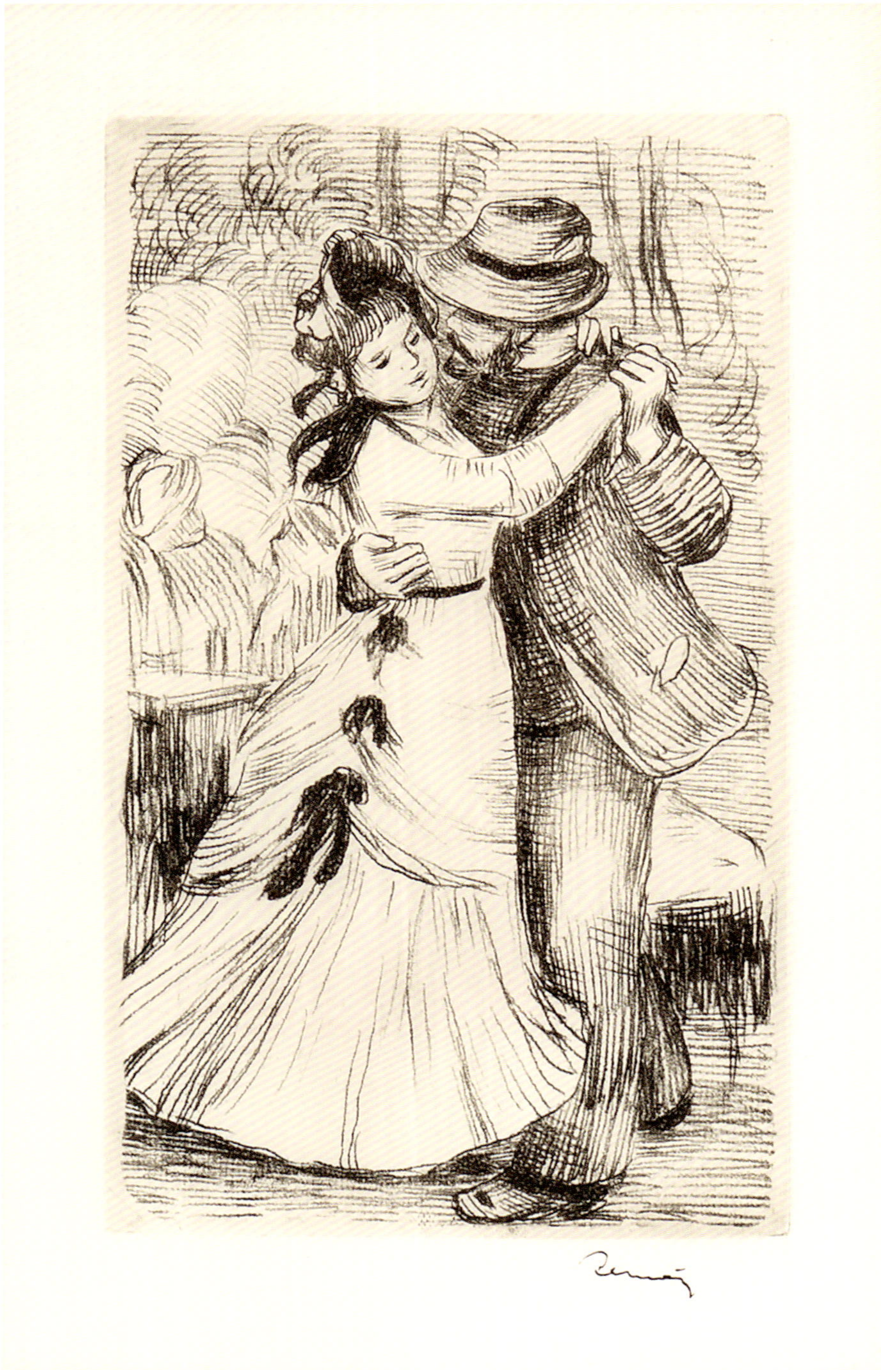

9. Pierre-Auguste Renoir
*Still Life with Apples*
[*Nature morte aux fruits*], c. 1890
Oil on canvas
7 ½ x 20 ¾ in. (19.05 x 52.7 cm)

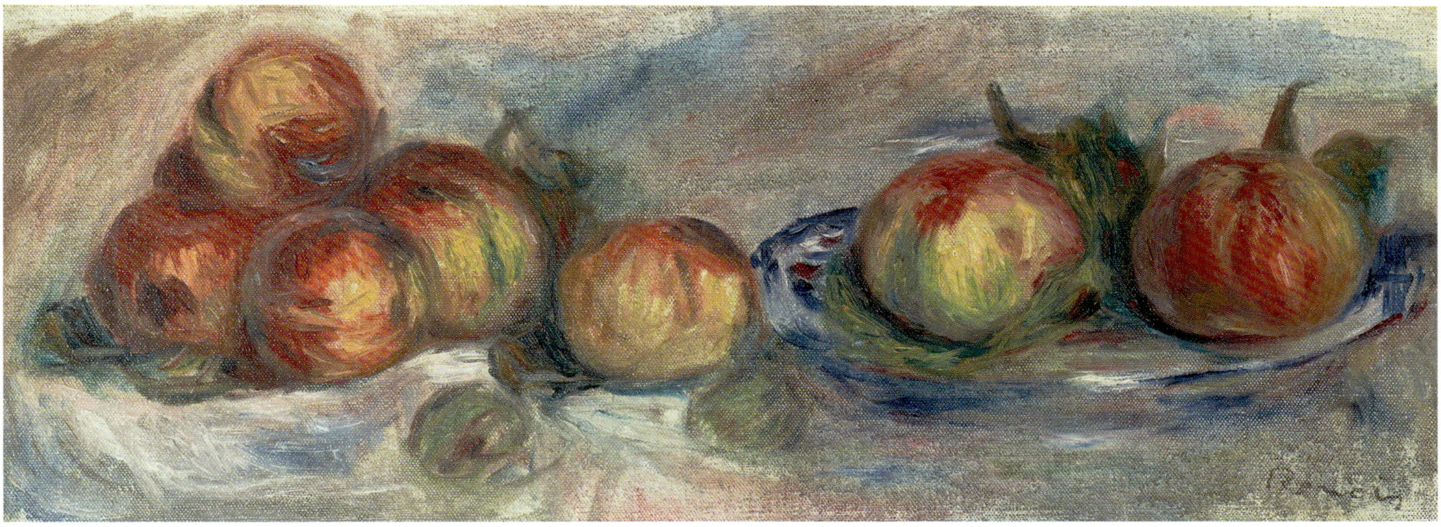

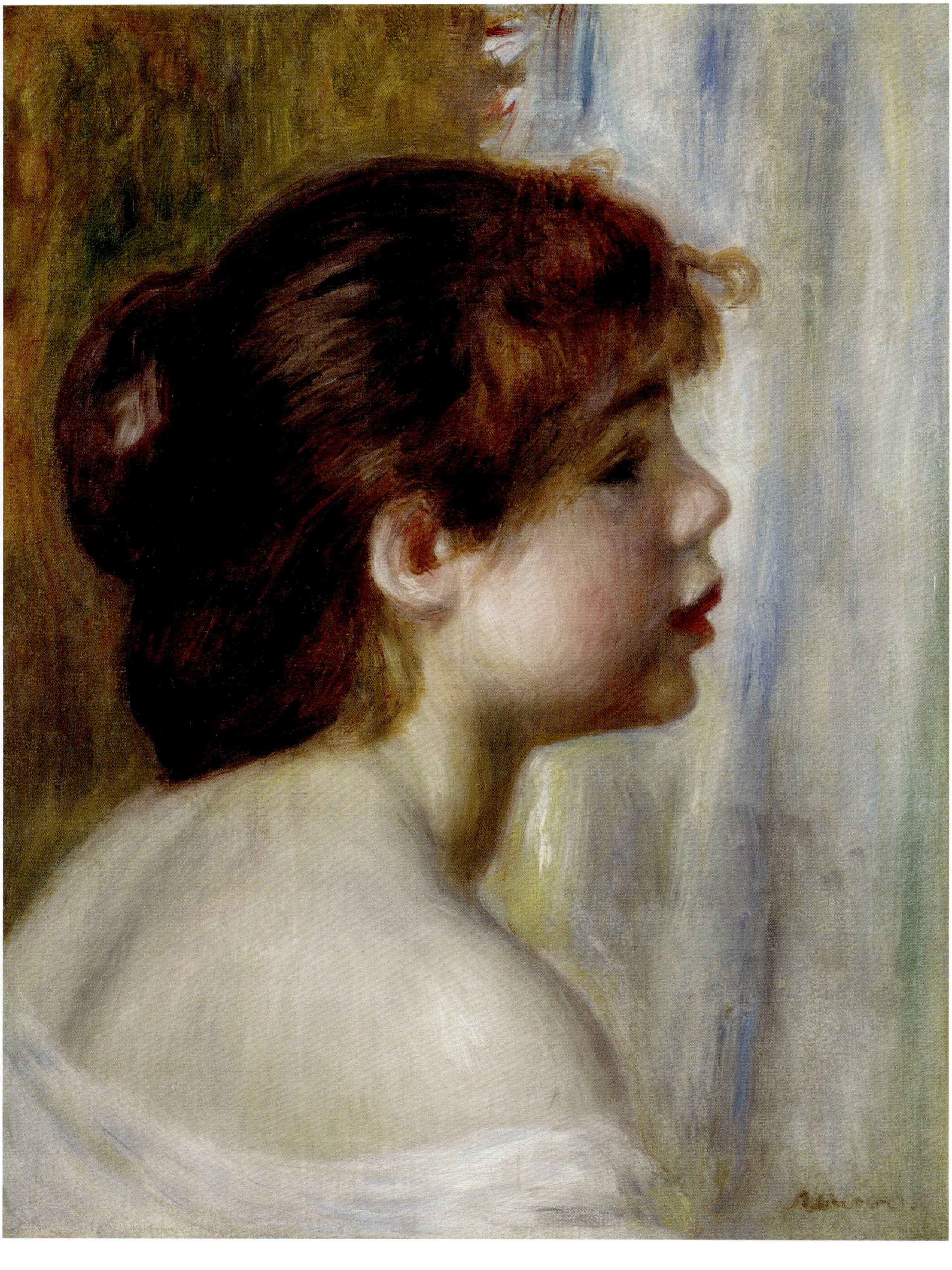

10. Pierre-Auguste Renoir
*Head of a Young Woman*
[*Tête d'une jeune femme*],
late nineteenth century
Oil on canvas
16 3/8 x 12 3/4 in. (41.6 x 32.4 cm)

11. Pierre-Auguste Renoir
*Woman Arranging Her Hat*
[*Femme arrangeant son chapeau*],
c. 1890
Oil on canvas
10 5/8 x 9 in. (27 x 22 cm)

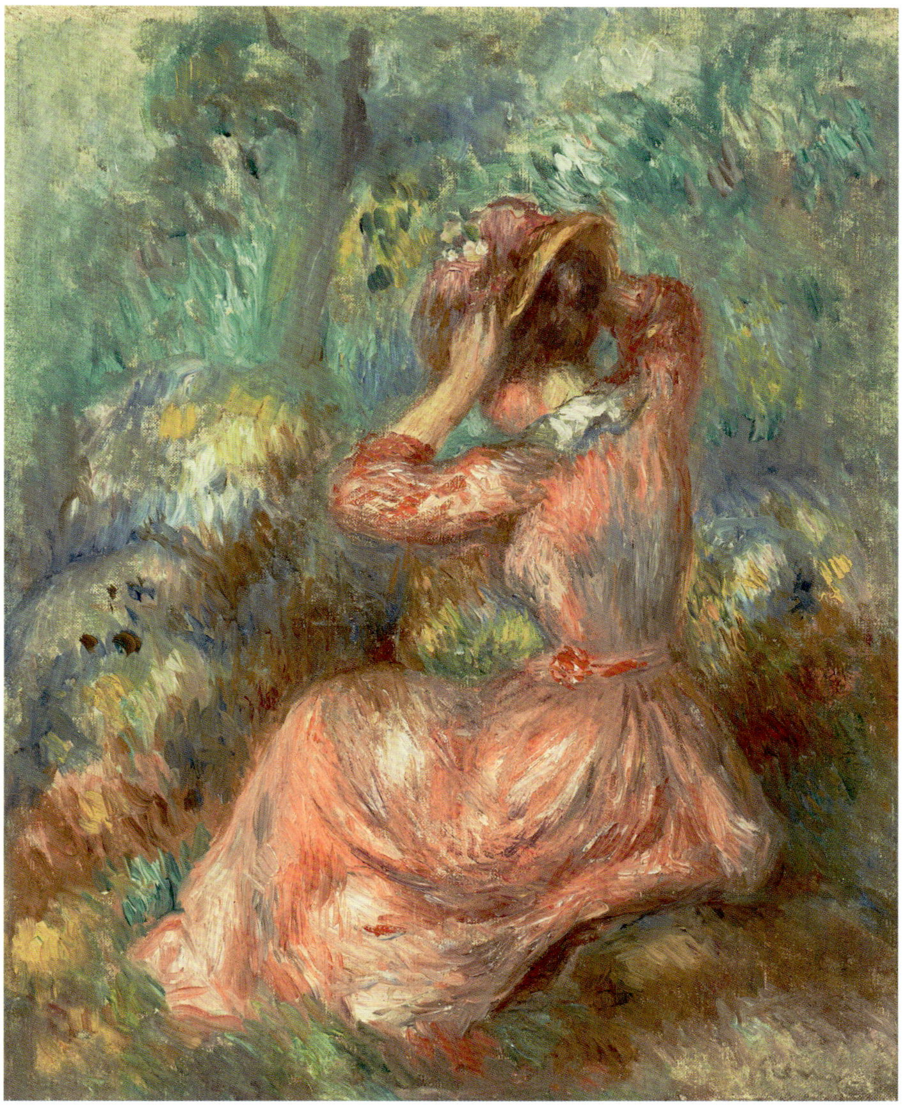

12. Pierre-Auguste Renoir
*Portrait of Jean* [*Portrait de Jean Renoir en rouge*], c. 1897
Oil on canvas
16 ⅜ x 13 ¼ in. (41.6 x 33.7 cm)

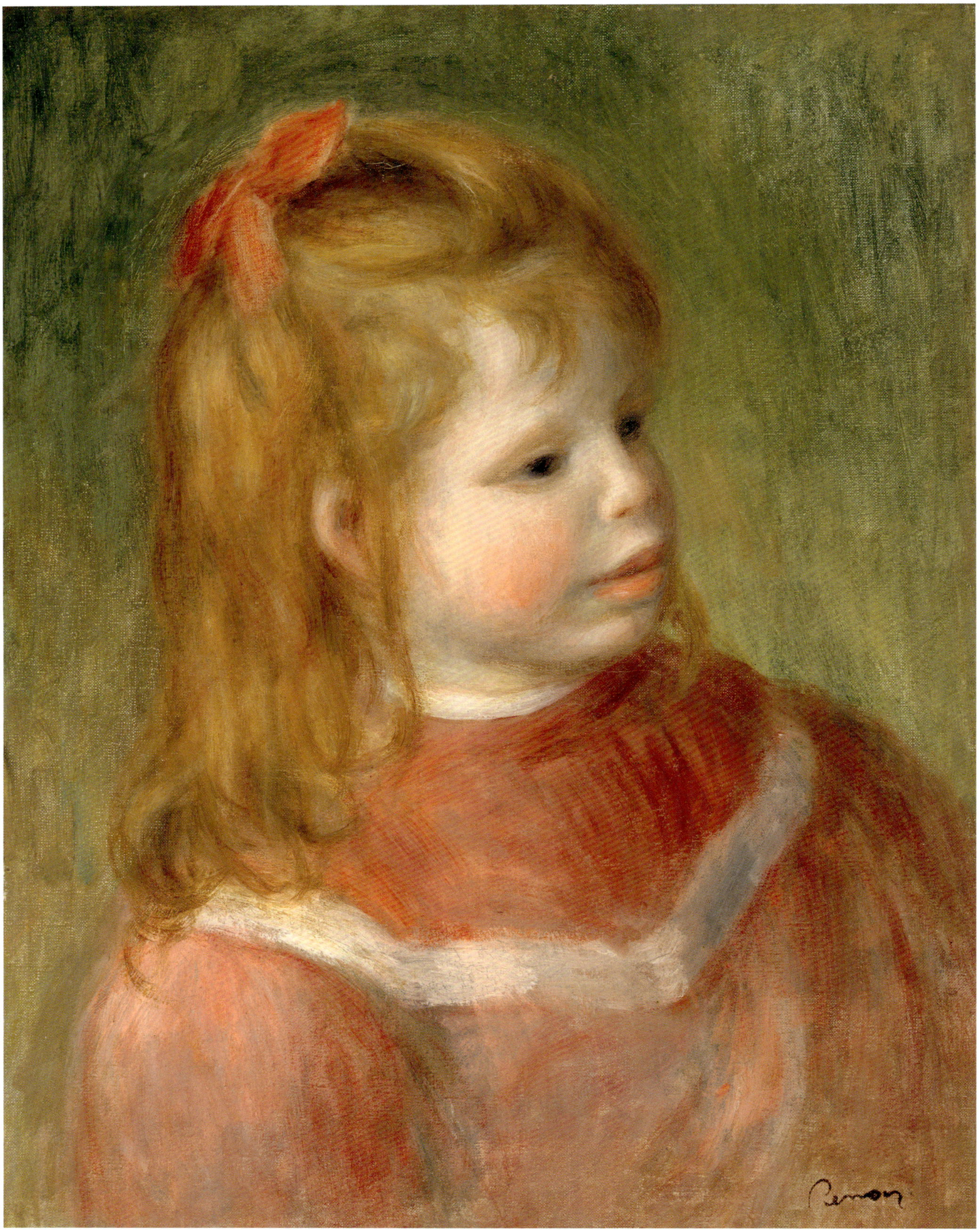

13. Pierre-Auguste Renoir
*Portrait of Jean Renoir*
[*Portrait de Jean Renoir*], 1899
Oil on canvas
15 ¾ x 12 ⅛ in. (40 x 32 cm)

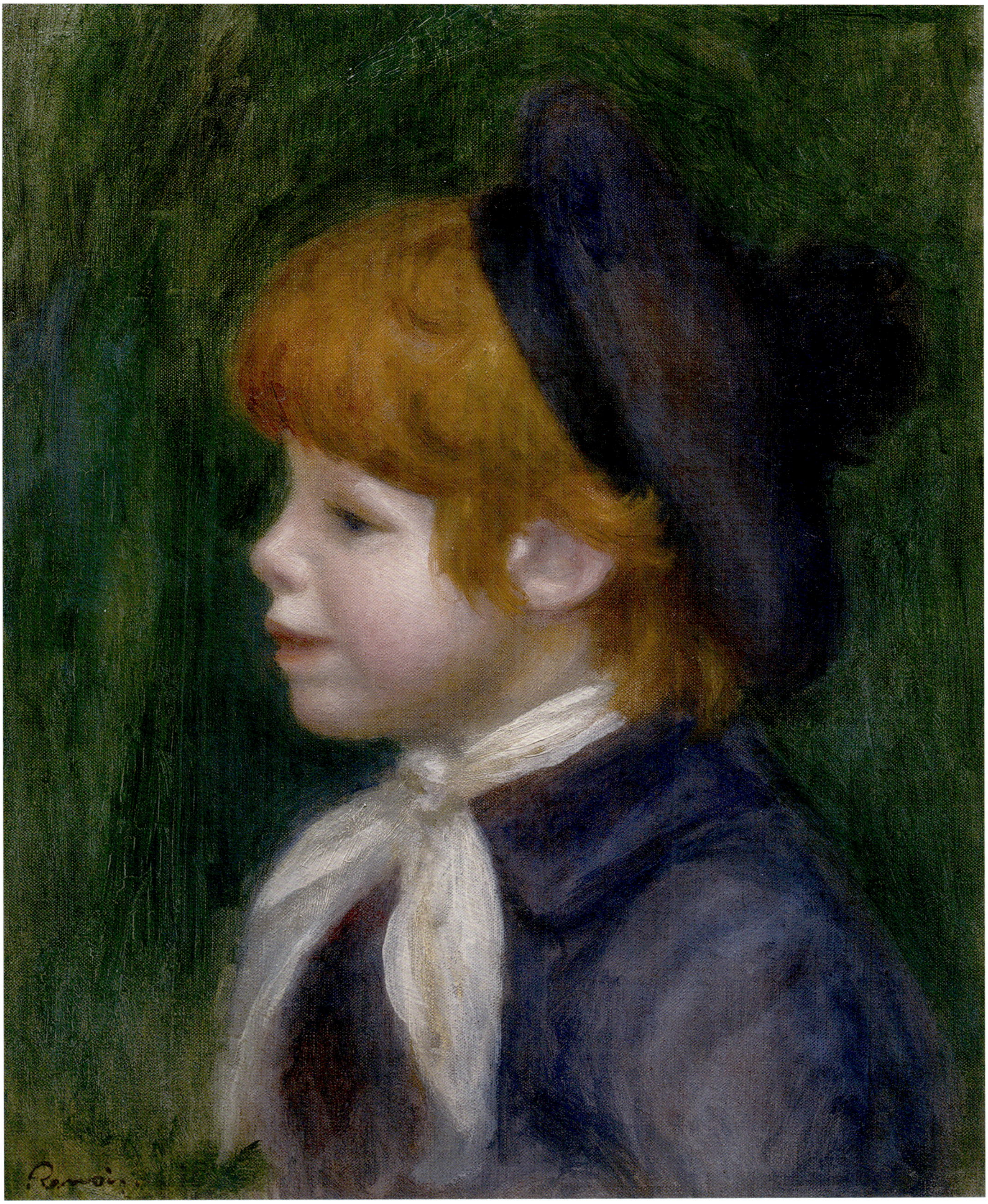

14. Pierre-Auguste Renoir
*Children Playing Ball* [*Enfants jouant à la balle*], c. 1900
Lithograph
23 ½ x 19 ¾ in. (60 x 51 cm)

15. Pierre-Auguste Renoir
*Girl in a Straw Hat* [*Femme assise, Gabrielle au chapeau de paille*], 1900
Oil on canvas
45 x 39 in. (81.5 x 65.5 cm)

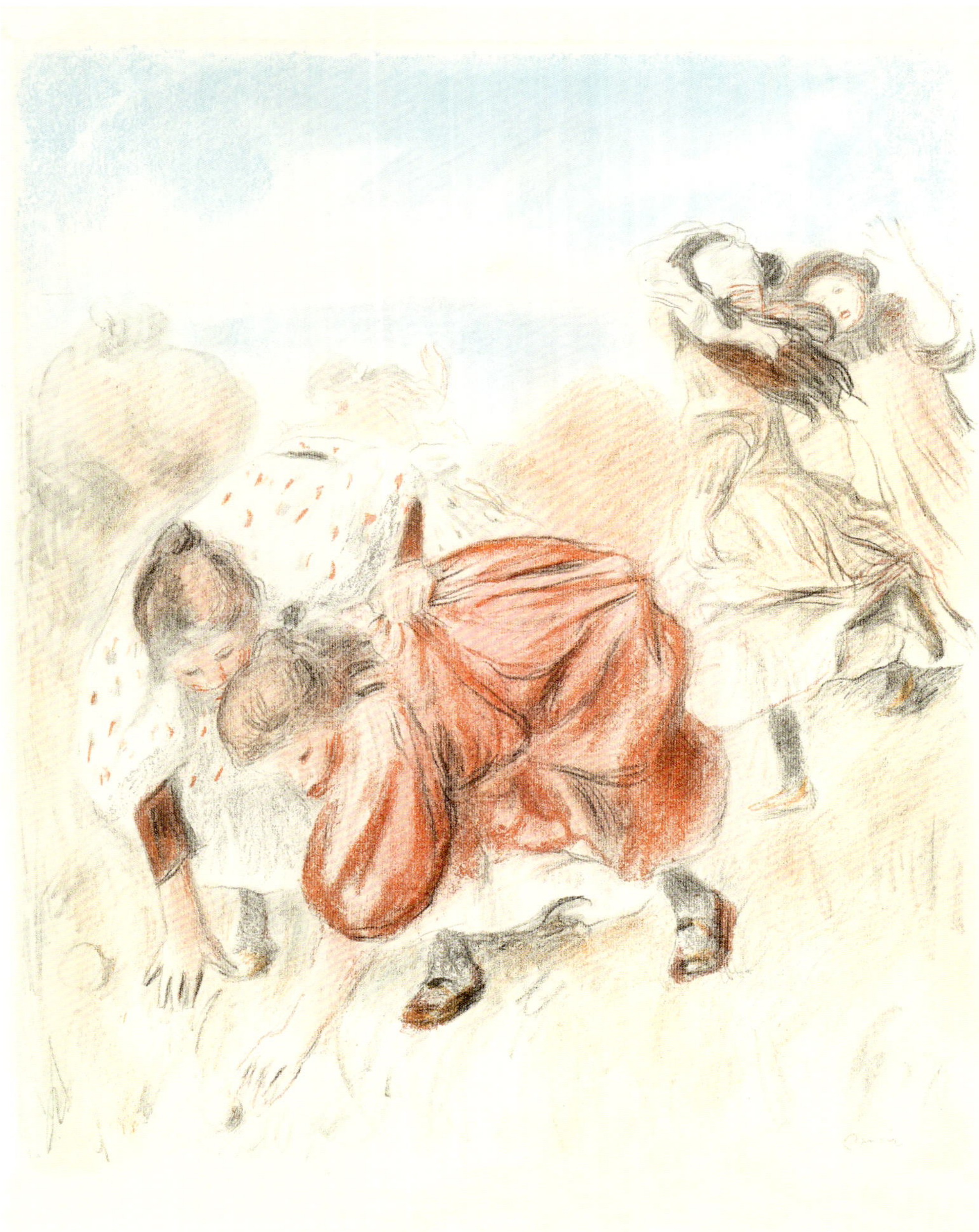

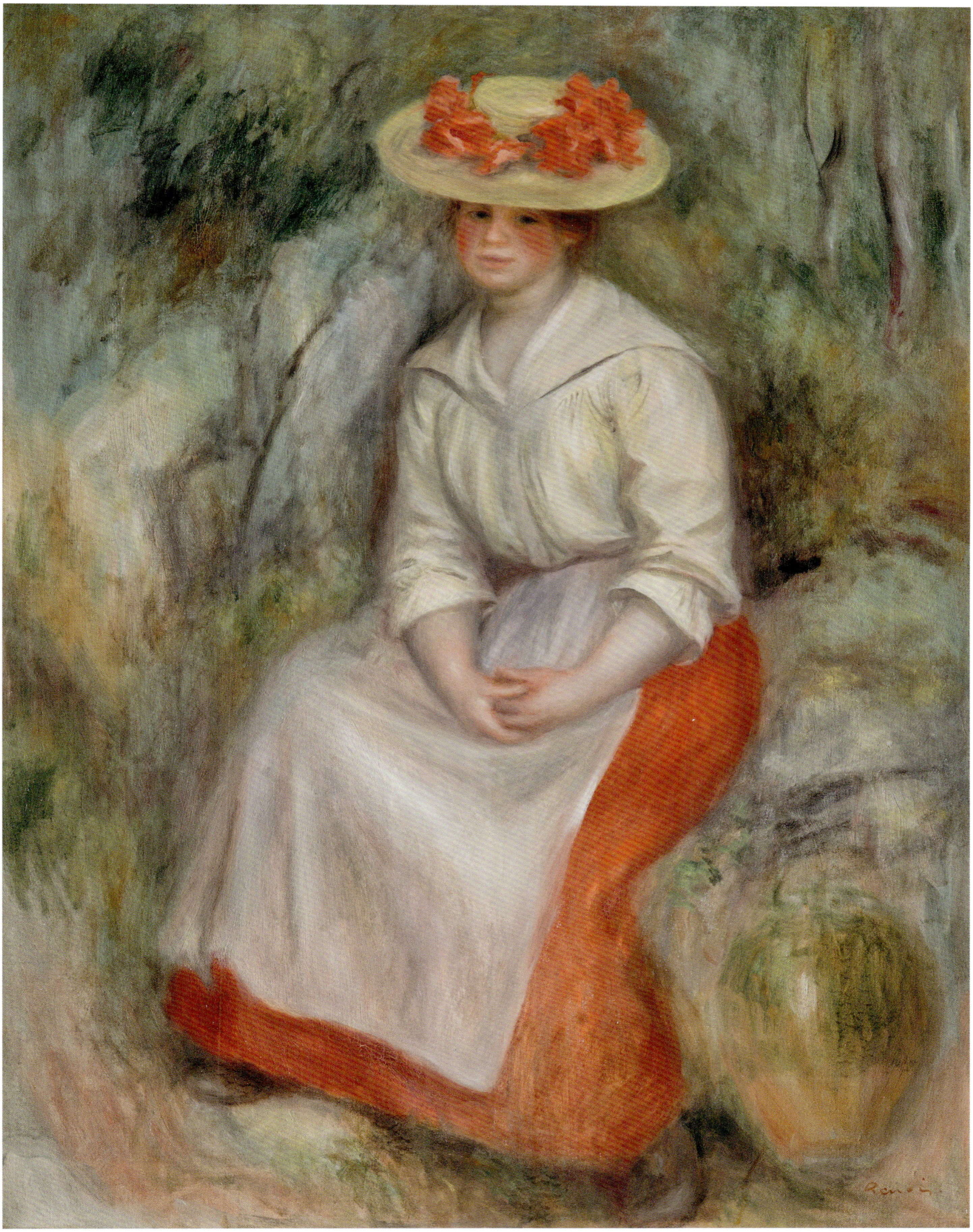

16. Pierre-Auguste Renoir
*Springtime in Essoyes*
[*Printemps à Essoyes*], c. 1900
Oil on canvas
19 ¾ x 24 ½ in. (50.16 x 62.23 cm)

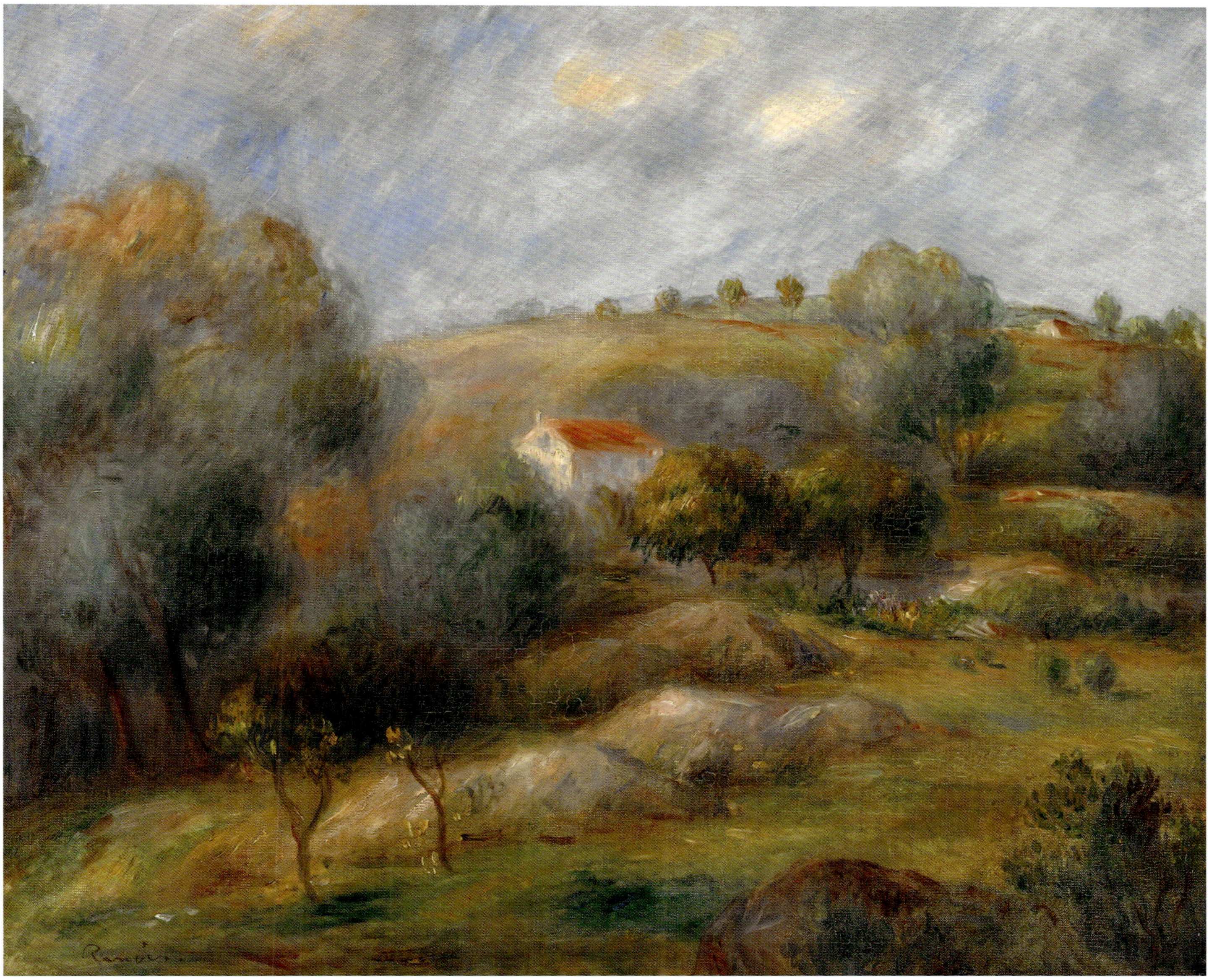

17. Pierre-Auguste Renoir
*Paul Cézanne*, c. 1902
Lithograph, second state
10 ¼ x 9 ½ in. (26 x 24 cm)

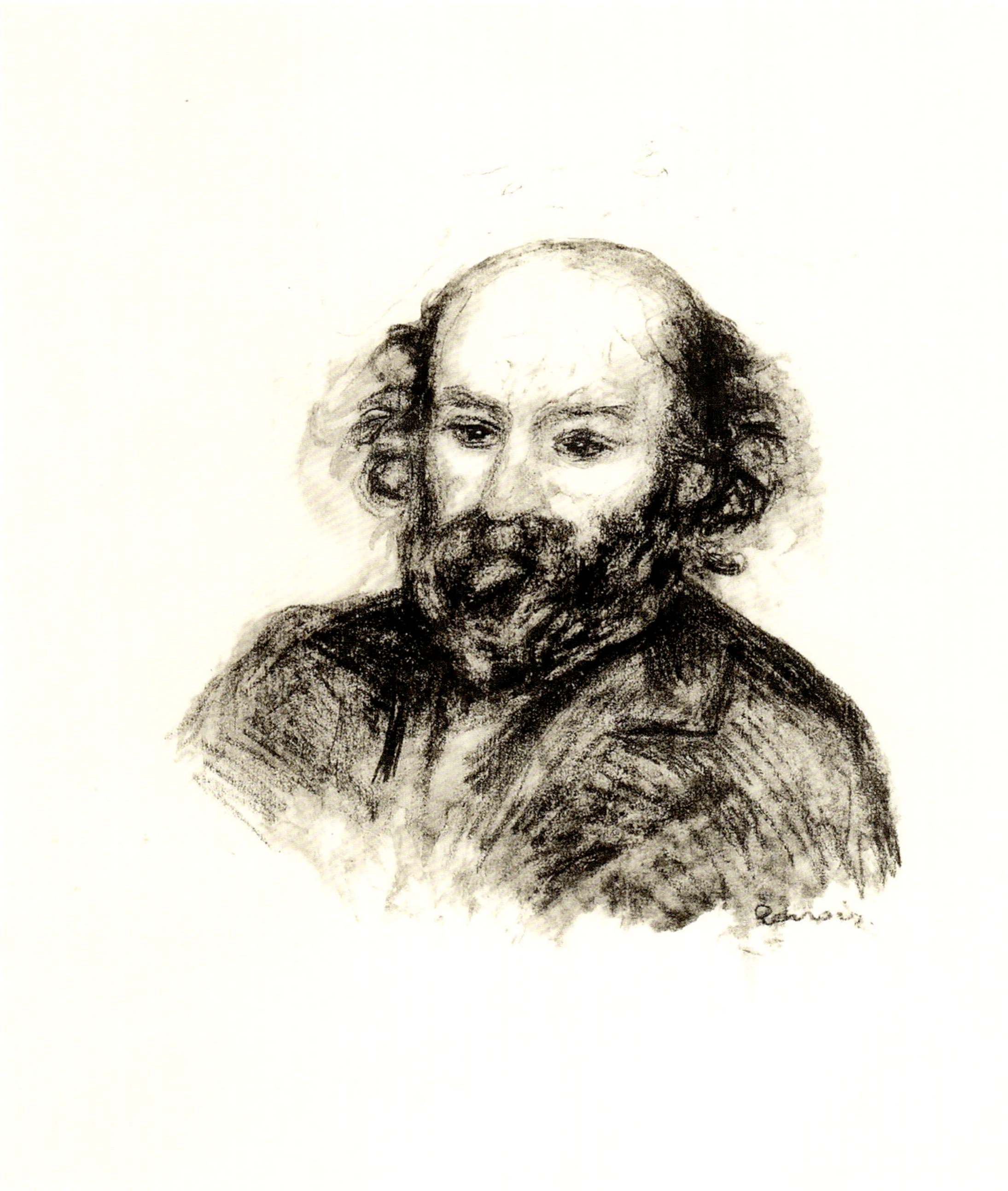

18. Pierre-Auguste Renoir
*Claude Renoir, Head Lowered*
[*Claude Renoir, la tête abaissée*],
c. 1904
Lithograph, second state
8 ½ x 7 ⅜ in. (21.5 x 18.8 cm)

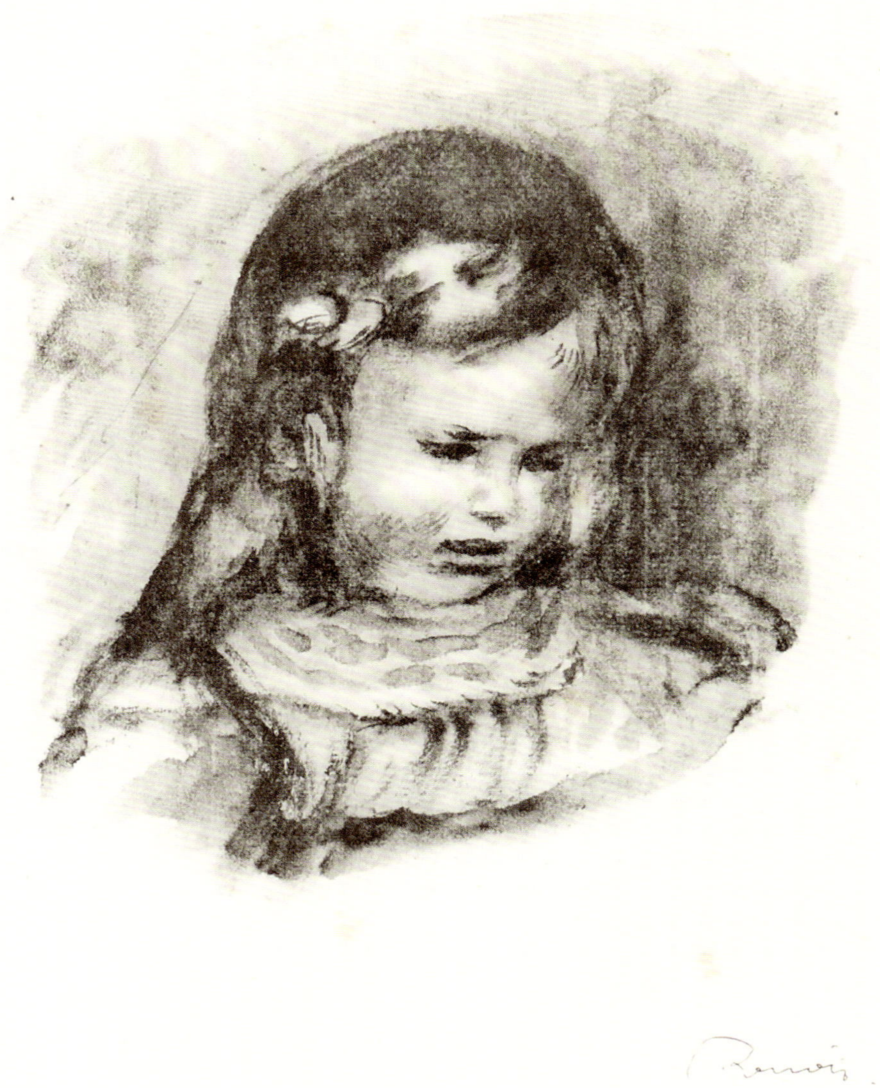

19. Pierre-Auguste Renoir
*Coco*, 1905
Oil on canvas
10 7/8 x 14 3/16 in. (27.62 x 36 cm)

20. Pierre-Auguste Renoir
*Portrait of Claude Renoir*
[*Buste d'enfant, Coco*], c. 1902
Oil on canvas
13 x 11 1/8 in. (32.5 x 28.5 cm)

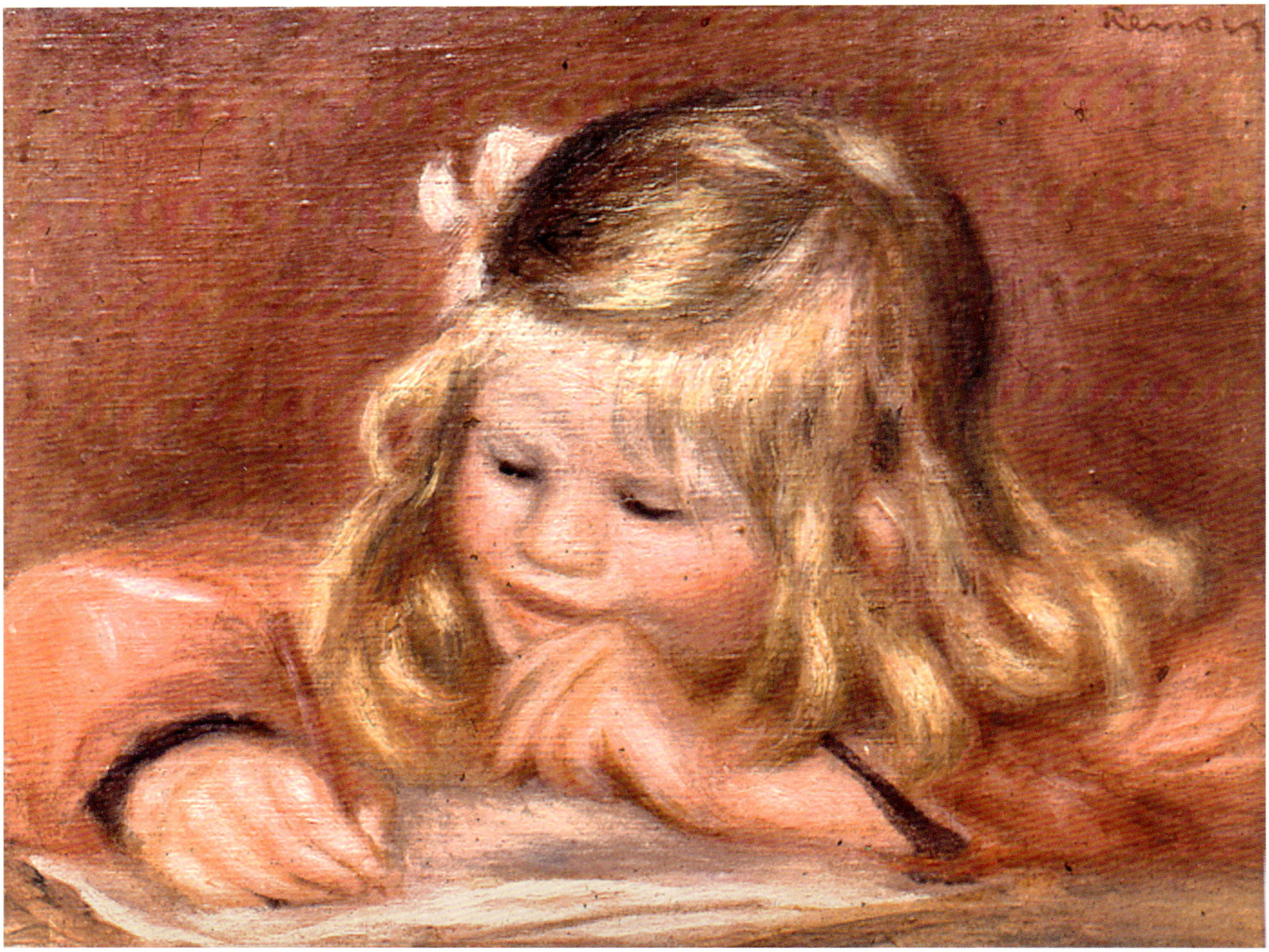

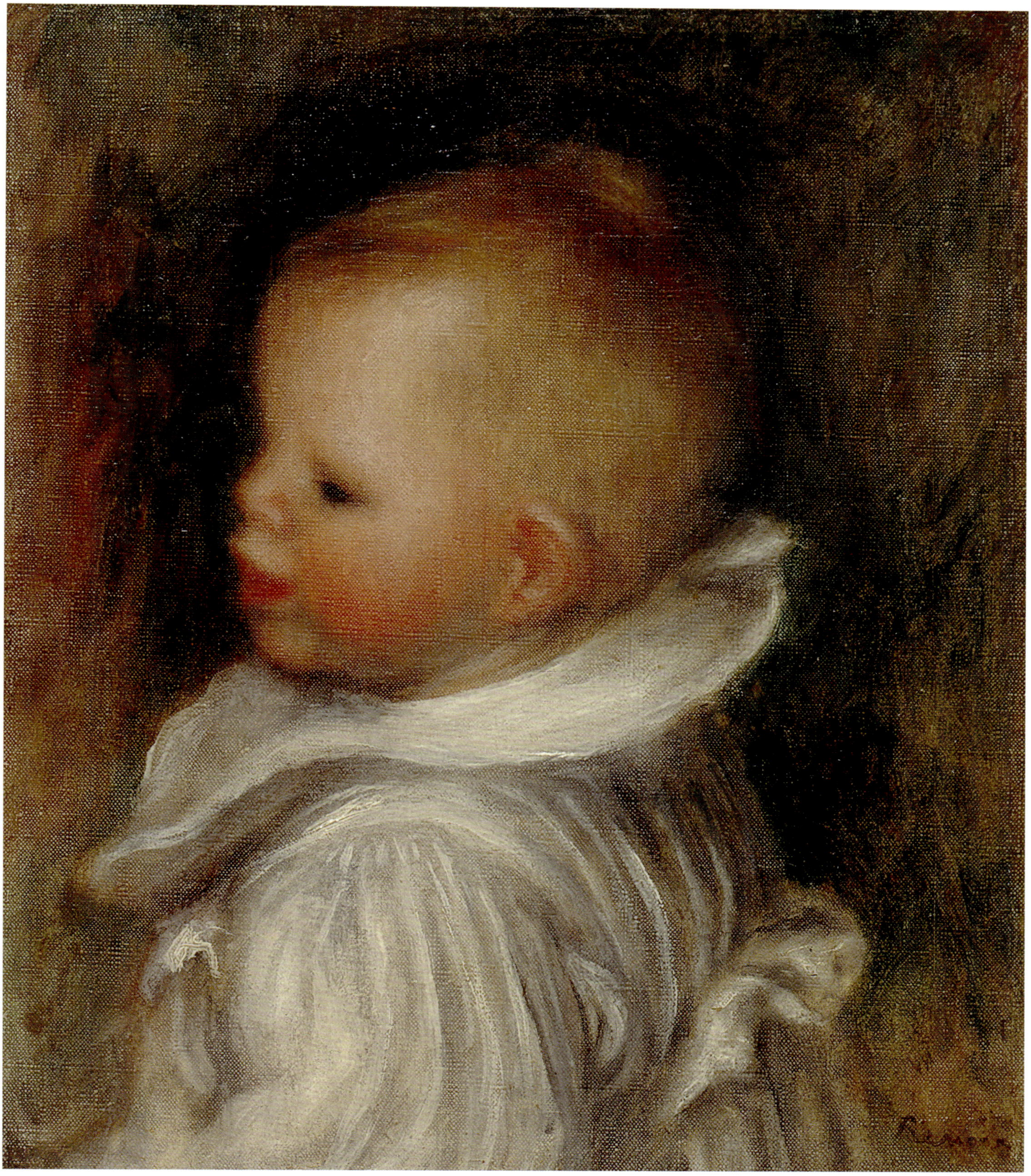

21. Pierre-Auguste Renoir
*Reclining Nude [Femme nue couchée, tournée à droite]*, c. 1906
Etching
5 3/8 x 7 13/16 in. (13.6 x 19.8 cm)

22. Pierre-Auguste Renoir
*Reclining Nude [Femme nue couchée; Le modèle allongé]*, c. 1906
Oil on canvas
12 3/4 x 11 in. (32.5 x 28.5 cm)

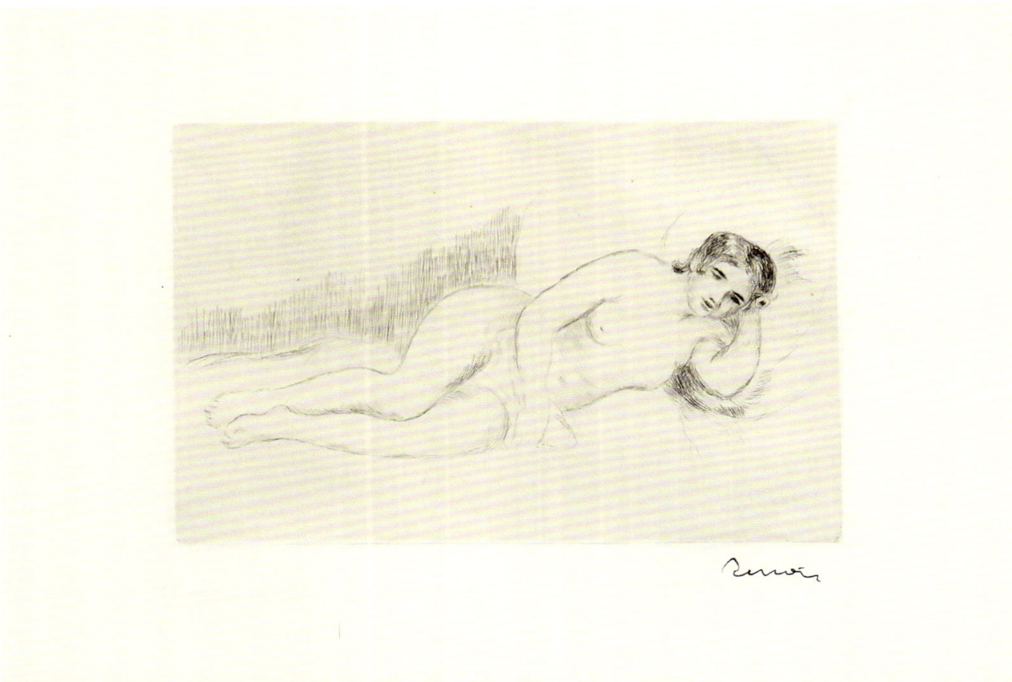

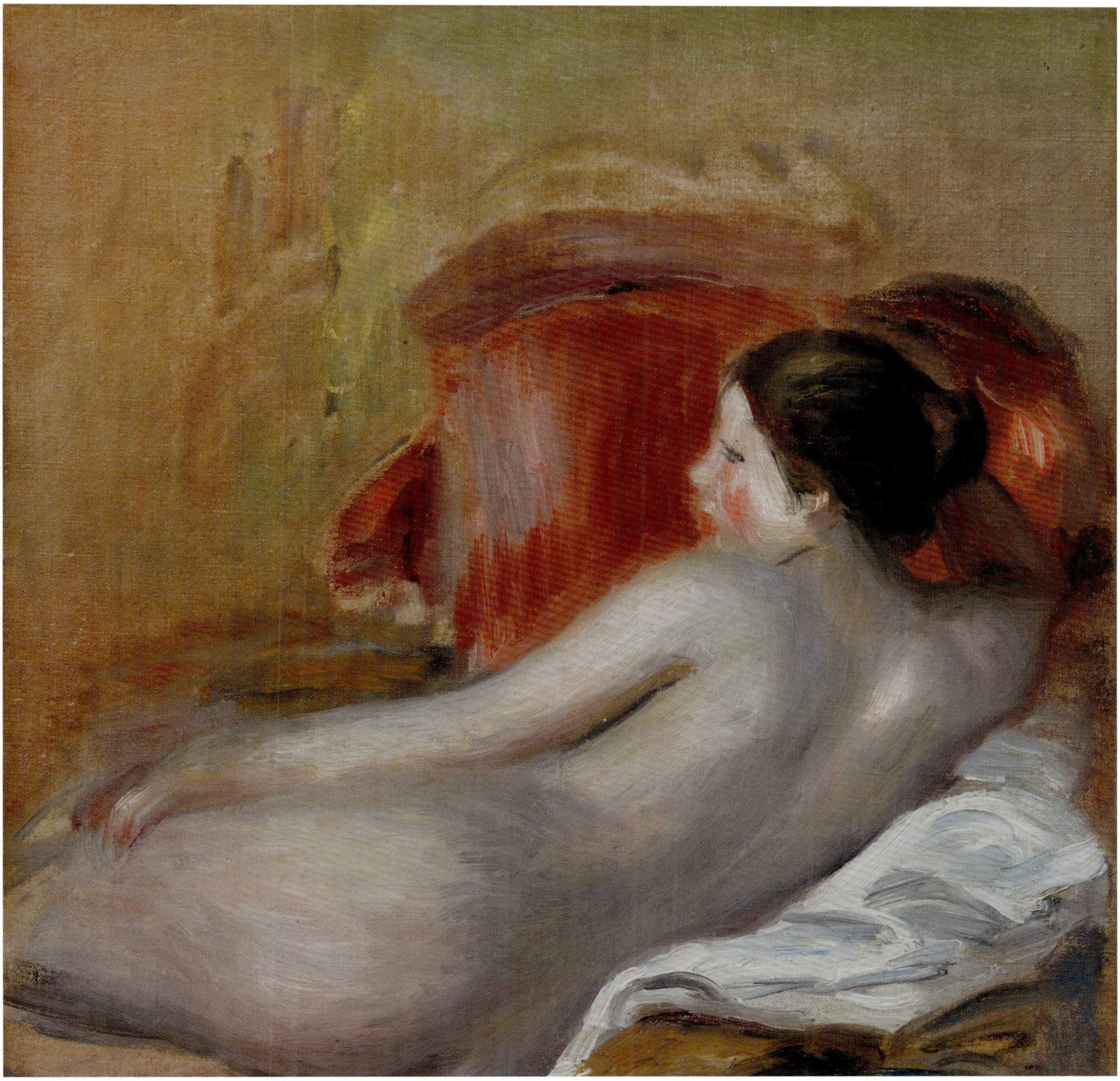

23. Pierre-Auguste Renoir
*Seated Nude* [*Femme nue assise*],
c. 1906
Etching
7 3/8 x 5 7/8 in. (18.8 x 14.9 cm)

24. Pierre-Auguste Renoir
*Woman in White Blouse*
[*Femme en blouse blanche (Gabrielle)*], c. 1907
Oil on canvas
9 1/2 x 8 3/8 in. (24.2 x 21.4 cm)

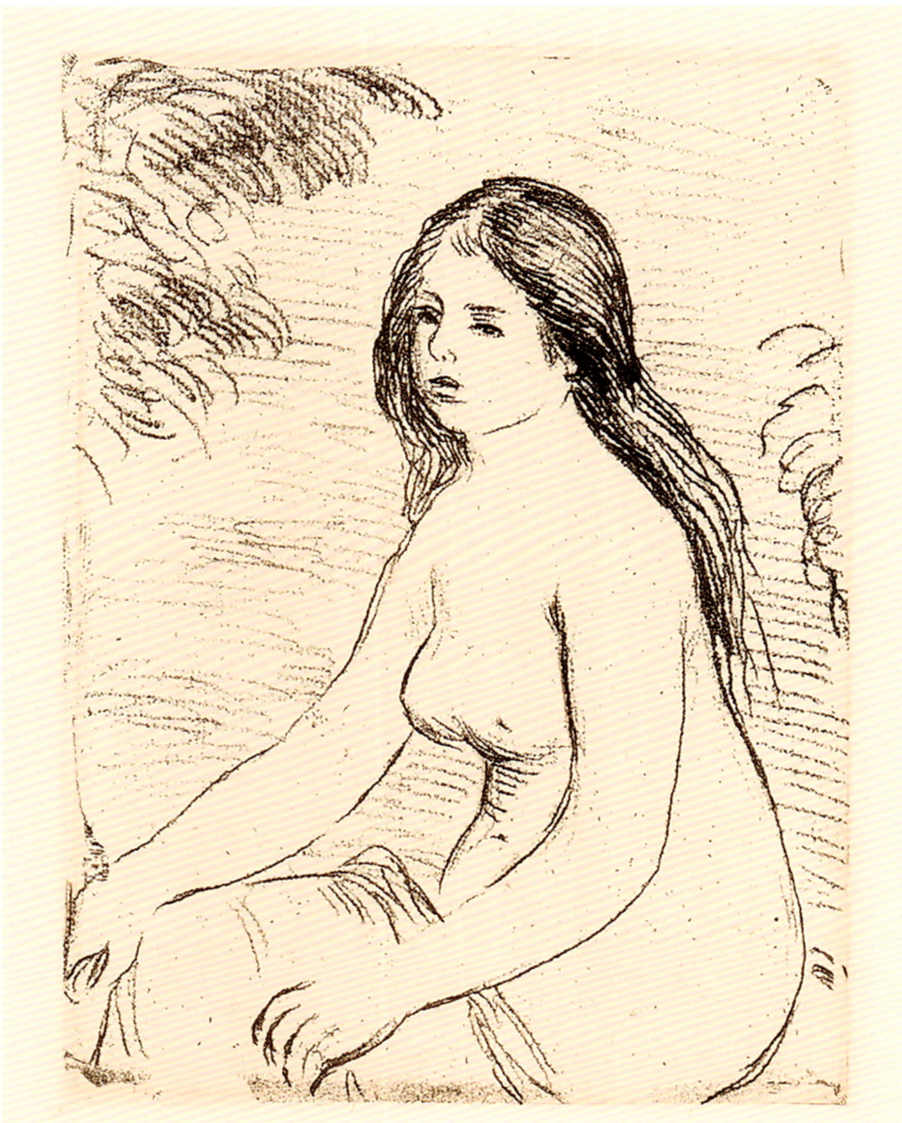

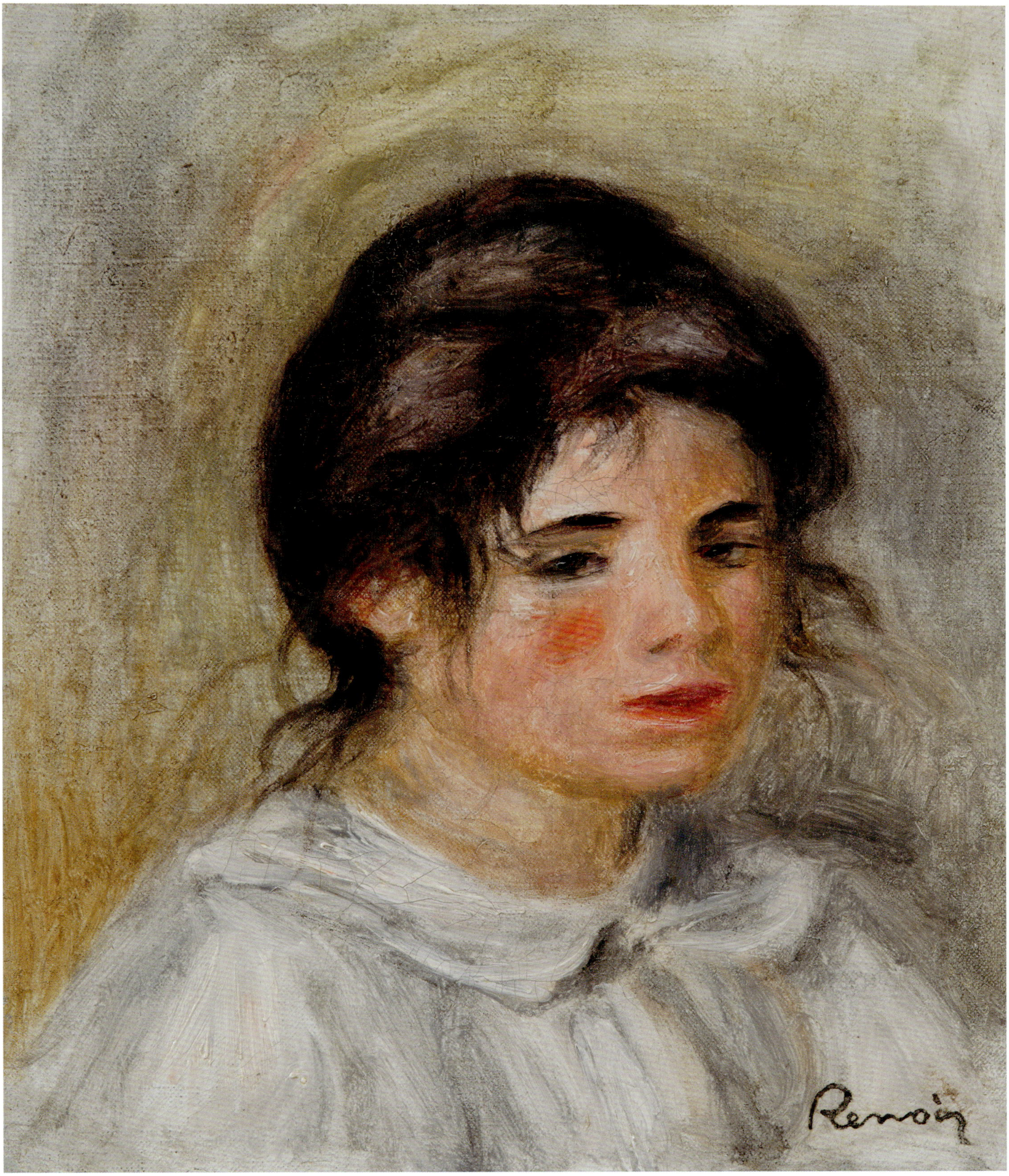
Renoir

25. Pierre-Auguste Renoir
*Seamstress at Window* [*Ravaudeuse à la fenêtre*], c. 1908–10
Oil on canvas
25 ½ x 21 ½ in. (64.77 x 54.61 cm)

26. Pierre-Auguste Renoir
*Portrait of Mme. Thurneyssen and Her Daughter* [*Mère et enfant*], 1910
Oil on canvas
39 ⅜ x 31 ⅝ in. (100.01 x 80.33 cm)

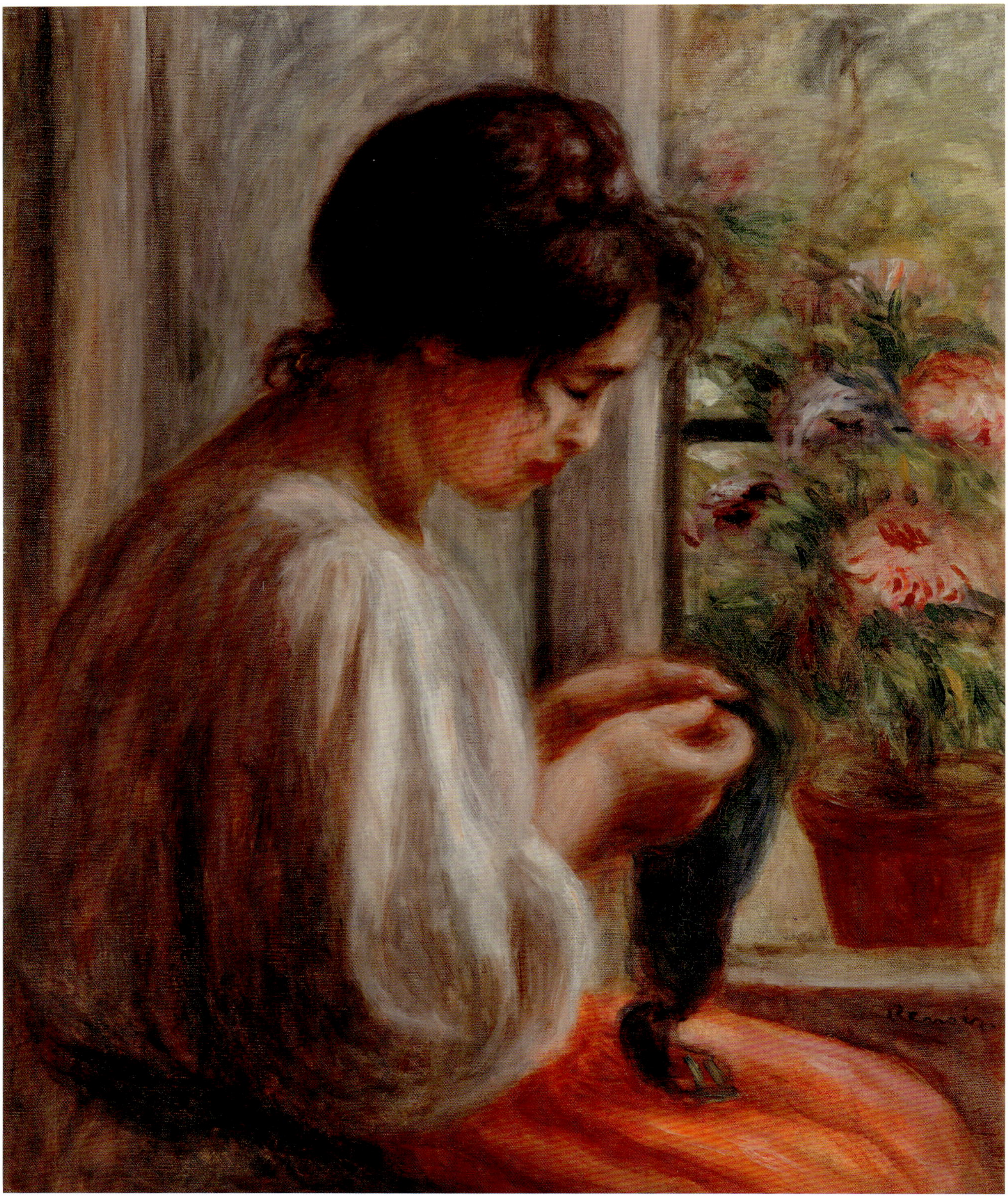

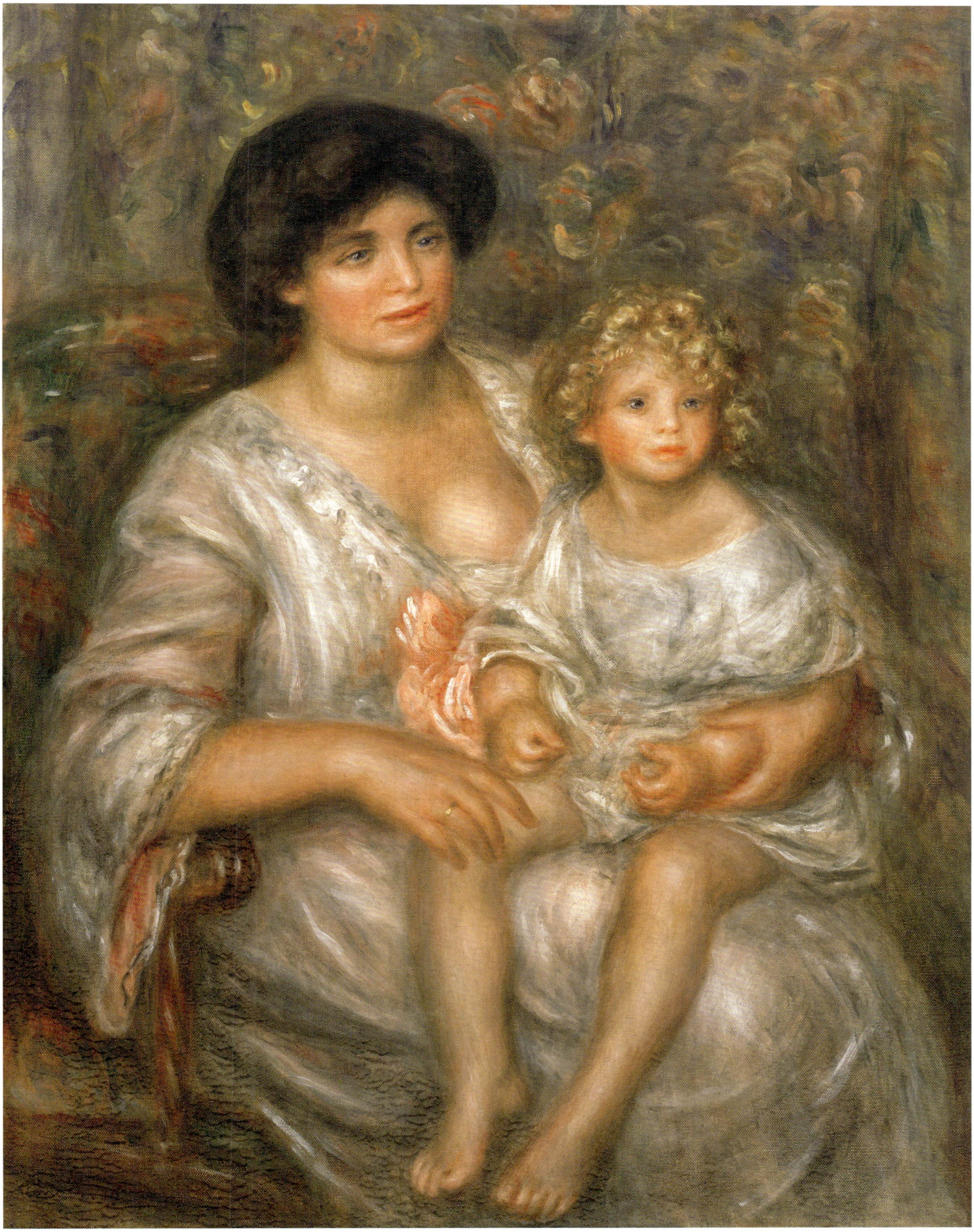

27. Pierre-Auguste Renoir
*Head of Coco* [*Tête de Coco*], 1908
Bronze
8 ½ in. (21.59 cm) in diameter

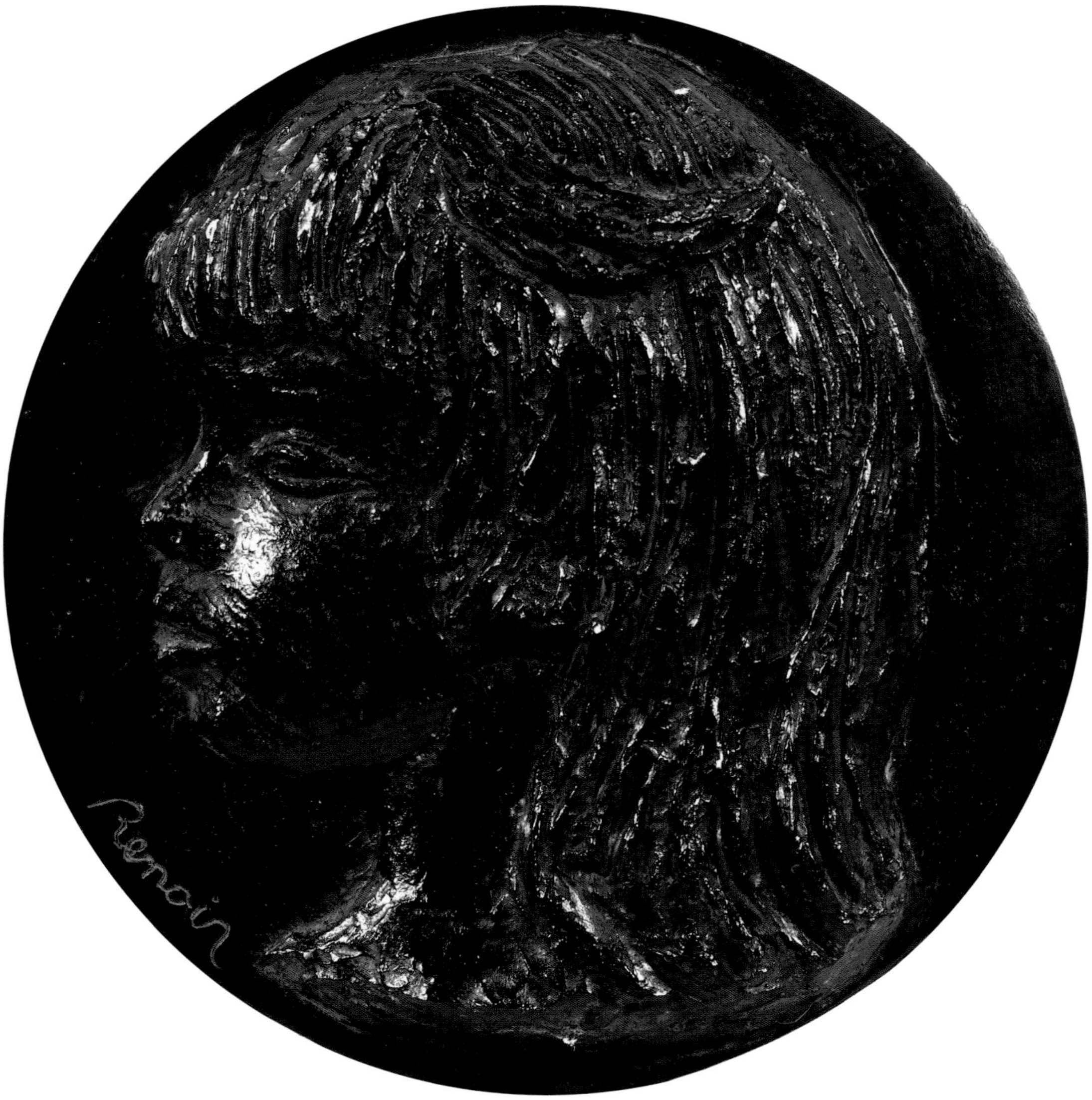

28. Pierre-Auguste Renoir
*Landscape at Cagnes*
[*Paysage à Cagnes*], 1910
Oil on canvas
10 ¾ x 13 ⅞ in. (27.3 x 35.24 cm)

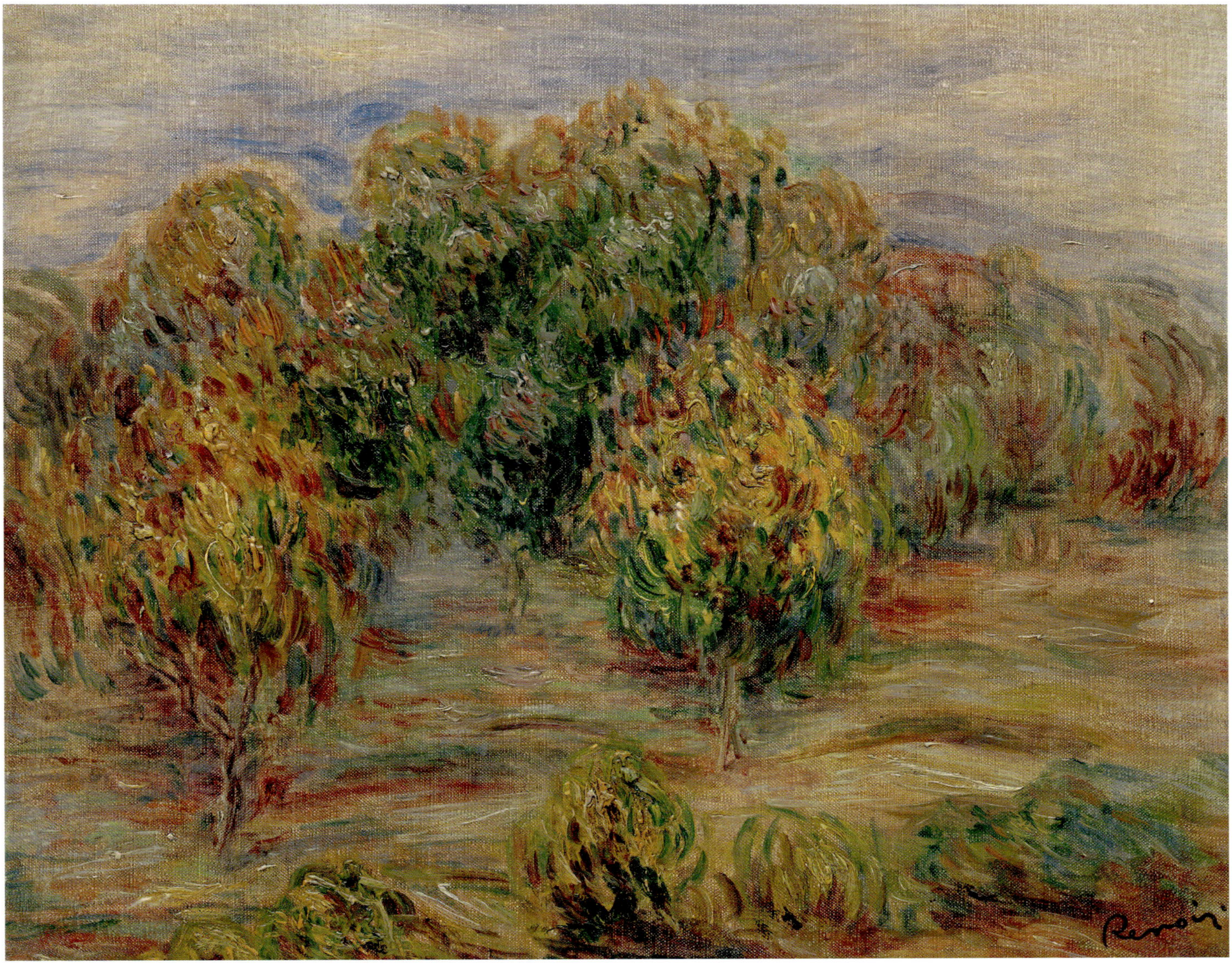

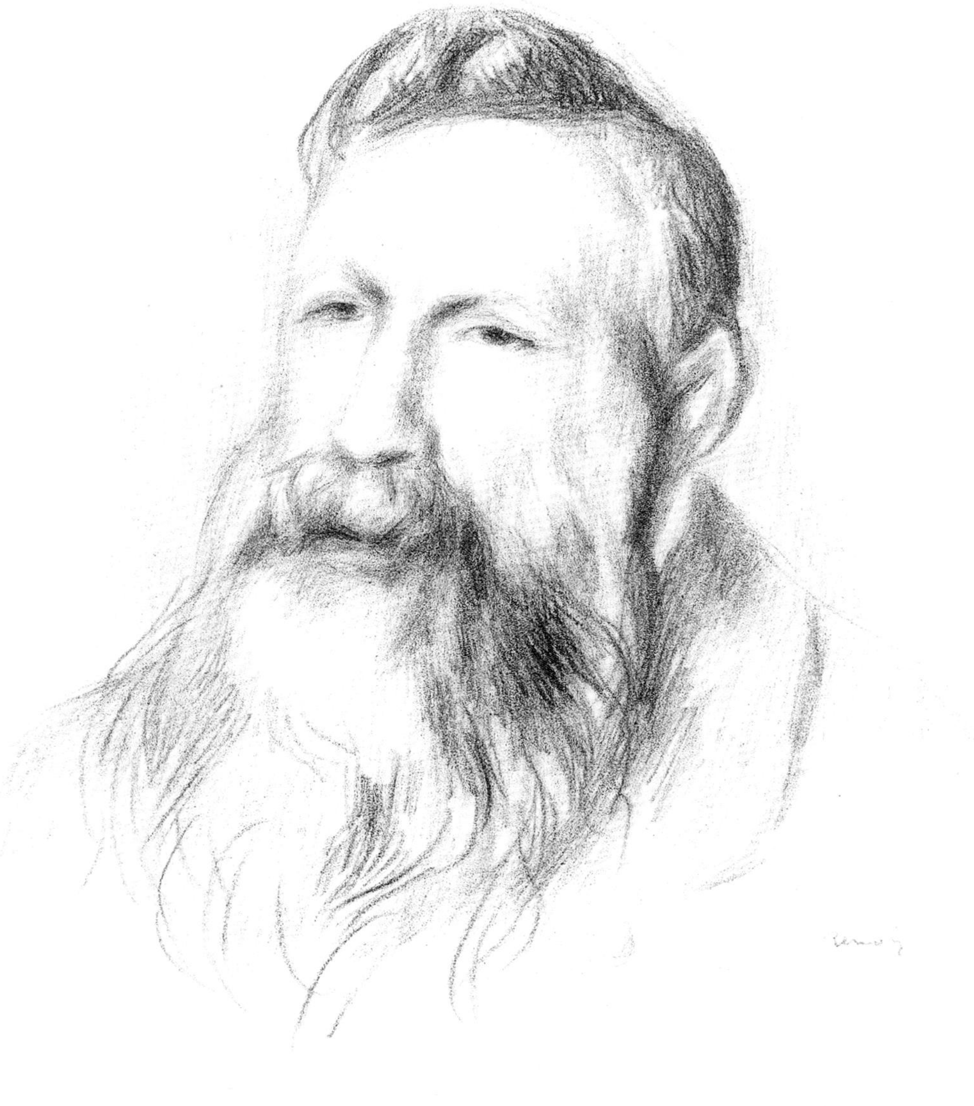

29. Pierre-Auguste Renoir
*Auguste Rodin*, c. 1910
Lithograph
$15\frac{3}{4}$ x $15\frac{3}{8}$ in. (40 x 38.5 cm)

30. Pierre-Auguste Renoir
*The Washers, 2nd State*
[*Les laveuses, $2^{e}$ Pensée*], c. 1910
Lithograph
$18\frac{1}{2}$ x $23\frac{13}{16}$ in. (46.8 x 60.5 cm)

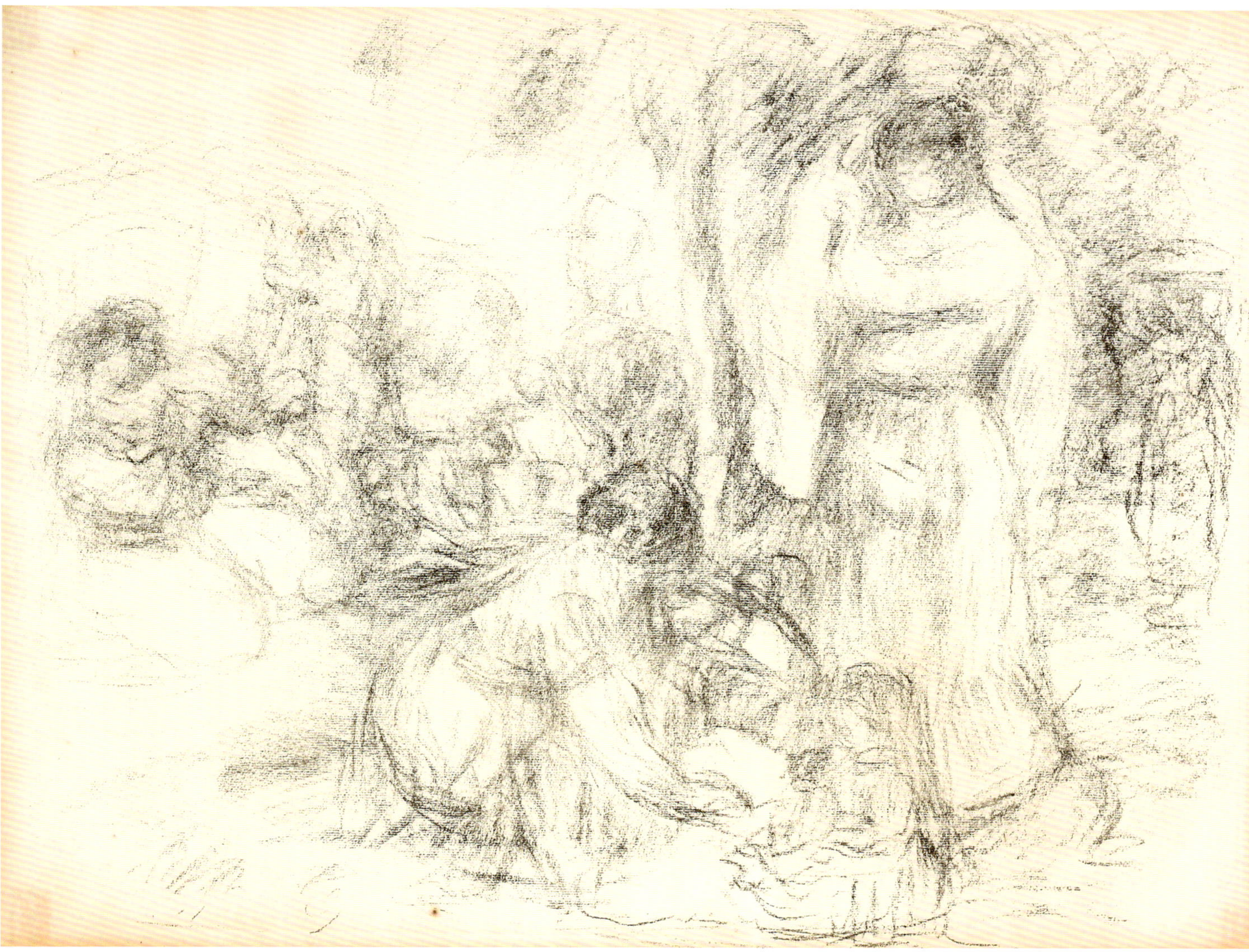

31. Pierre-Auguste Renoir
*Woman at the Corner Stove*
[*Femme au coin du poêle*], 1912
Oil on canvas
18 ⅛ x 19 ¾ in. (46 x 50 cm)

32. Pierre-Auguste Renoir
*Bather* [*Baigneuse*], 1912
Oil on canvas
25 ¾ x 22 in. (65.4 x 55.9 cm)

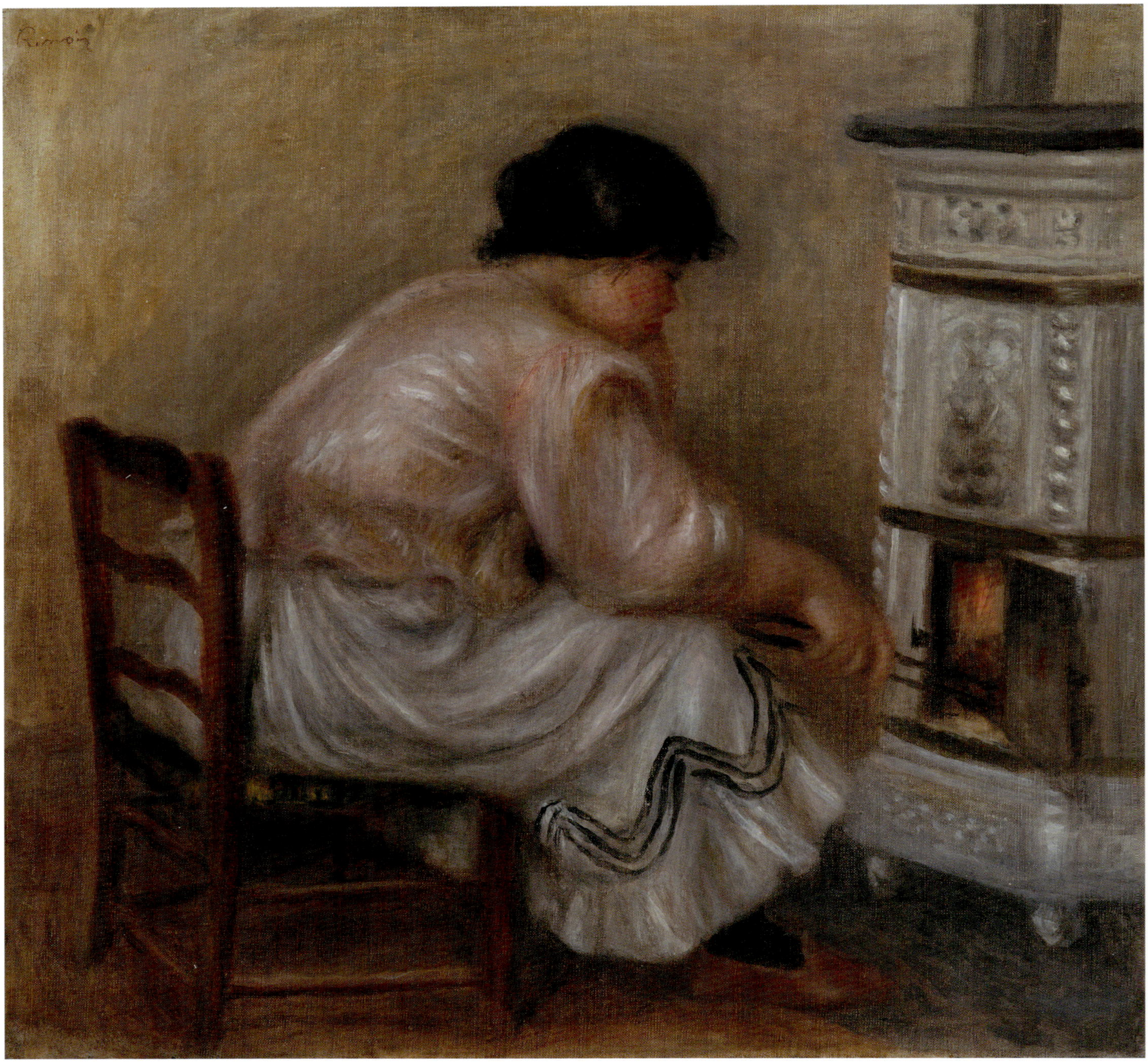

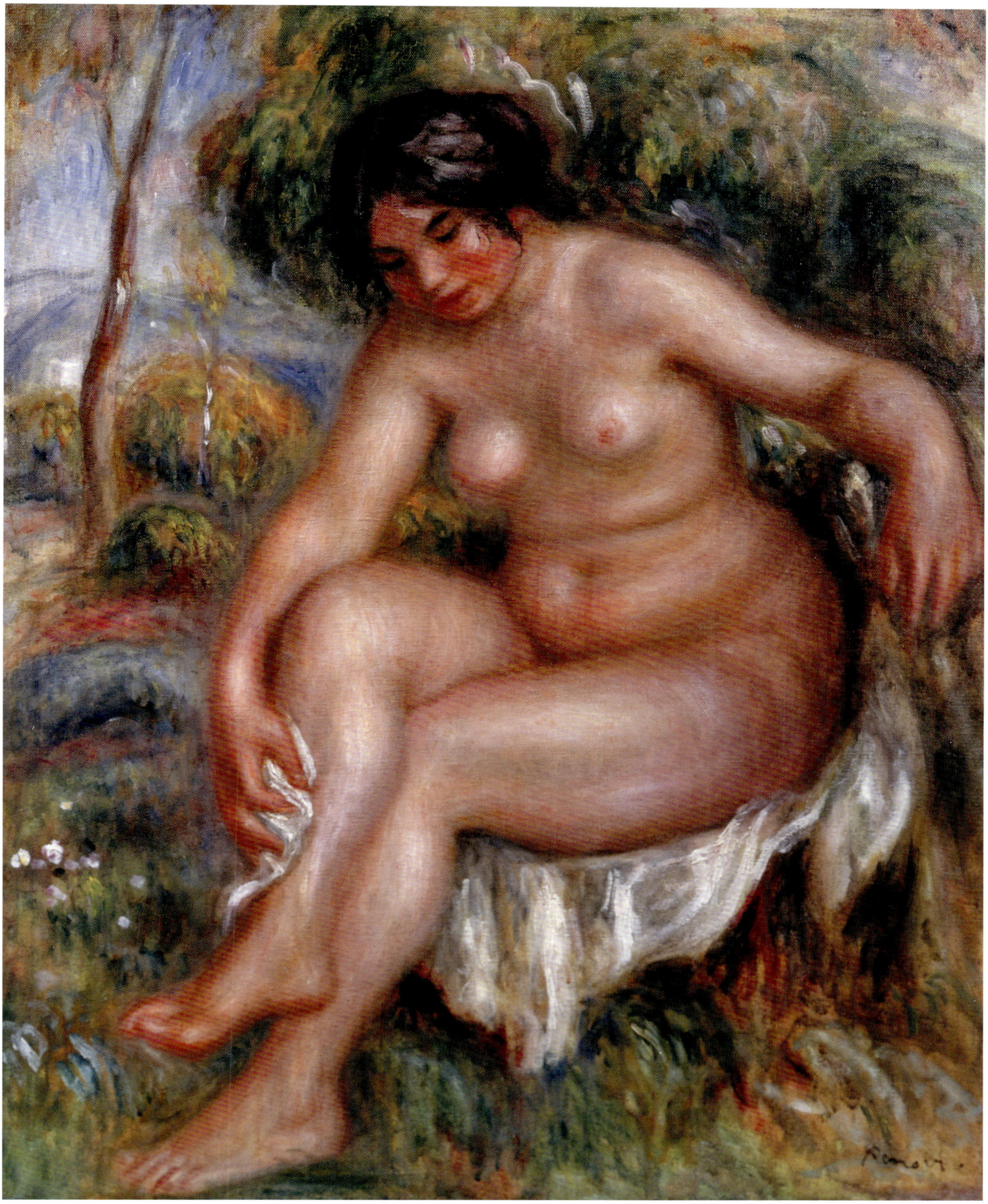

33. Pierre-Auguste Renoir
*Mlle. Estable*, 1912
Oil on canvas
16 5/16 x 12 3/8 in. (41.4 x 31.4 cm)

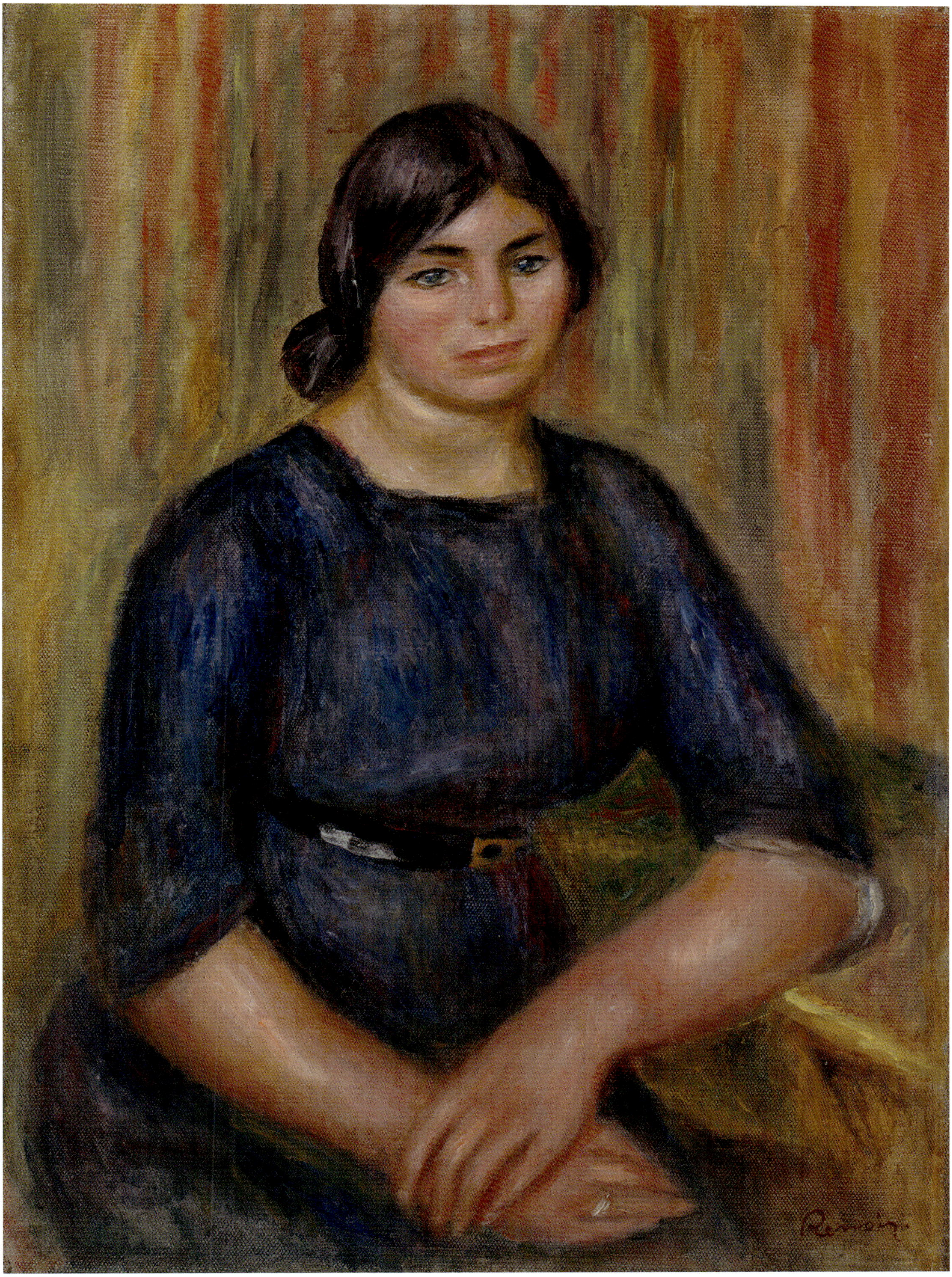
Renoir.

34. Pierre-Auguste Renoir
*Flowers* [*Fleurs*], 1915–19
Oil on canvas
9 ½ x 9 ¾ in. (24.13 x 24.77 cm)

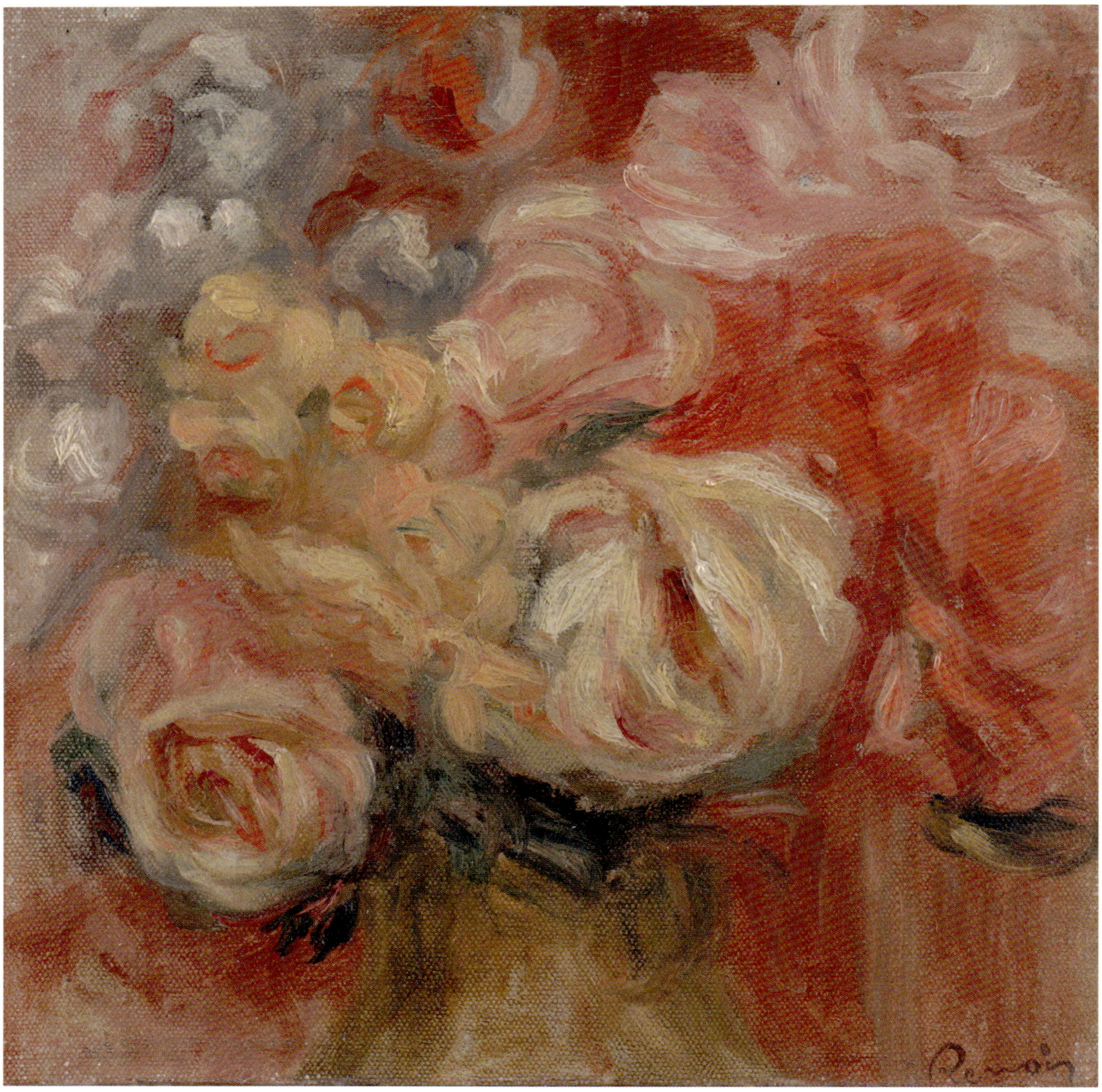

35. Pierre-Auguste Renoir
*Bare-Breasted Sleeping Woman*
[*Femme à la poitrine nue endormie*],
1919
Oil on canvas
15 ¾ x 20 ⅛ in. (40 x 51 cm)

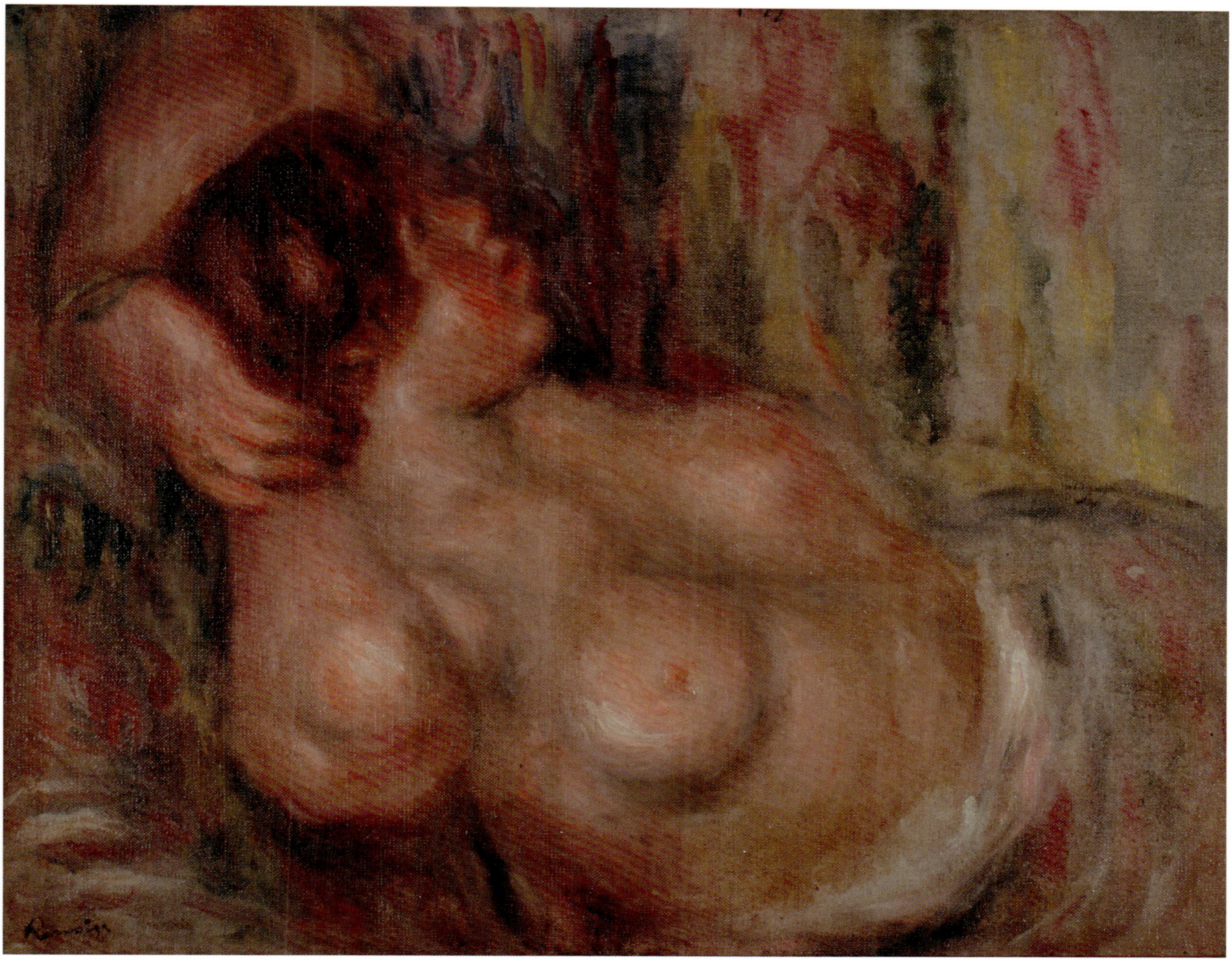

# William J. Glackens

36. William J. Glackens
*Outside the Guttenberg Race Track*,
1897
Oil on canvas
12 x 17 in. (30.48 x 43.18 cm)

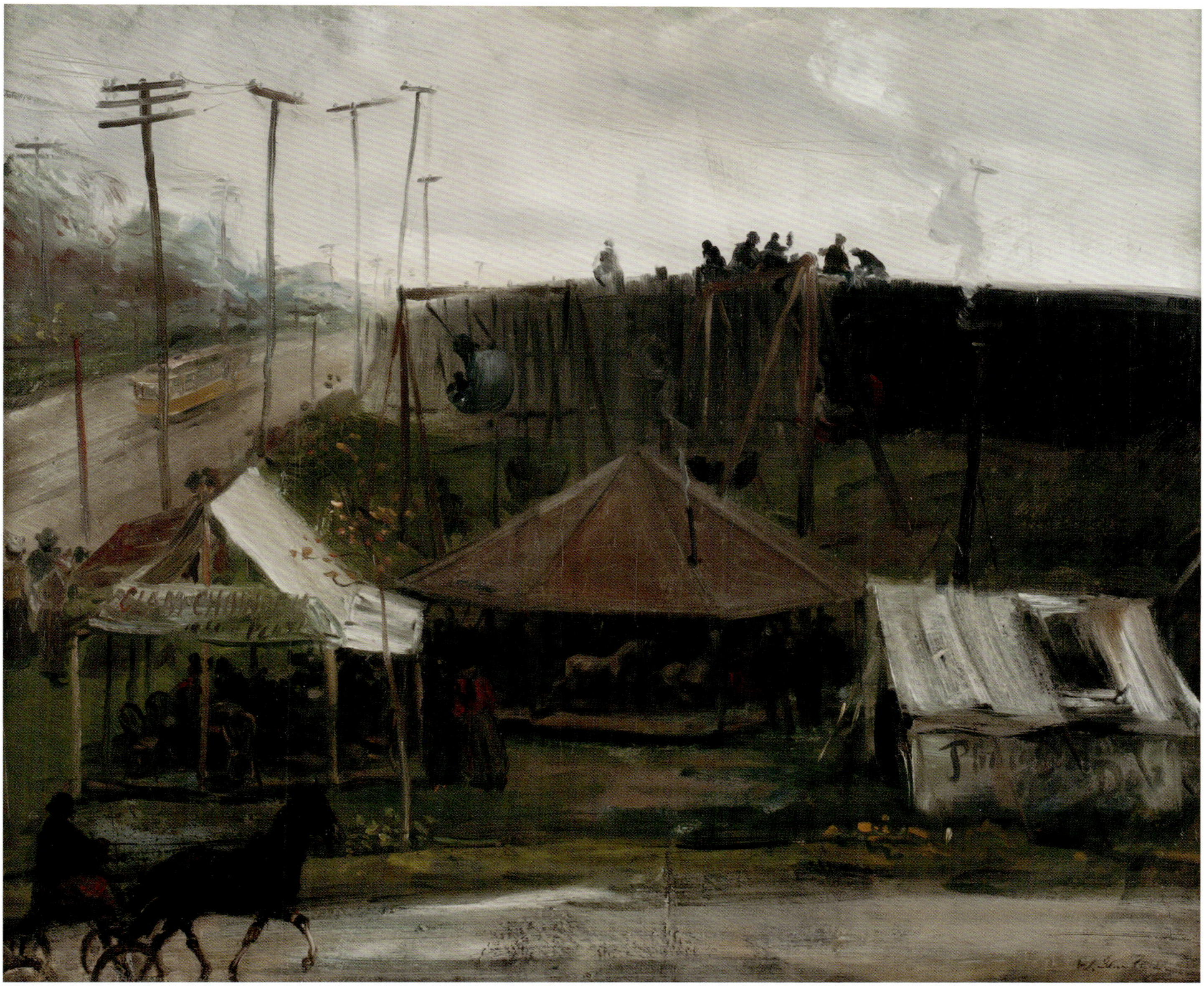

37. William J. Glackens
*Nude Dressing Her Hair*, 1909
Oil on canvas
30 x 25 in. (76.2 x 63.5 cm)

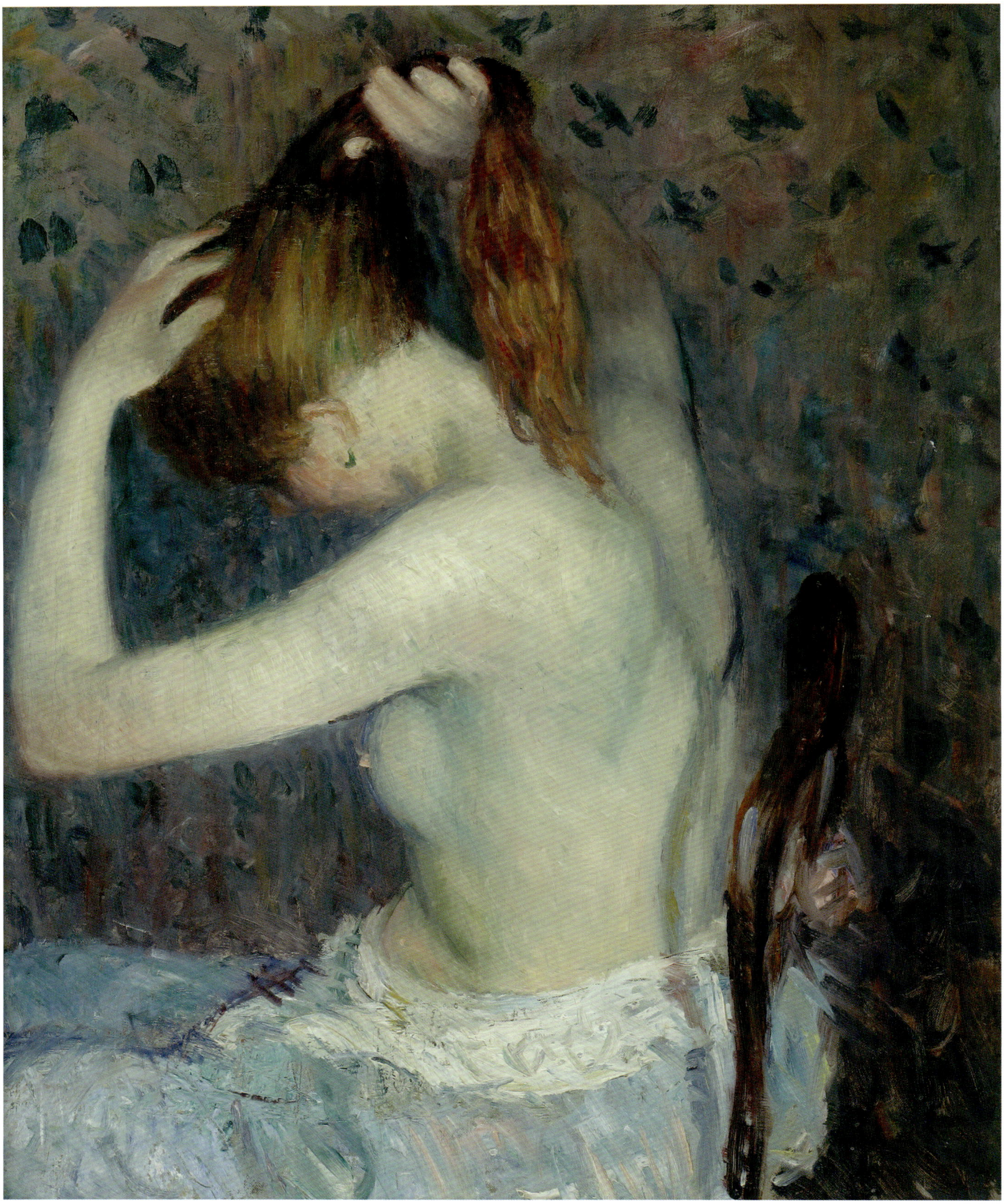

38. William J. Glackens
*Semi-Nude with Hat*, c. 1909
Oil on canvas
32 x 25 in. (81.28 x 63.5 cm)

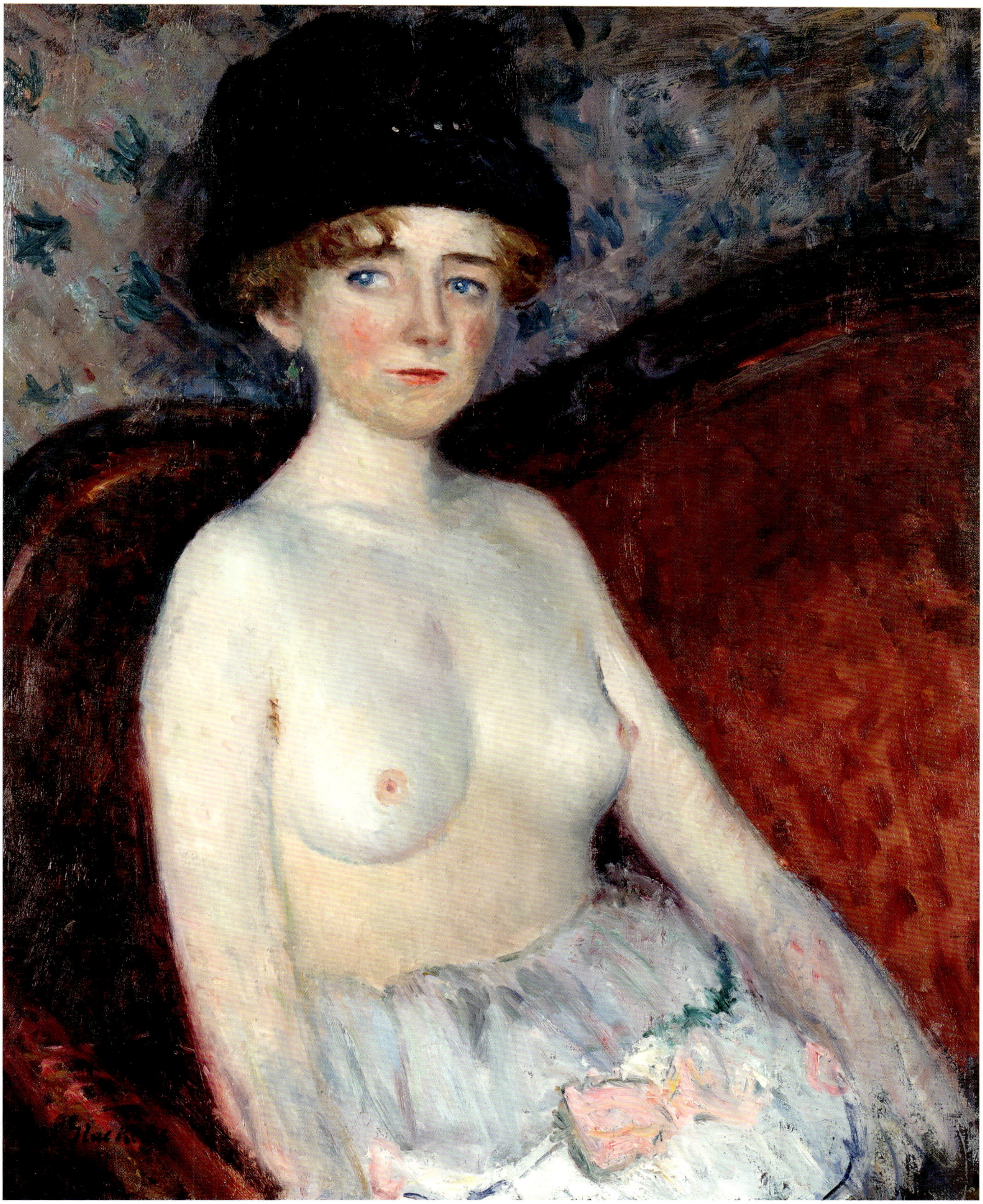

39. William J. Glackens
*Reclining Nude*, 1910
Oil on canvas
32 ⅛ x 54 ¼ in. (81.6 x 137.8 cm)

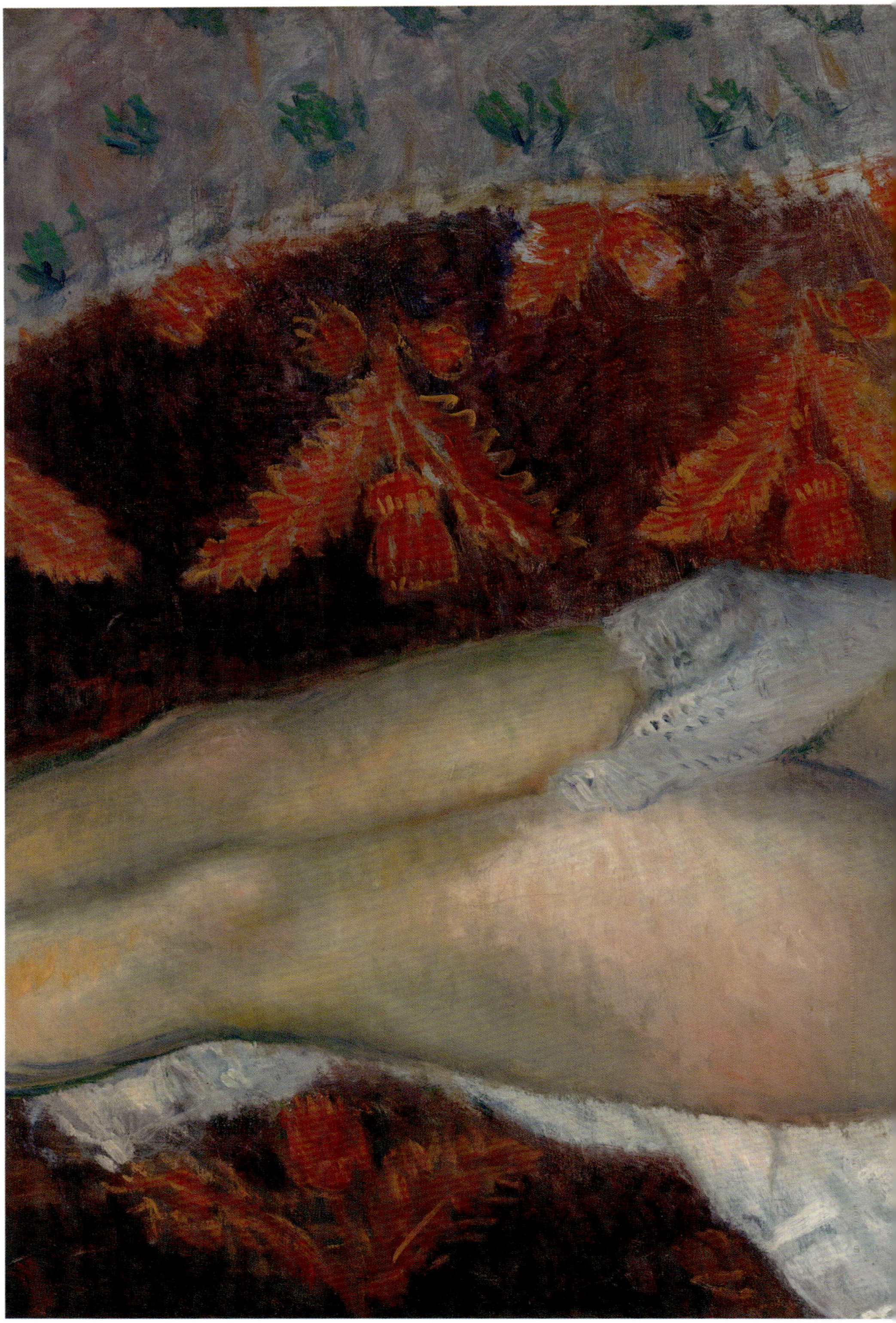

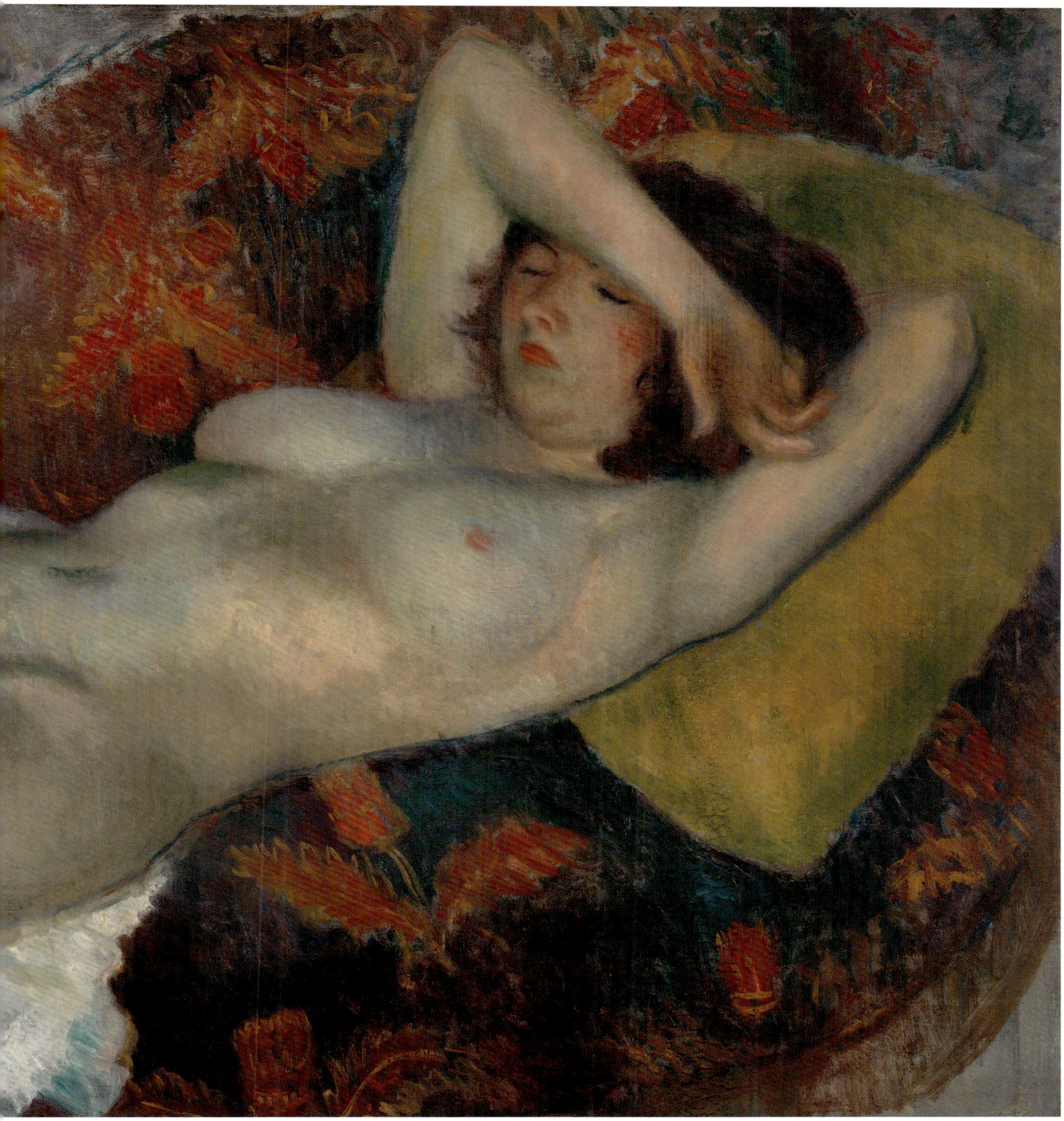

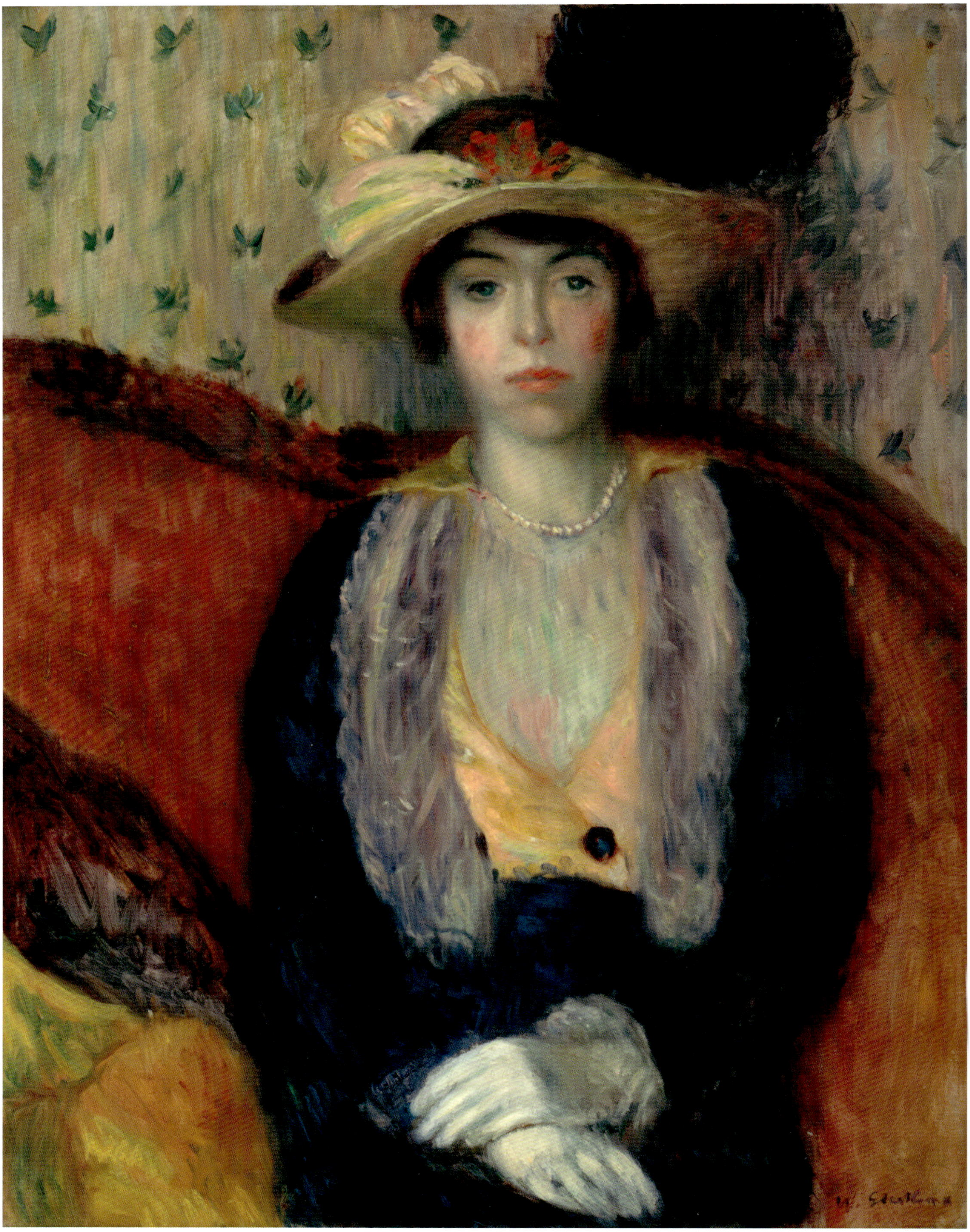

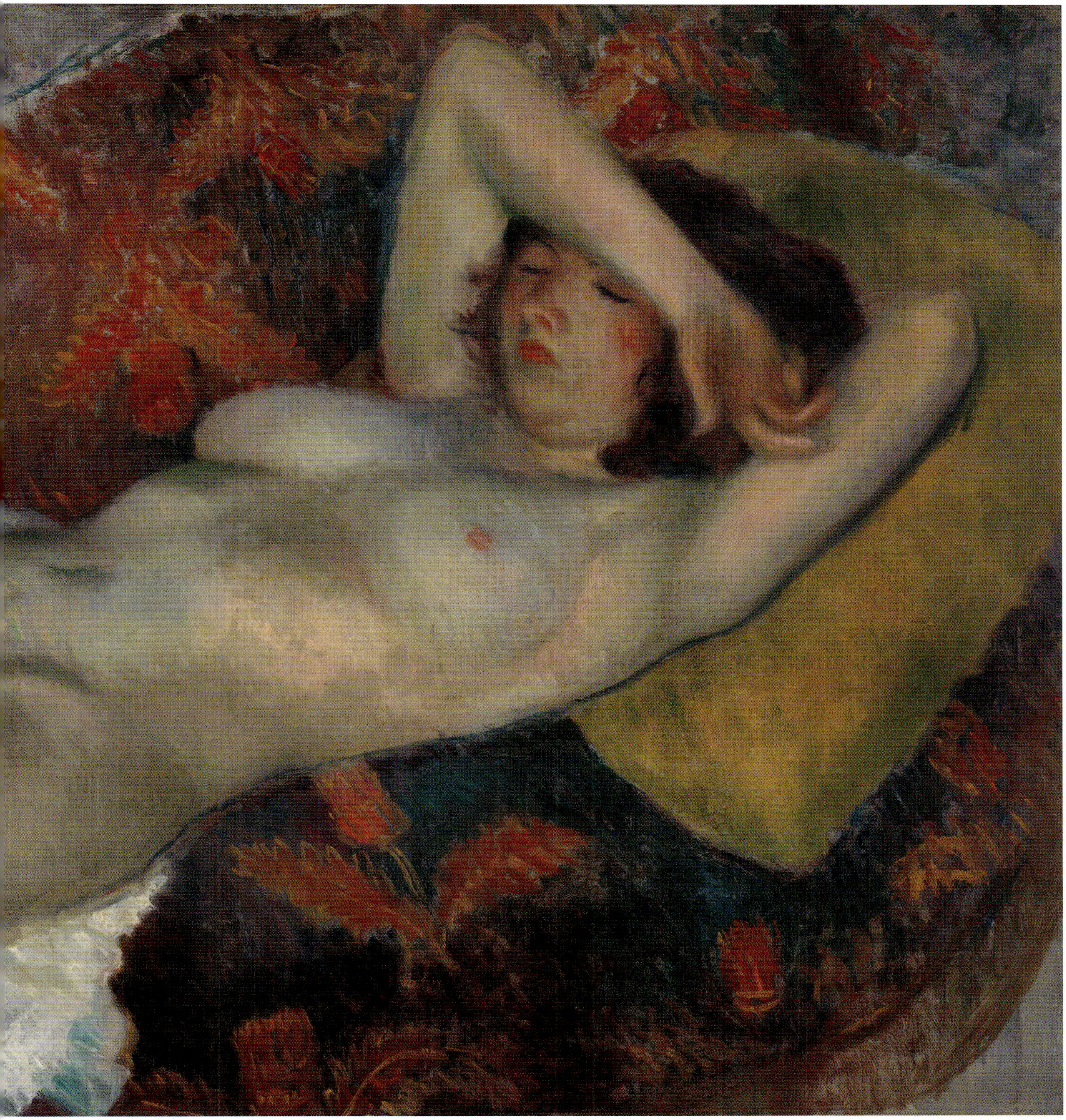

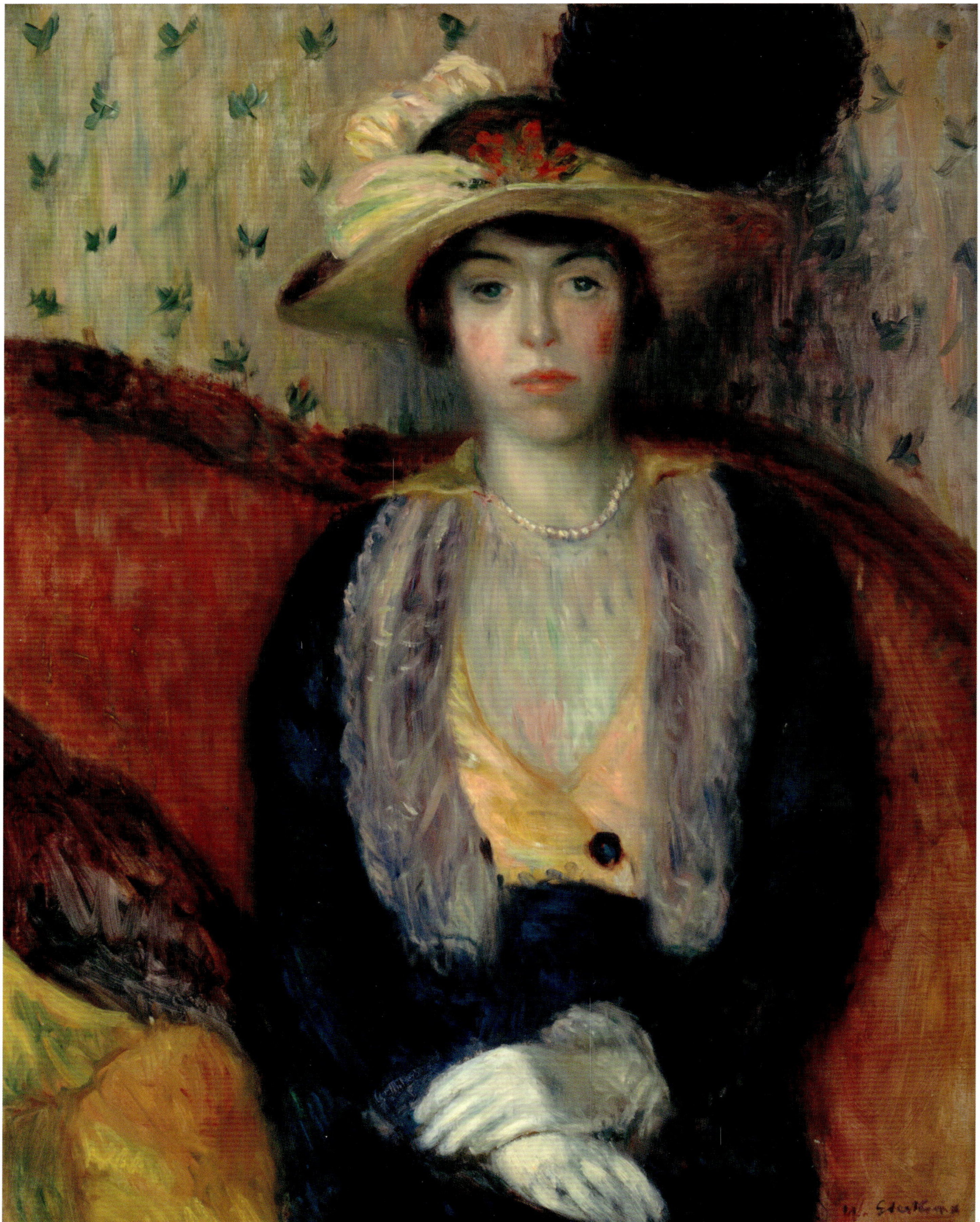

40. William J. Glackens
*Miss Olga D.*, 1910
Oil on canvas
32 x 26 in. (81.28 x 66.04 cm)

41. William J. Glackens
*Lenna at One Year*, 1914
Oil on canvas
14 ¾ x 11 ½ in. (37.4 x 29.2 cm)

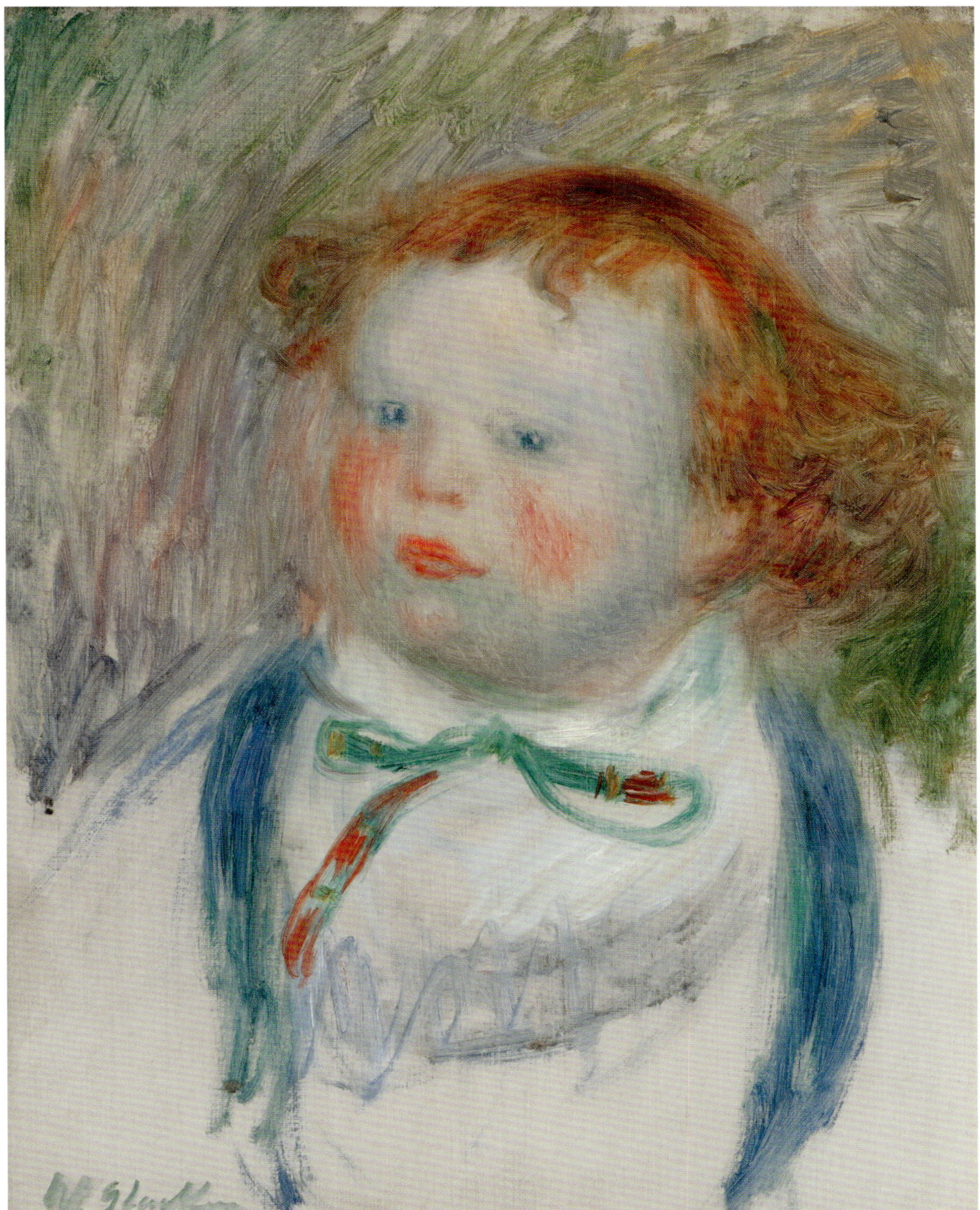

42. William J. Glackens
*The Little Pier*, 1914
Oil on canvas
25 x 30 in. (63.5 x 76.2 cm)

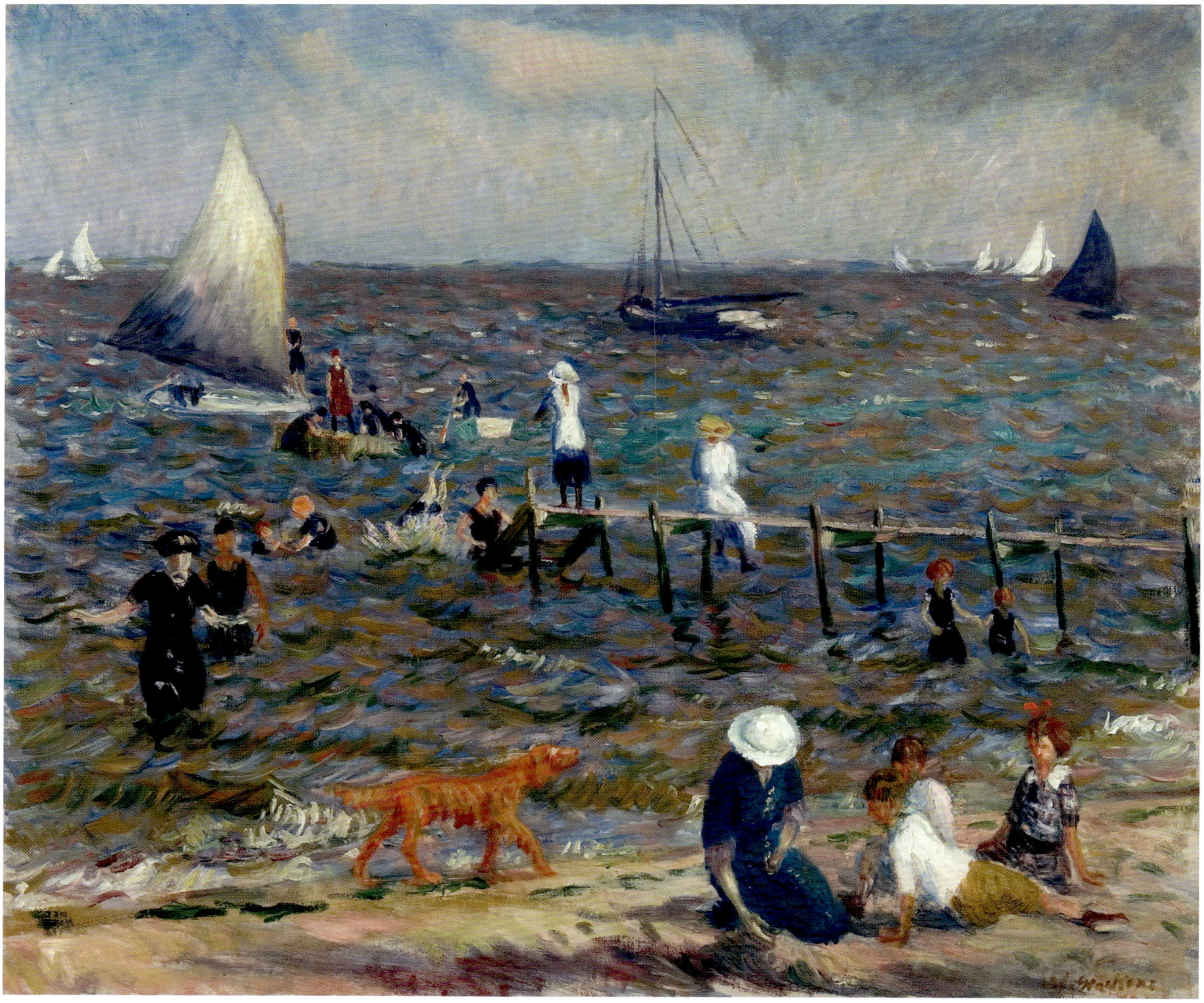

43. William J. Glackens
*Pier at Blue Point*, 1914
Oil on canvas
25 ⅞ x 32 in. (65.72 x 81.28 cm)

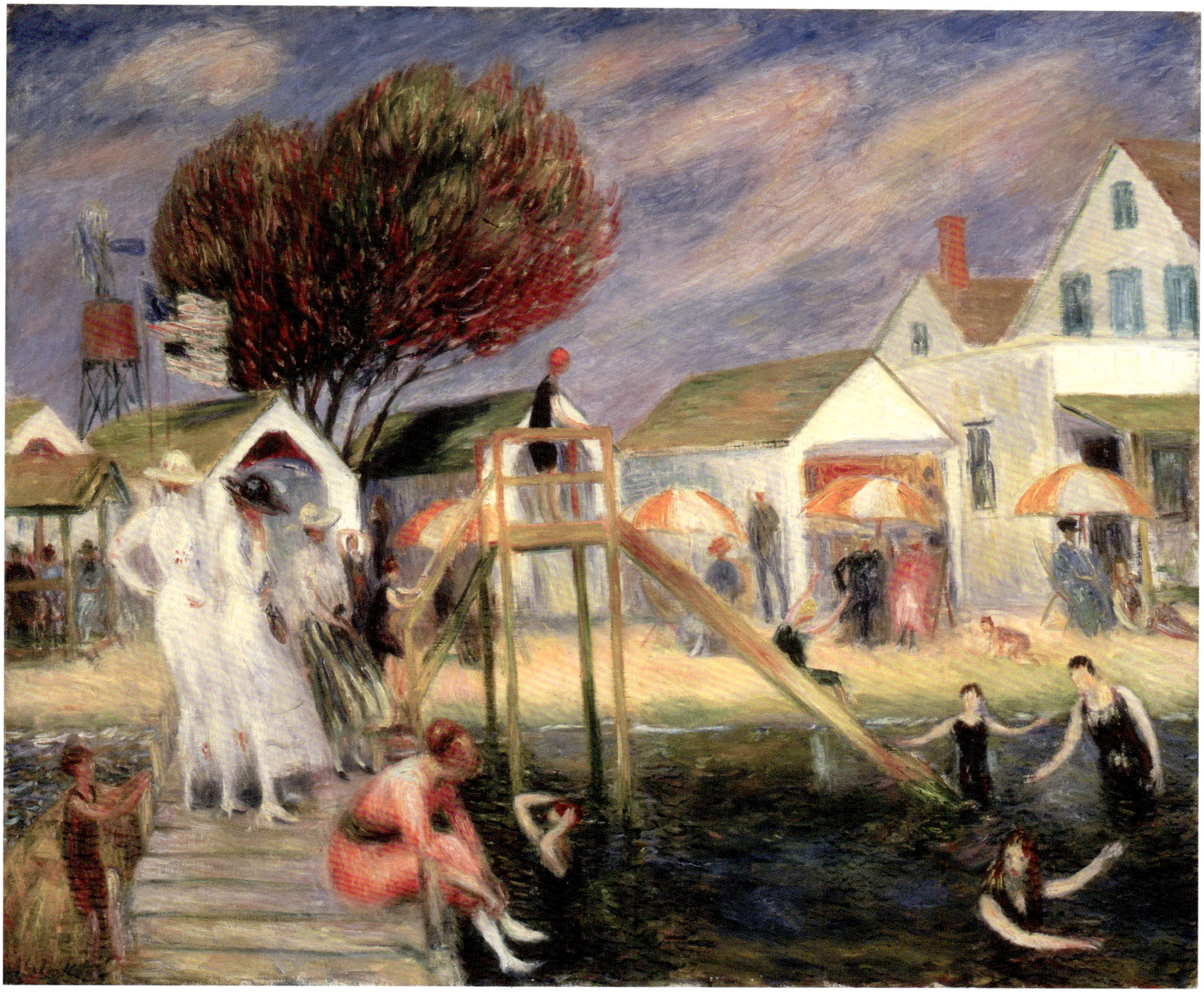

44. William J. Glackens
*Summer*, 1914
Oil on canvas
26 x 32 in. (66.04 x 81.28 cm)

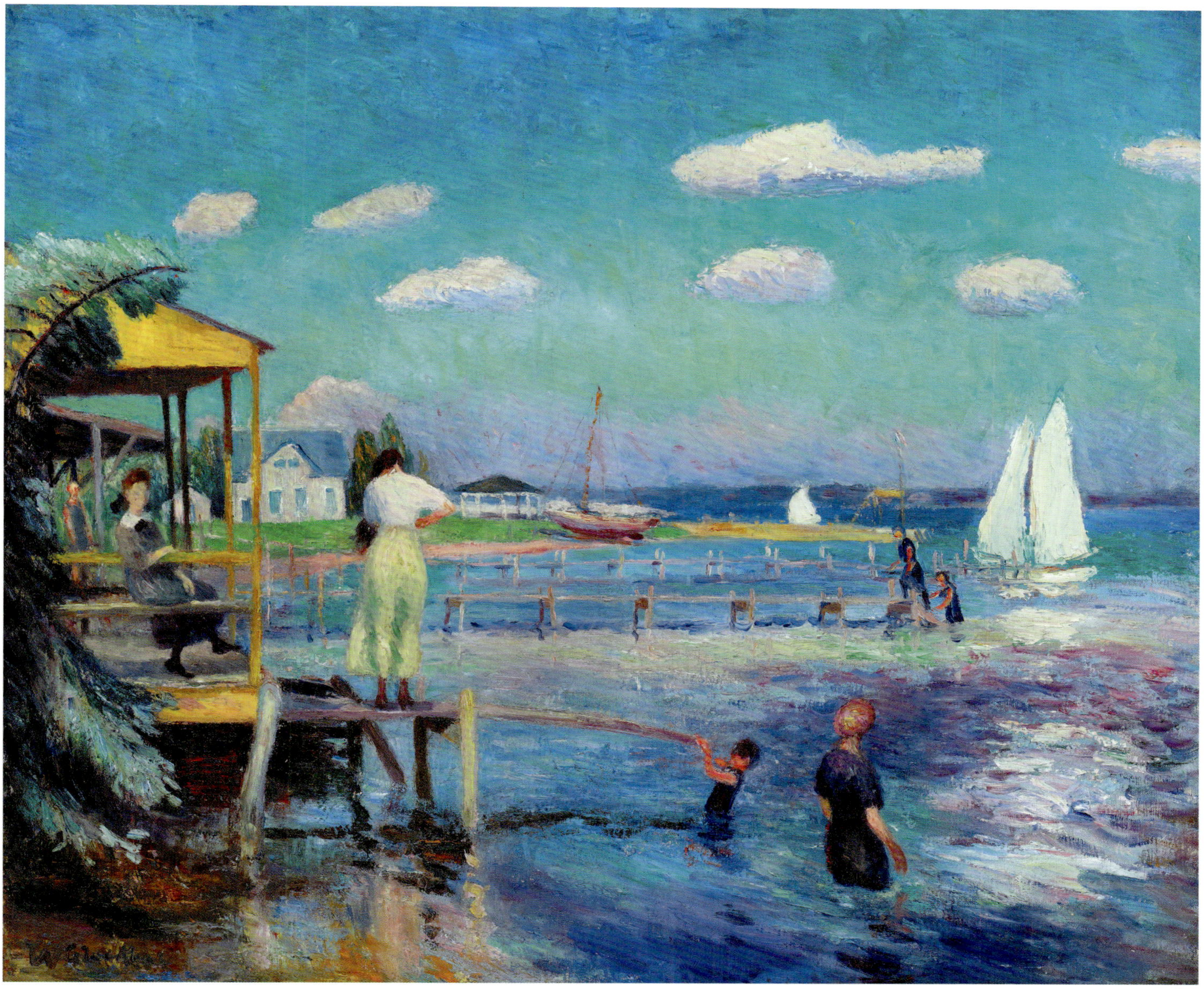

45. William J. Glackens
*Julia's Sister*, c. 1915
Oil on canvas
32 ⅛ x 26 ⅛ in. (81.6 x 66.4 cm)

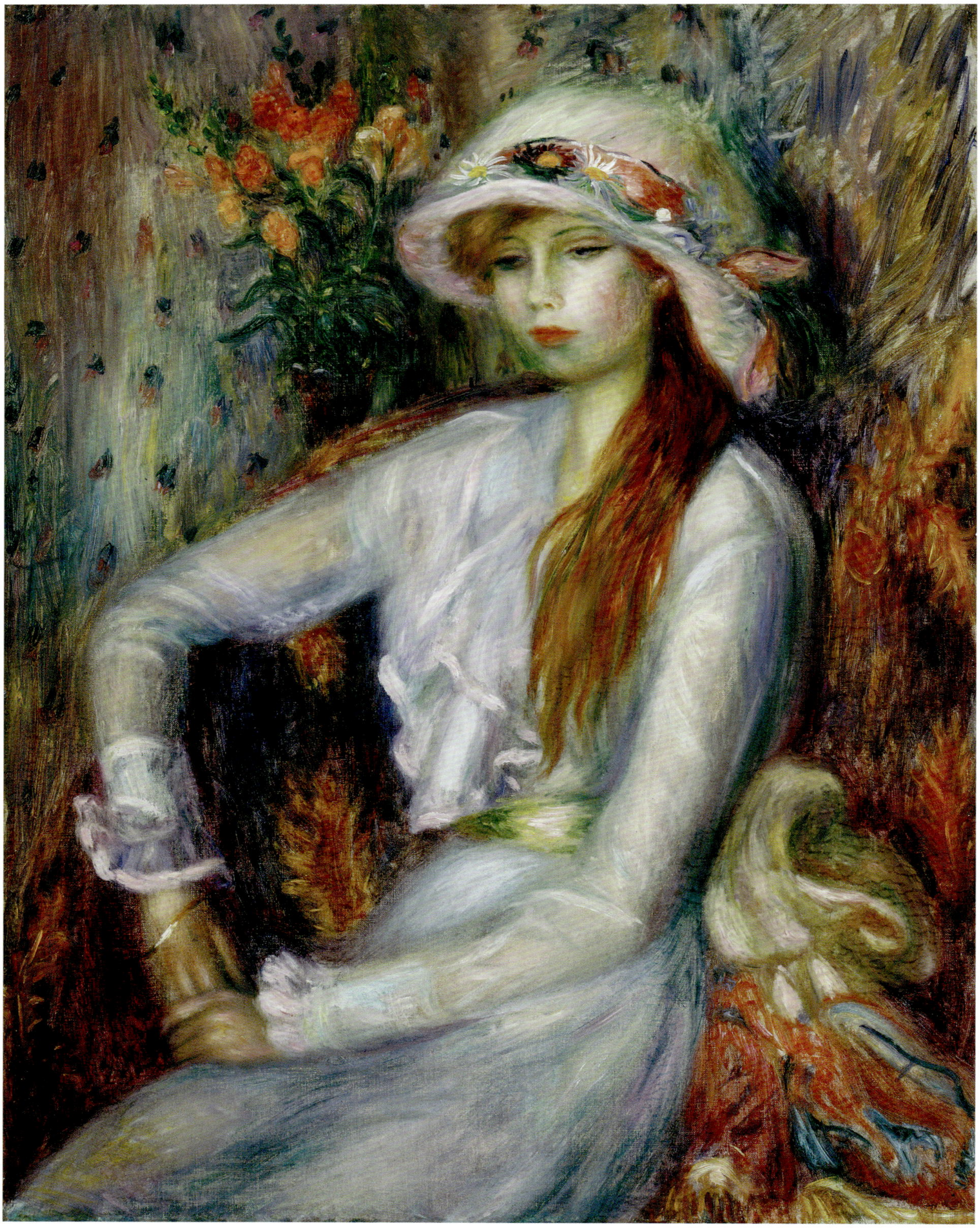

46. William J. Glackens
*Girl in Red Dress Pinning on Hat*,
c. 1915–16
Oil on canvas
31 ¾ x 26 in. (80.6 x 66 cm)

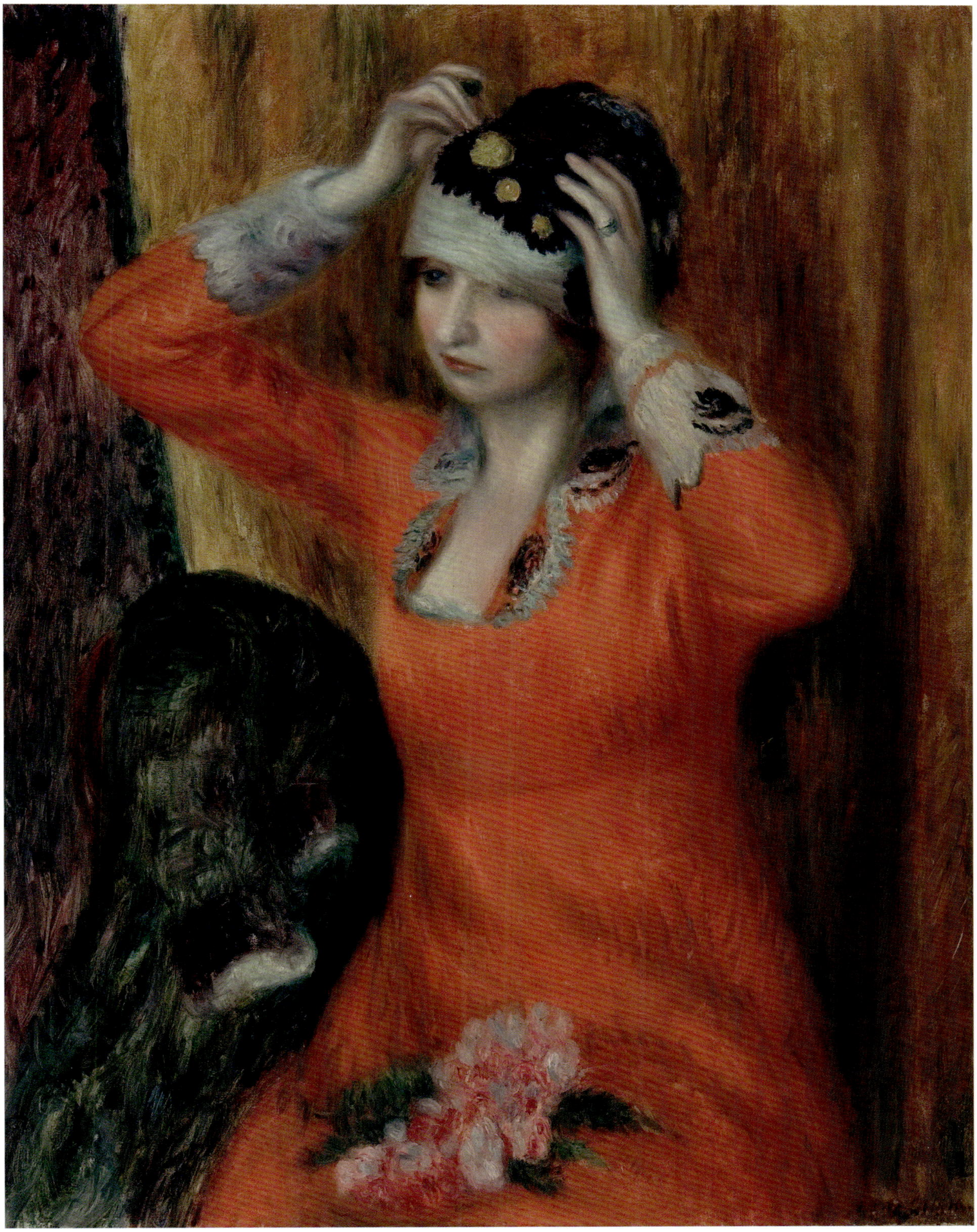

47. William J. Glackens
*Indian Series (Flautist on Peacock)*,
c. 1914–18
Oil on canvas
48 x 30 in. (121.92 x 76.2 cm)

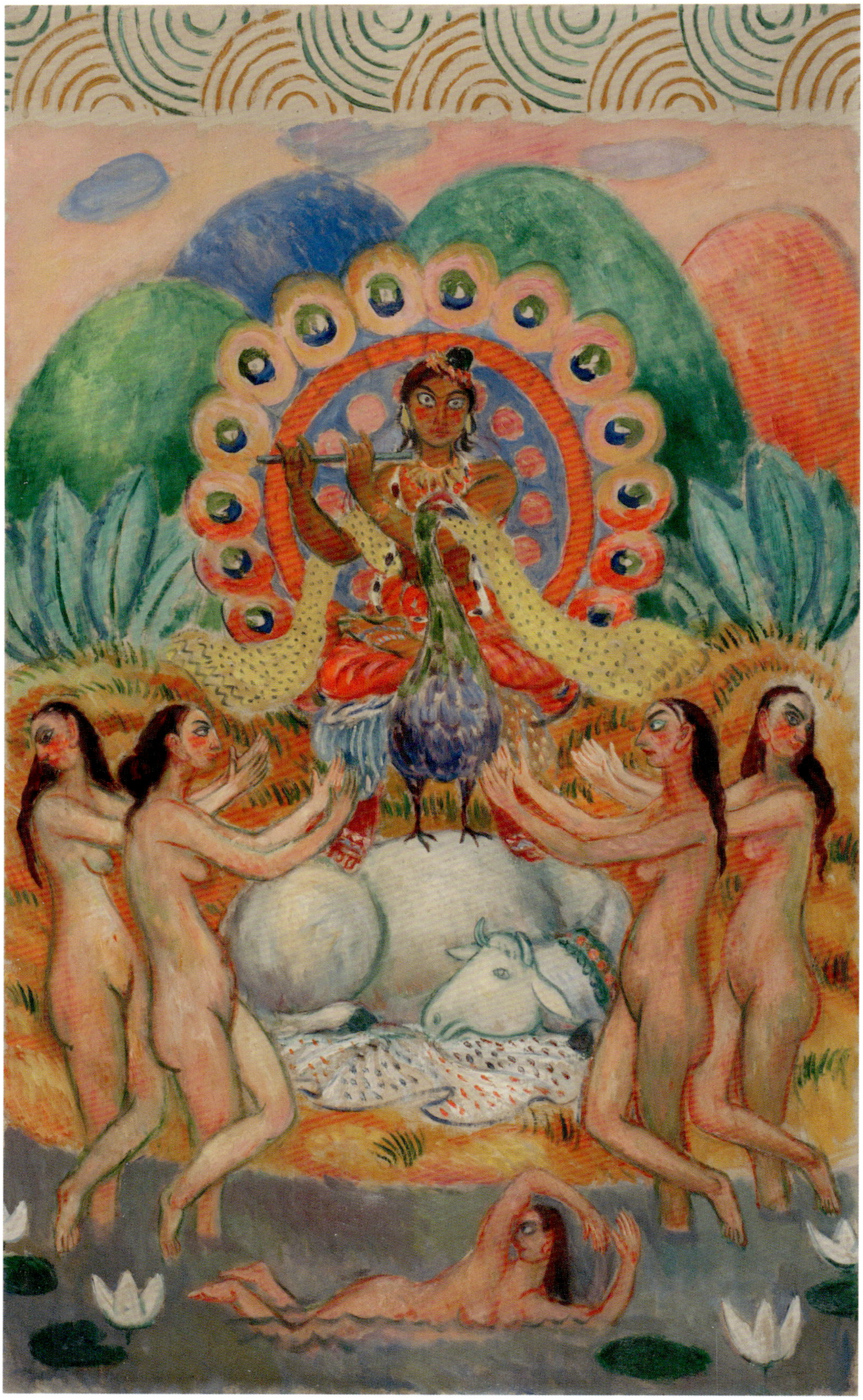

48. William J. Glackens
*Artist's Daughter in Chinese Costume*, 1918
Oil on canvas
48 3/16 x 30 1/16 in.
(122.39 x 76.35 cm)

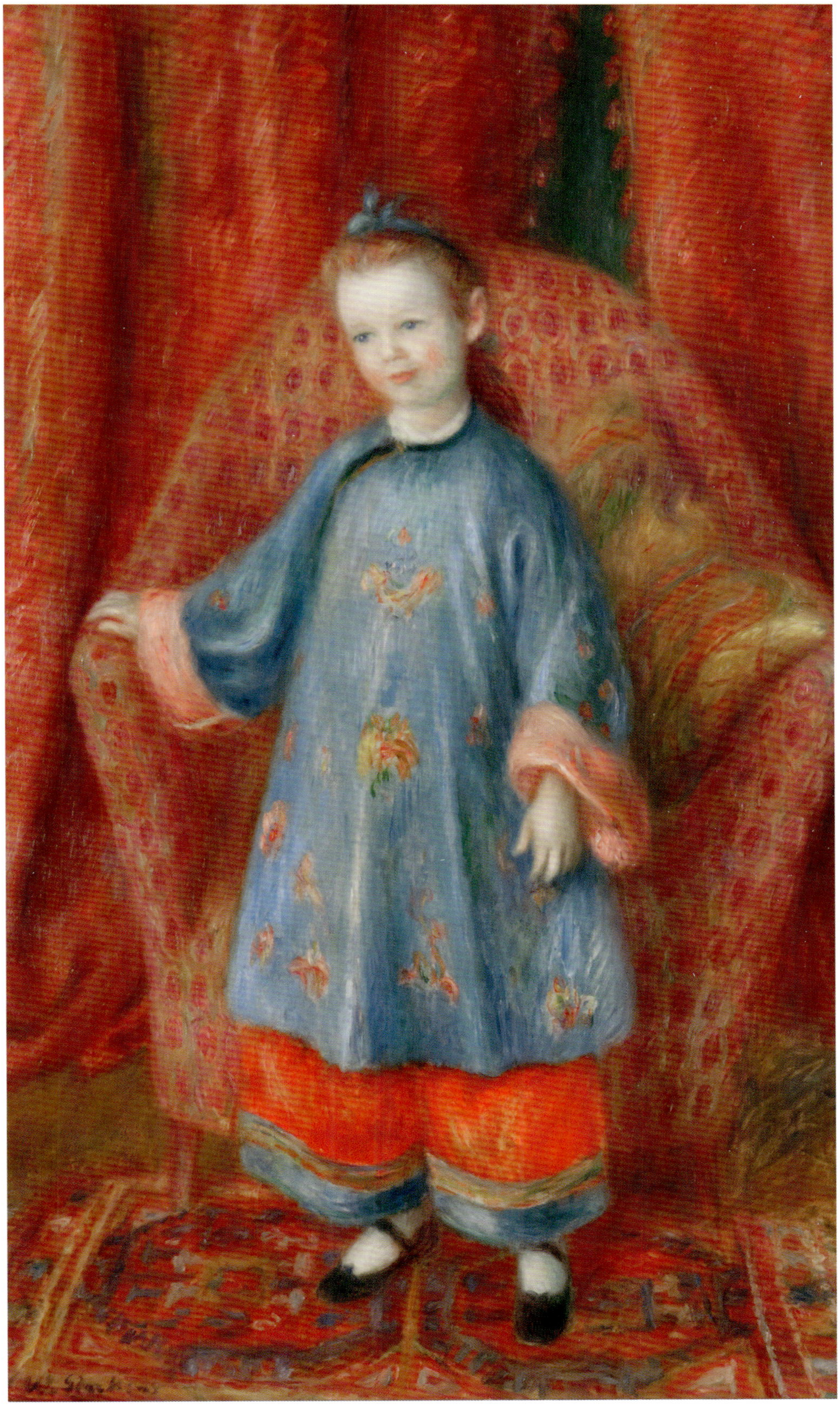

49. William J. Glackens
*Beach Scene, New London*, 1918
Oil on canvas
26 x 31 ⅞ in. (66.04 x 80.98 cm)

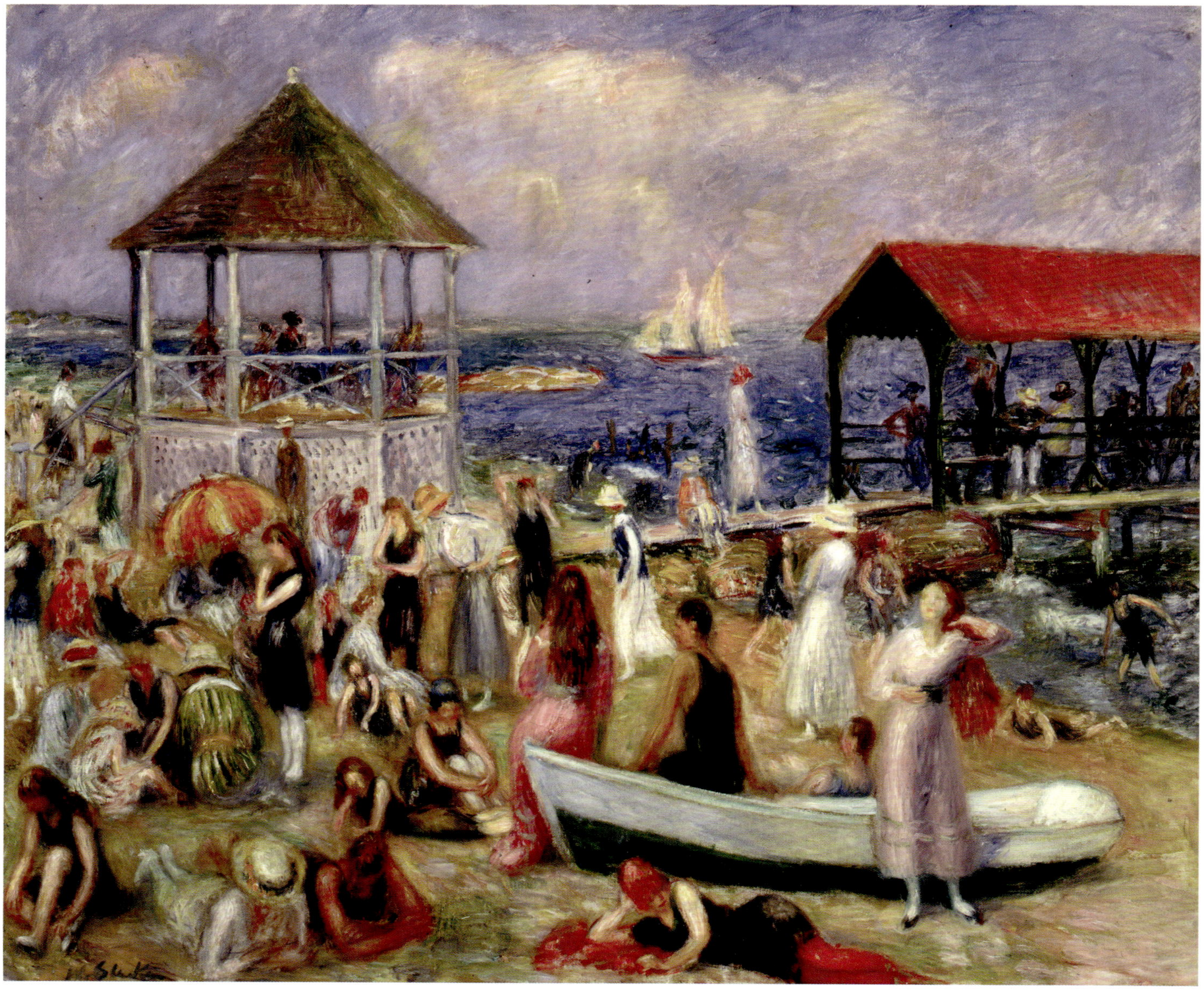

50. William J. Glackens
*Boat Landing at Gloucester*, c. 1918
Oil on canvas
25 ¼ x 31 in. (64.14 x 78.74 cm)

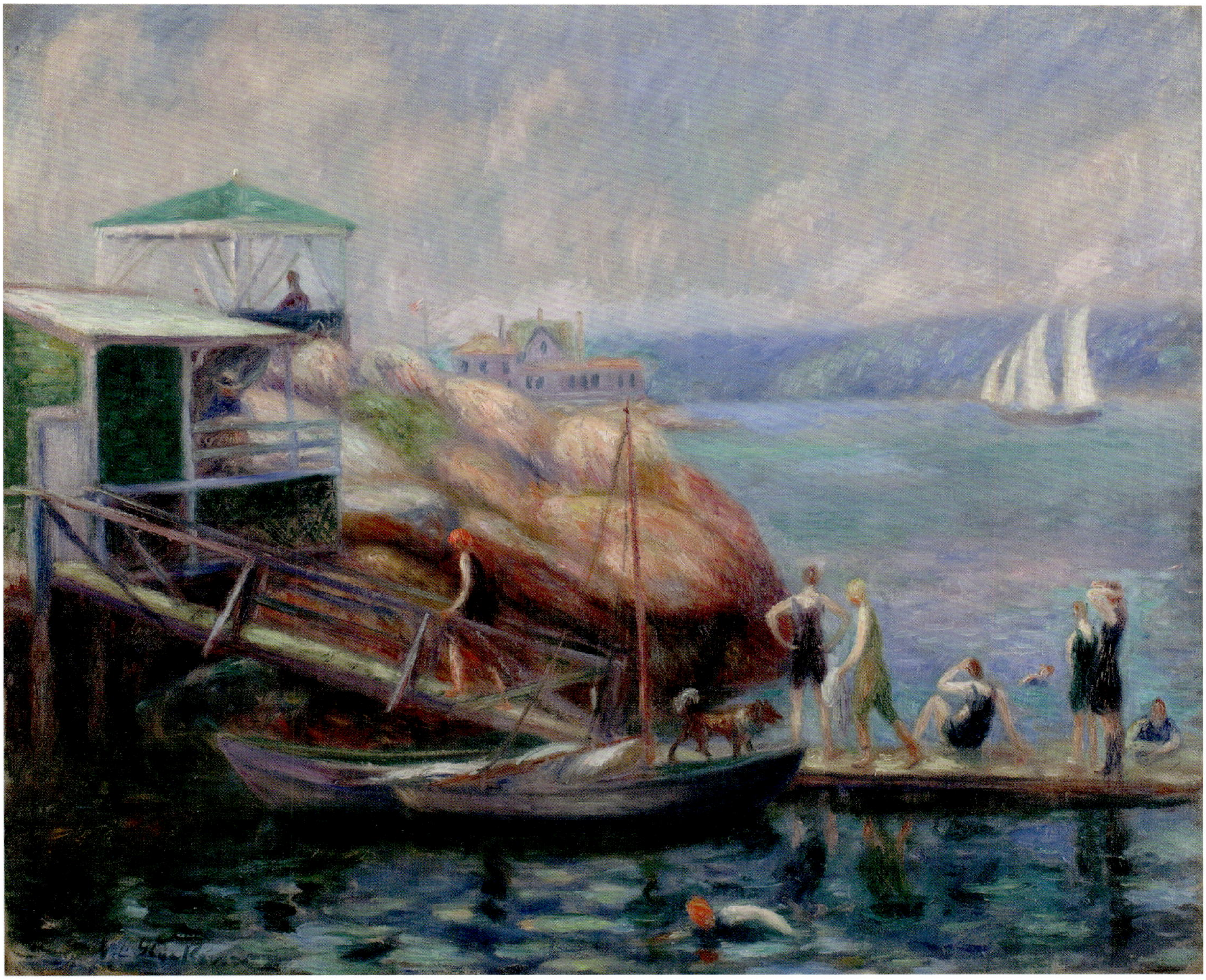

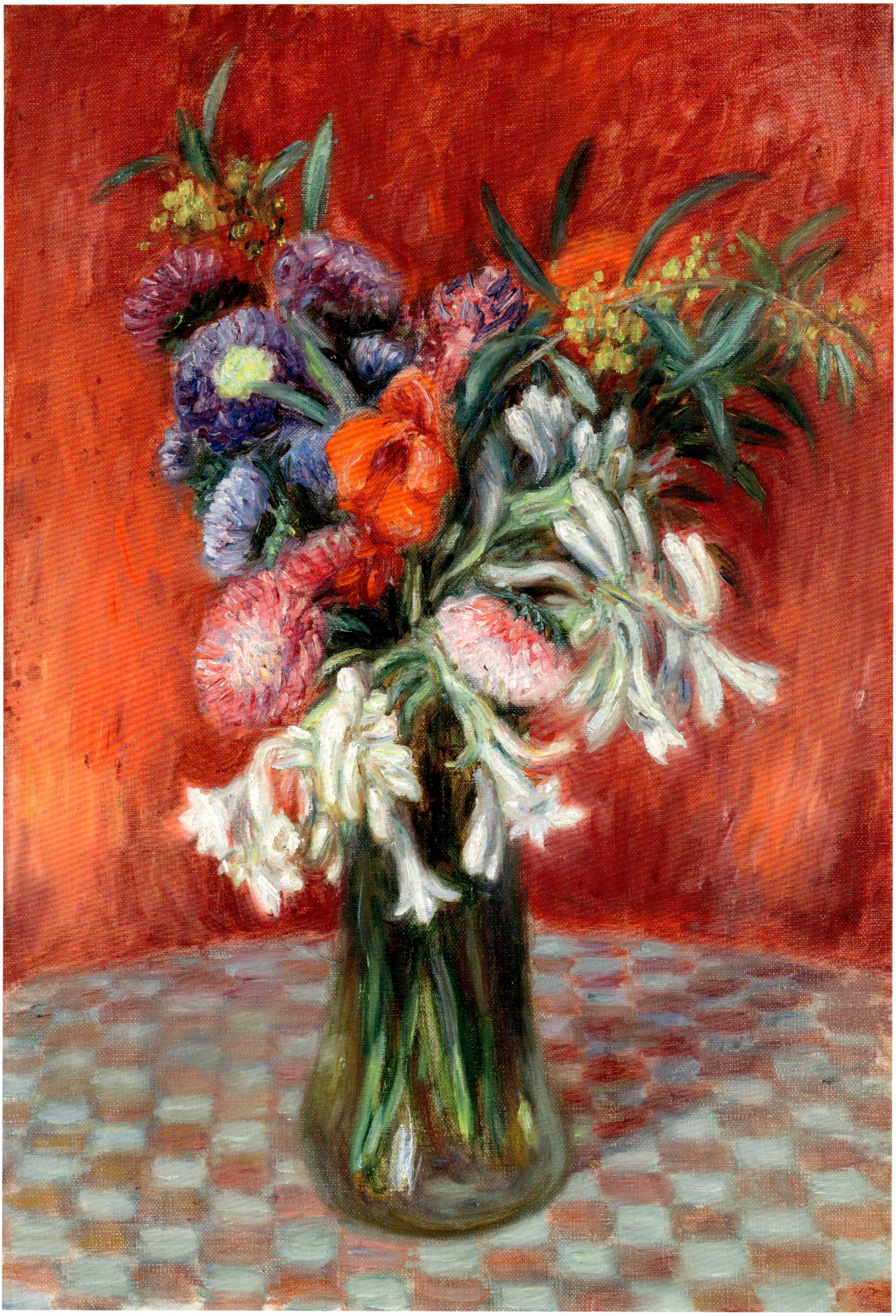

51. William J. Glackens
*Mixed Bouquet, Red Background*,
c. 1918
Oil on canvas
21 ¾ x 15 ⅛ in. (55.24 x 38.41 cm)

52. William J. Glackens
*Rose in a Glass*, c. 1918
Oil on canvas
11 ¼ x 8 ¼ in. (28.57 x 20.95 cm)

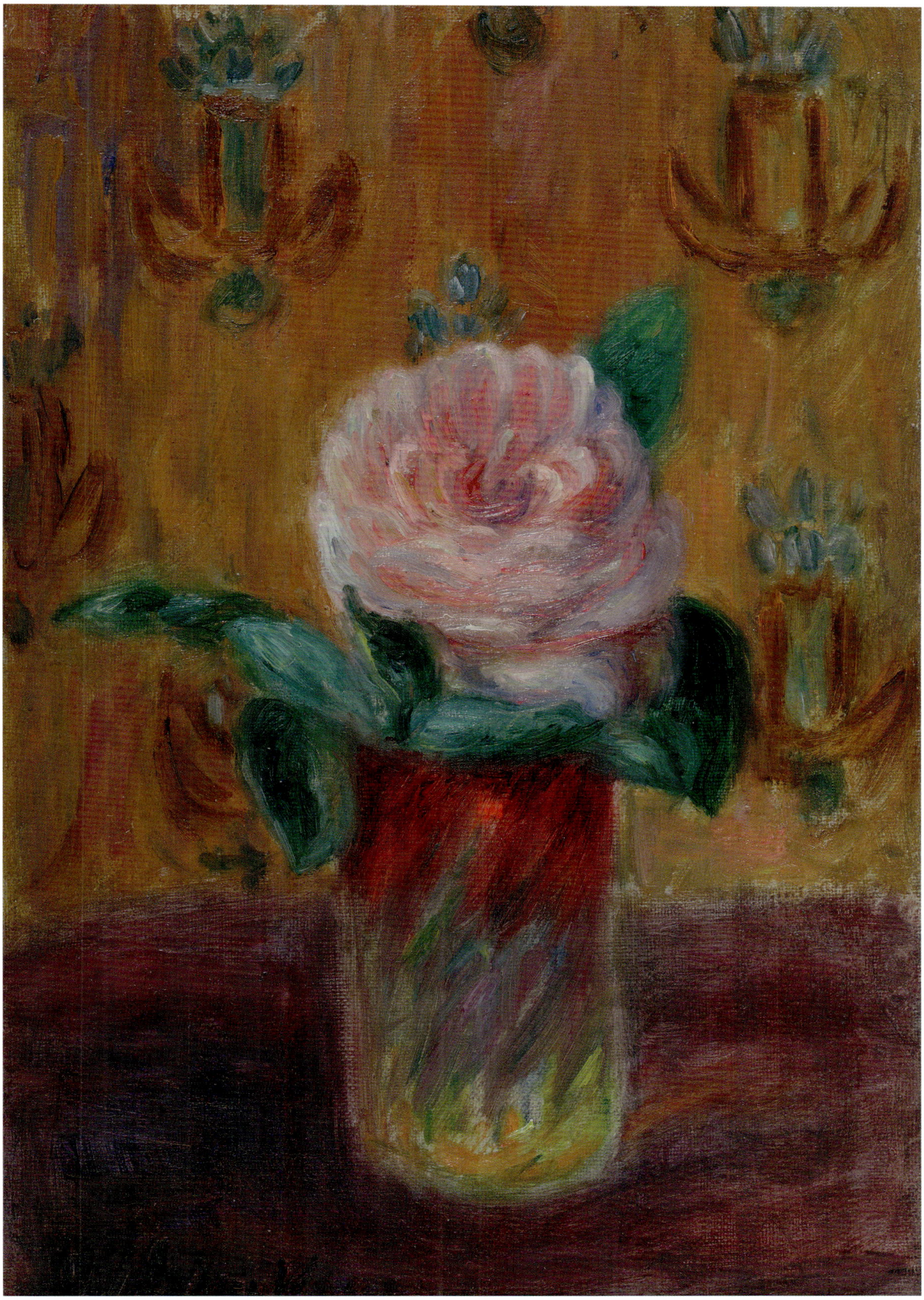

53. William J. Glackens
*Lenna Painting*, c. 1918
Oil on canvas
12 x 15 in. (30.48 x 38.1 cm)

54. William J. Glackens
*Finnish Woman*, 1920
Oil on canvas
32 x 26 in. (81.28 x 66.04 cm)

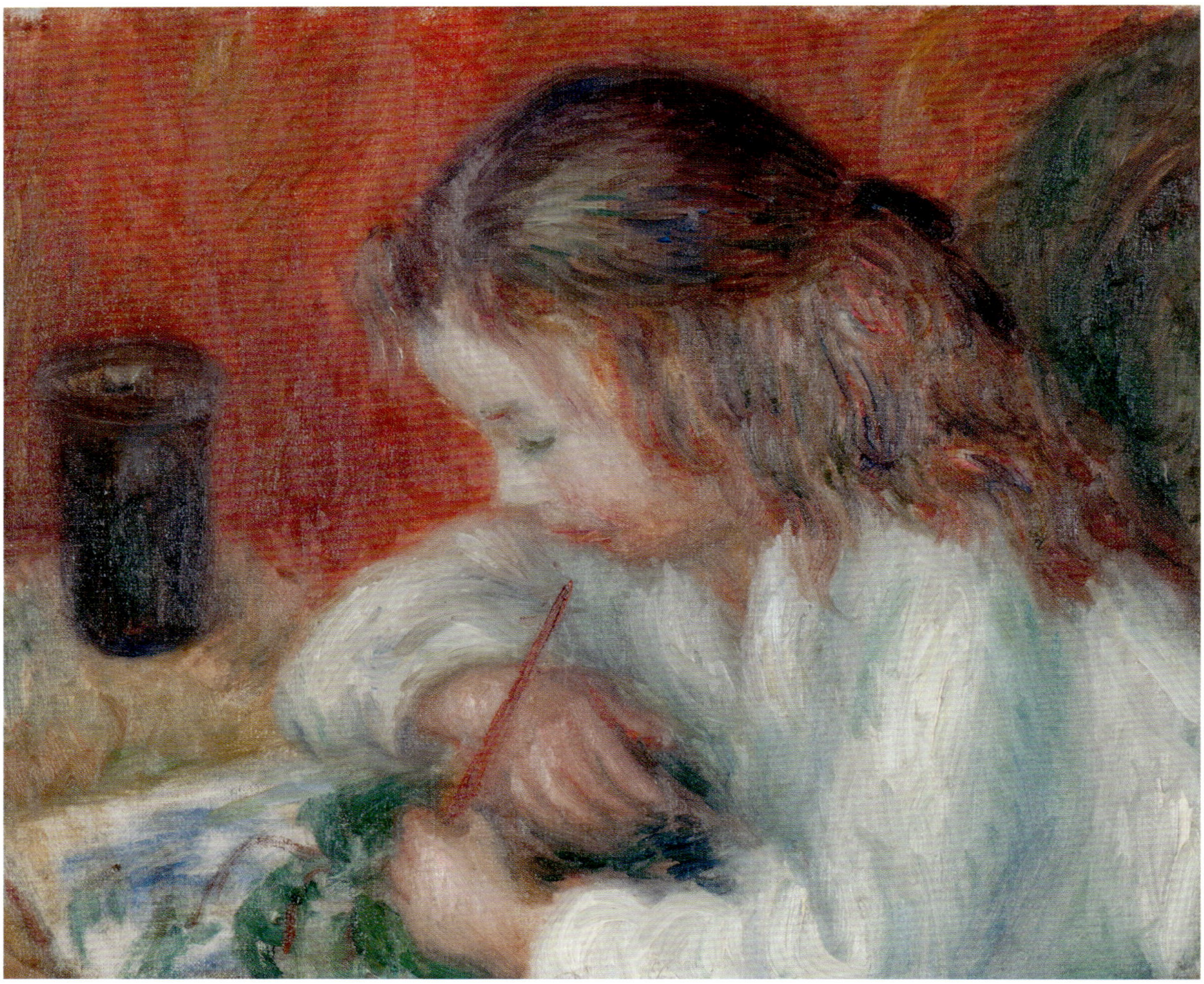

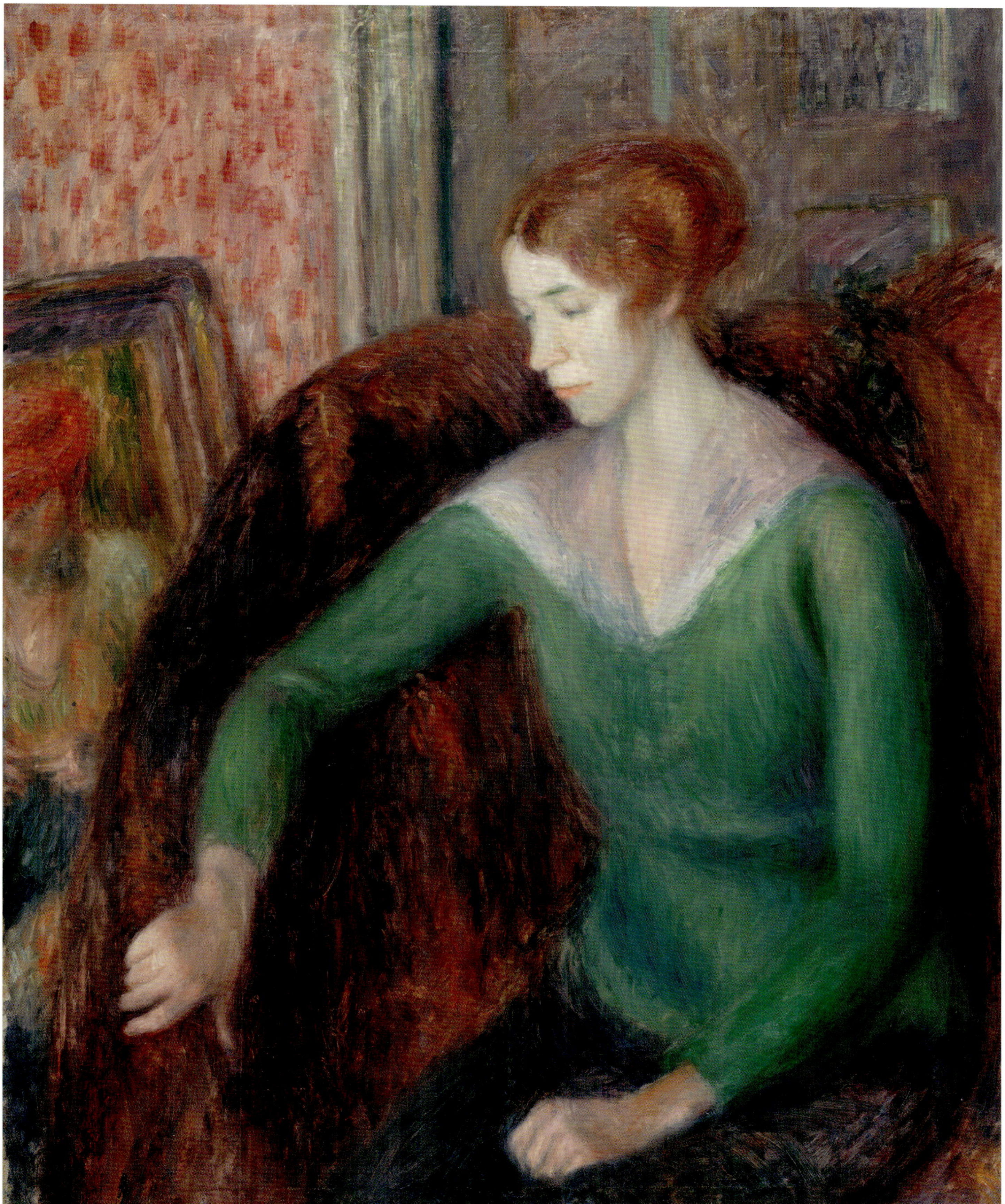

55. William J. Glackens
*Hallie Knitting in Red Hat*, c. 1920
Oil on canvas
24 x 18 in. (60.96 x 45.72 cm)

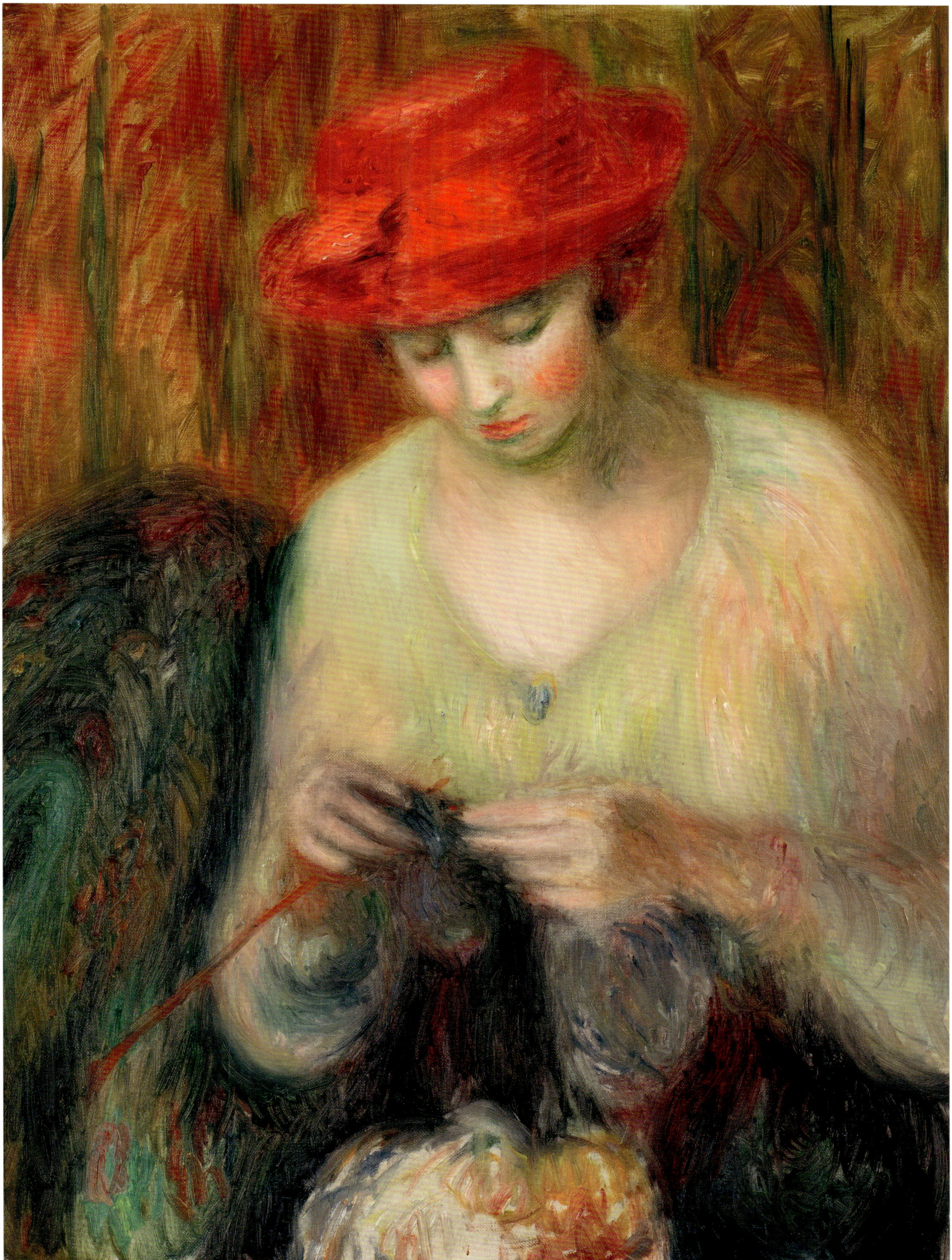

56. William J. Glackens
*Lenna with Rabbit Hound*, c. 1922
Oil on canvas
35 ½ x 31 ¼ in. (90.17 x 79.37 cm)

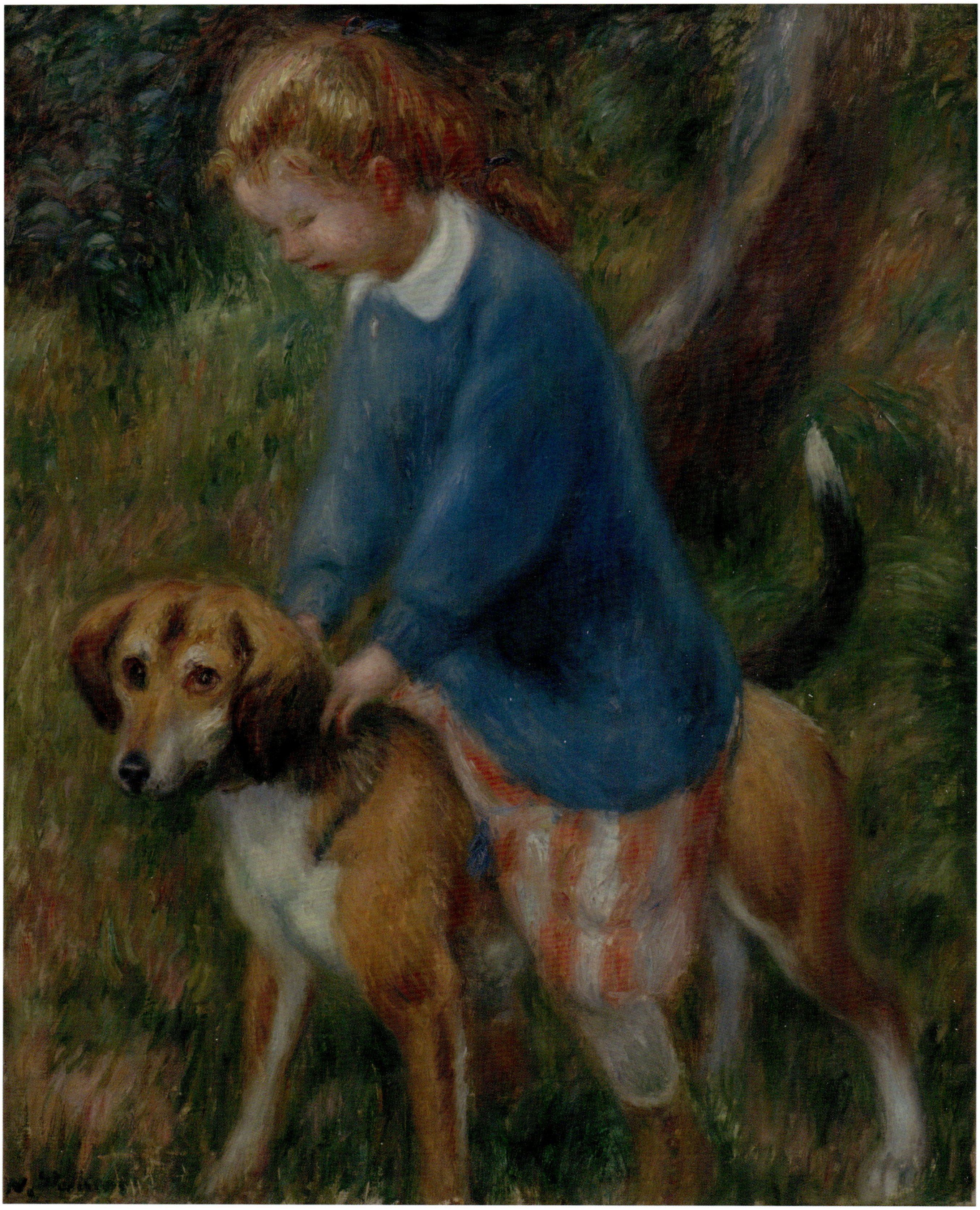

57. William J. Glackens
*Lenna Dressed as Toy Soldier*,
c. 1923
Oil on canvas
25 ¼ x 12 ¾ in. (64.13 x 32.38 cm)

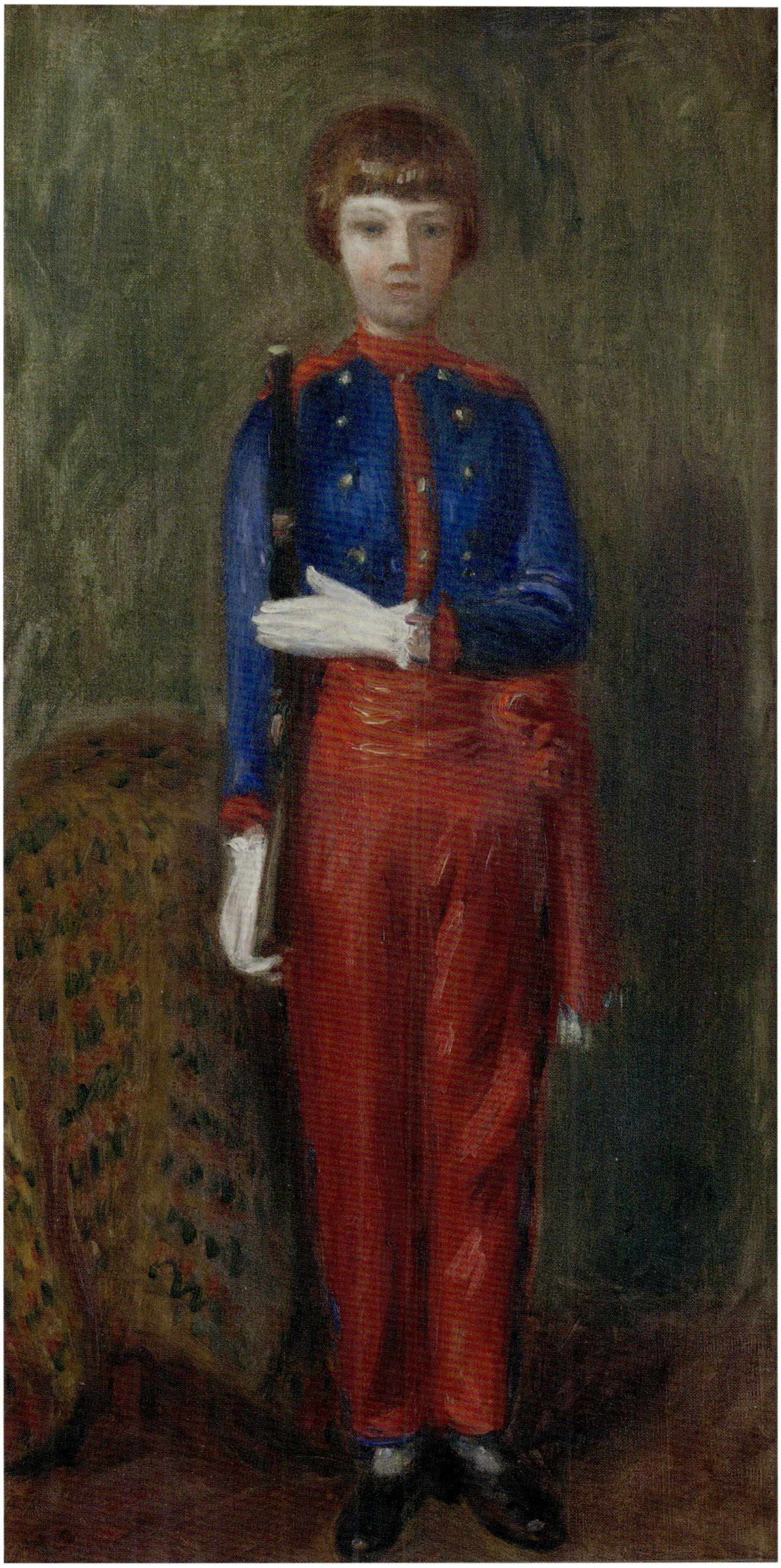

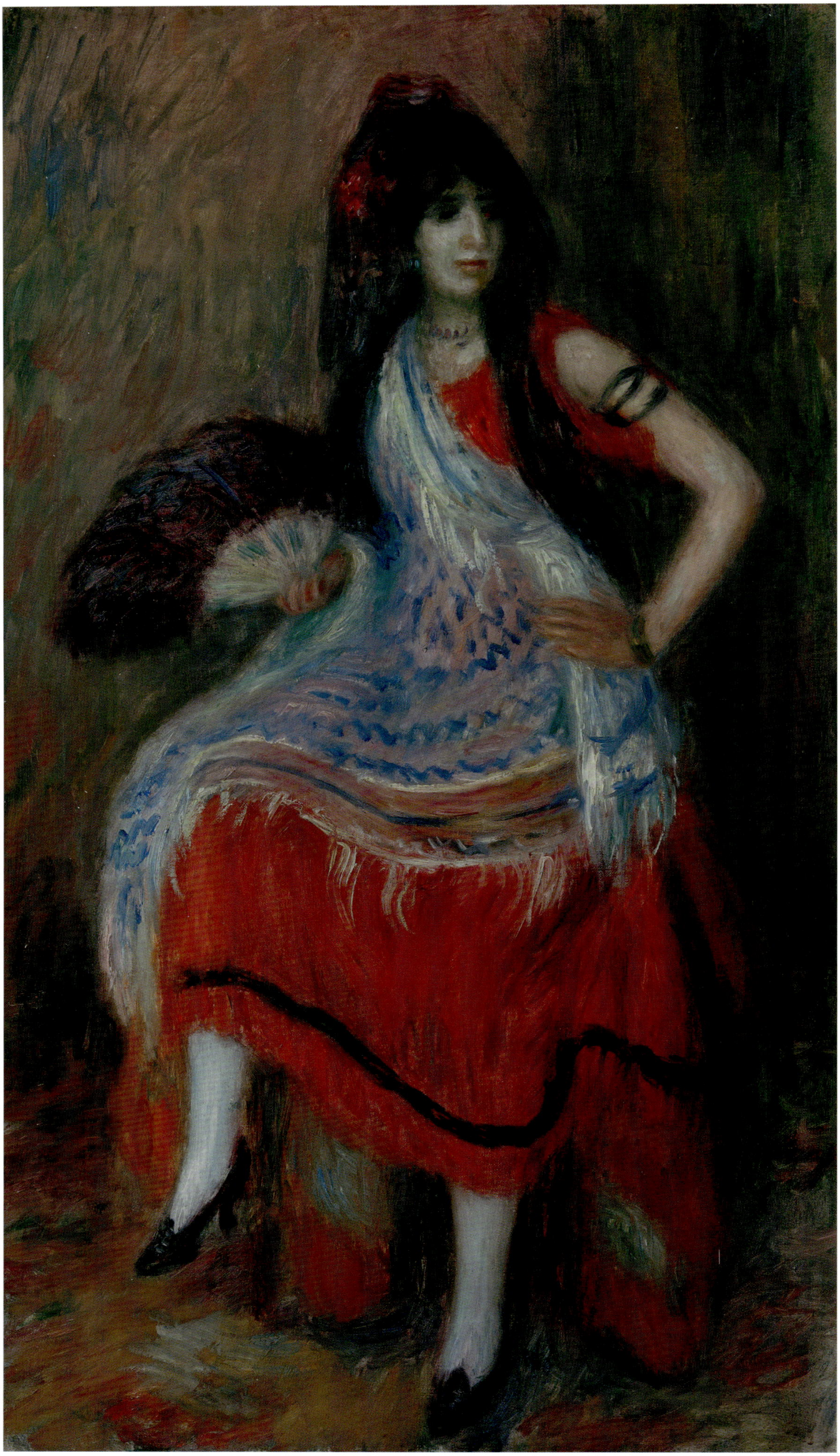

58. William J. Glackens
*Andalusian Woman,* c. 1920s
Oil on canvas
30 x 18 in. (76.2 x 45.72 cm)

59. William J. Glackens
*Turkish Lady Seated*, c. 1920s
Oil on canvas
24 x 17 in. (60.96 x 43.18 cm)

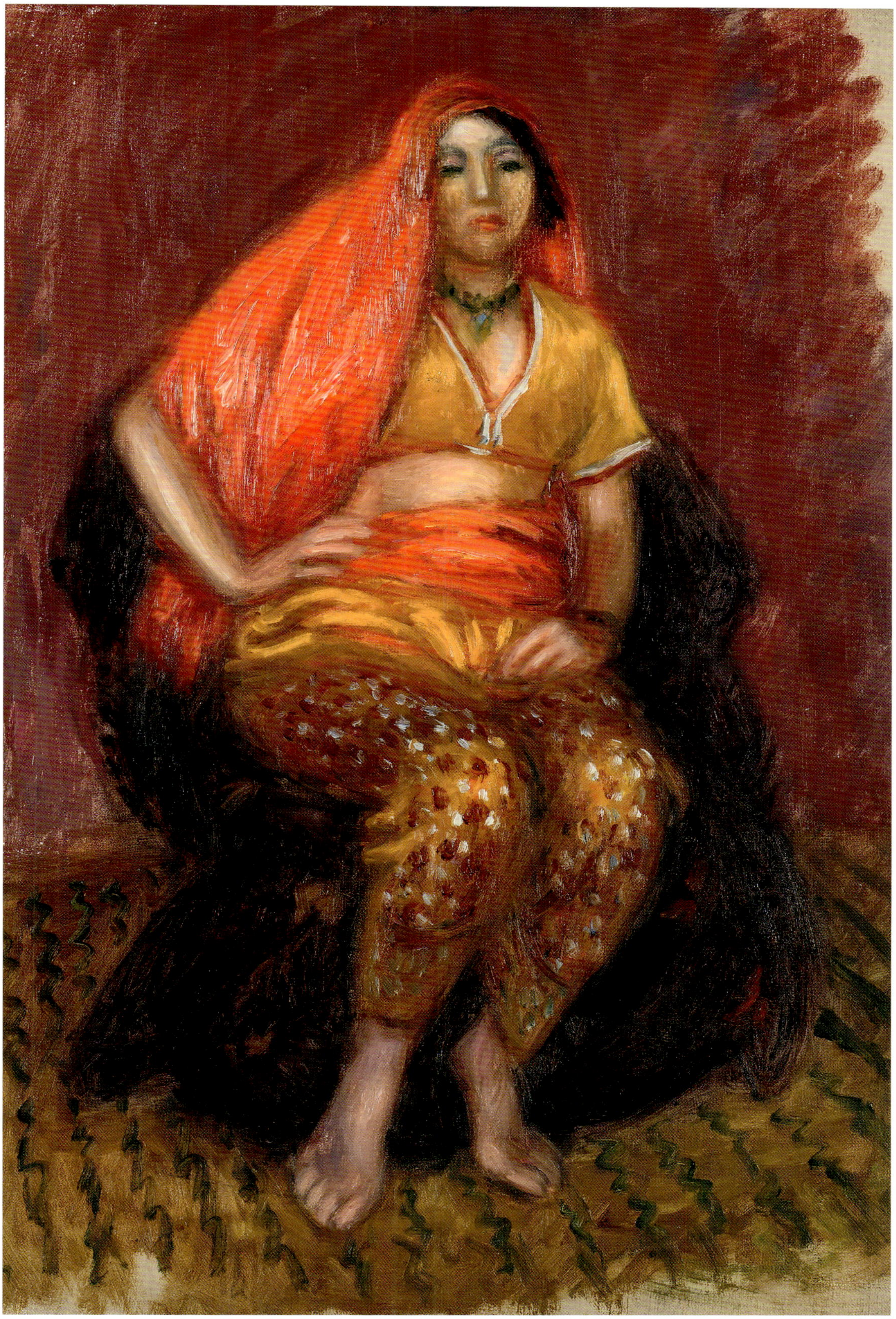

60. William J. Glackens
*Negress in Oriental Costume*,
c. 1923
Oil on canvas
32 x 26 in. (81.28 x 66.04 cm)

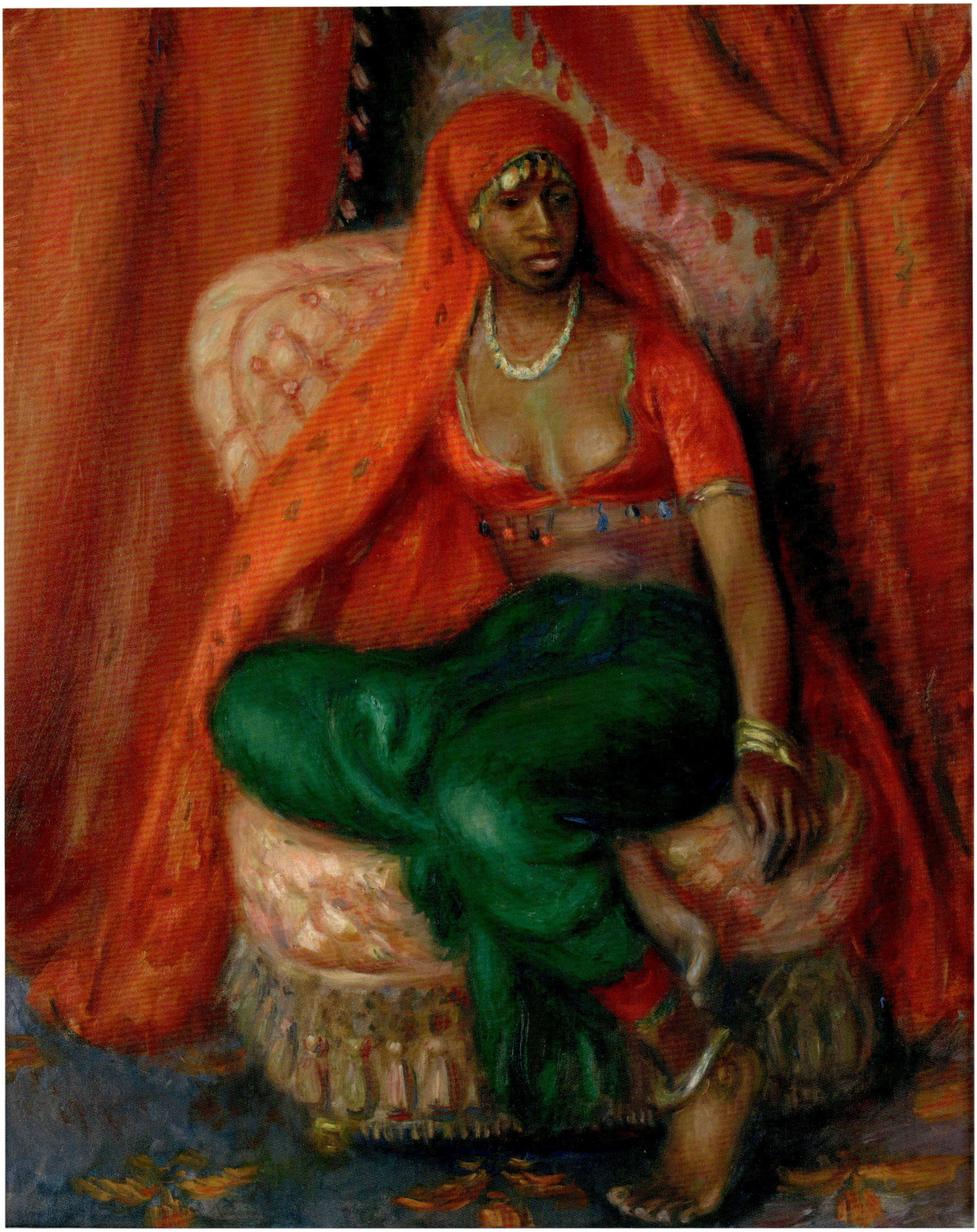

61. William J. Glackens
*Breakfast Porch*, 1925
Oil on canvas
31 x 25 in. (78.74 x 63.5 cm)

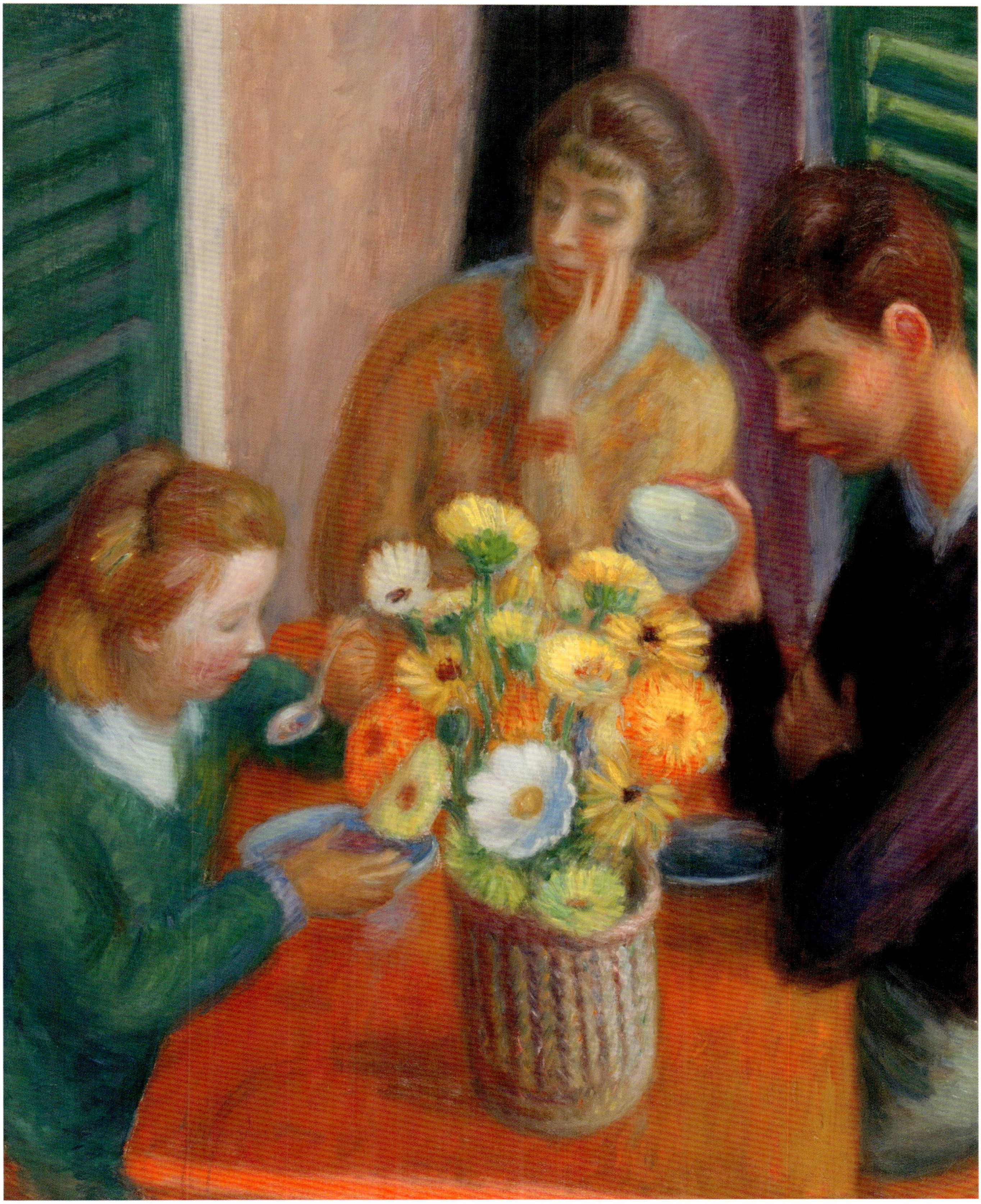

62. William J. Glackens
*The Promenade*, 1927
Oil on canvas
32 x 25 ¾ in. (81.3 x 65.4 cm)

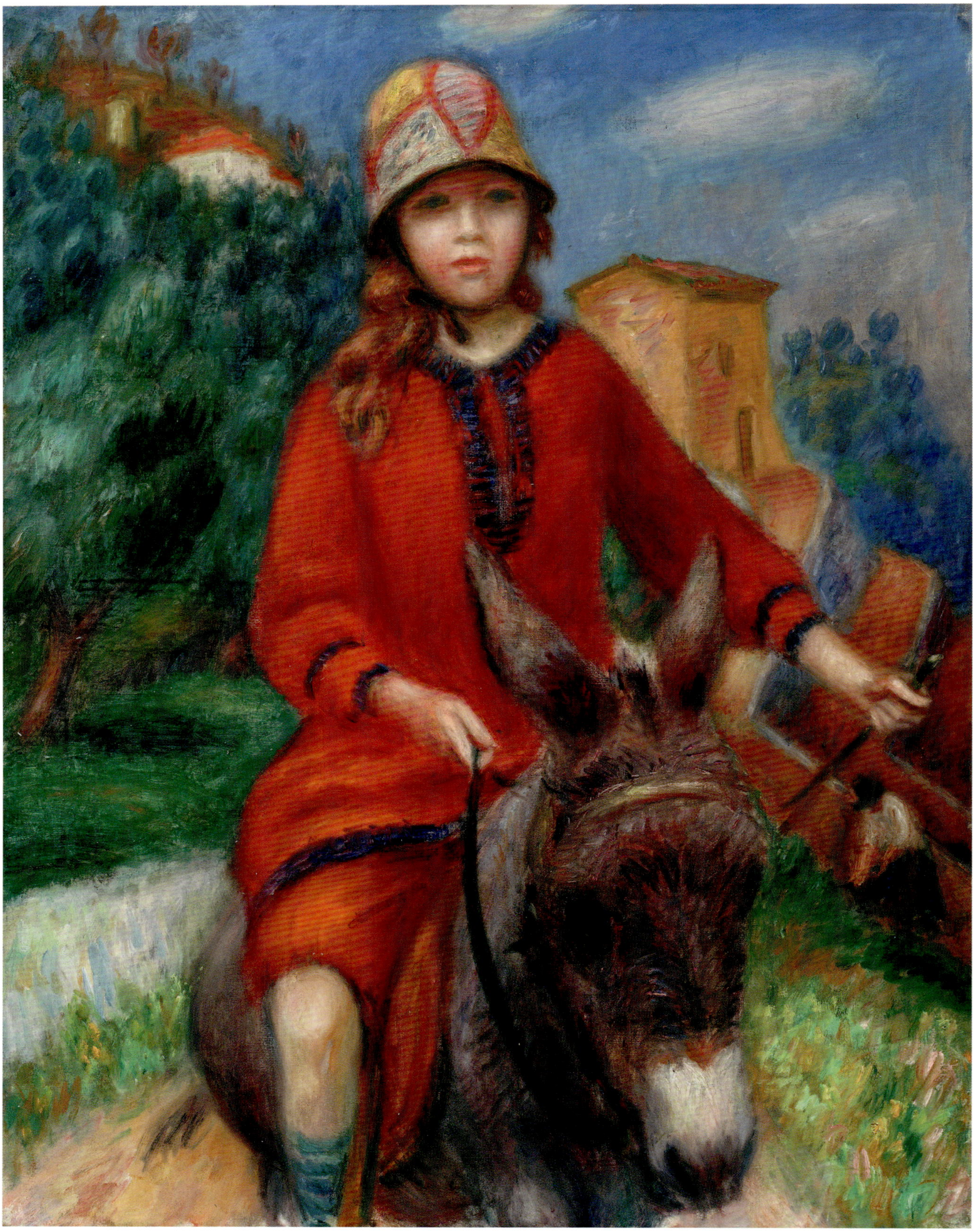

63. William J. Glackens
*Back of Nude*, c. 1930s
Oil on canvas
30 x 25 in. (76.2 x 63.5 cm)

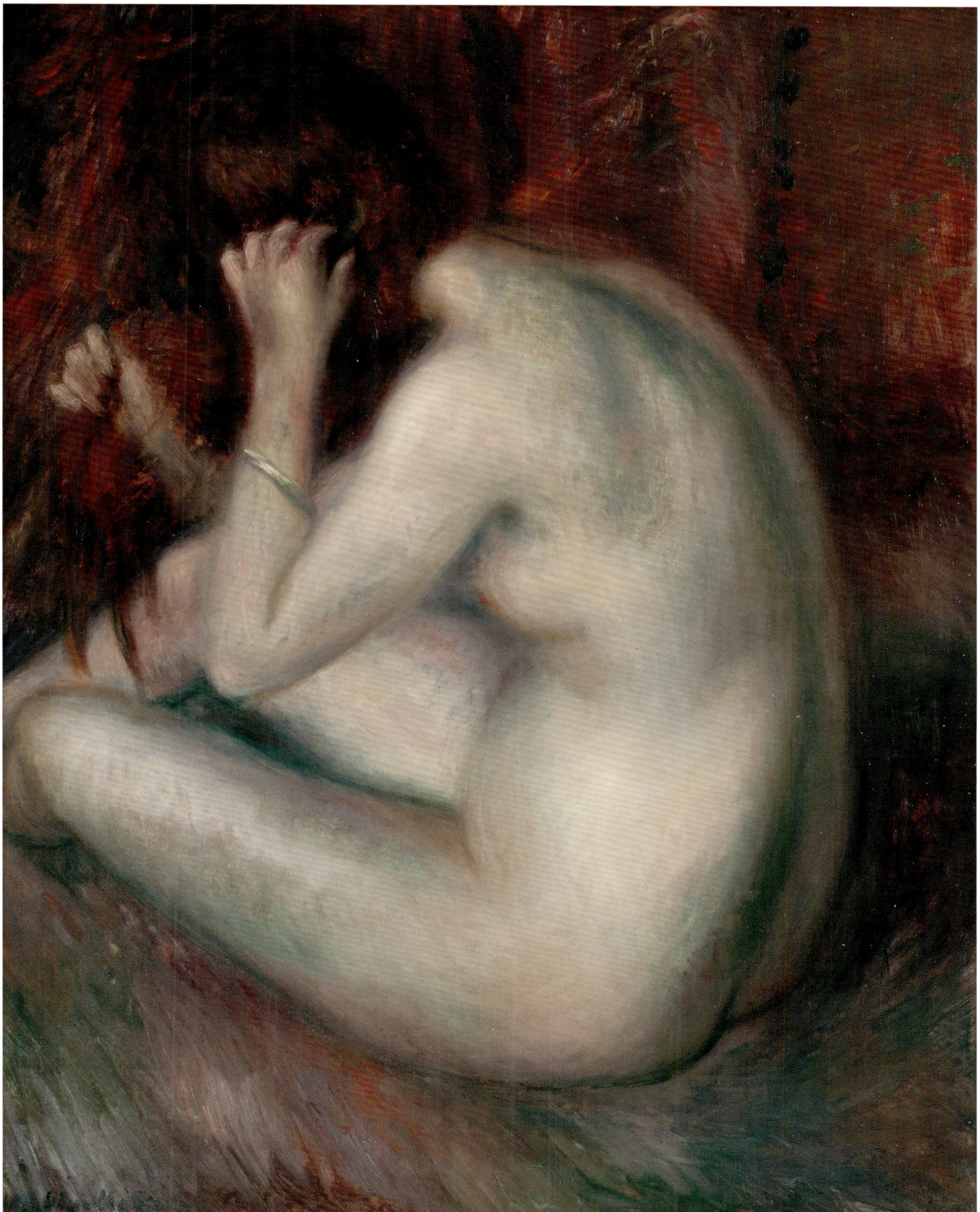

64. William J. Glackens
*Bowlers, La Ciotat*, 1930
Oil on canvas
22 ¼ x 31 in. (56.51 x 78.74 cm)

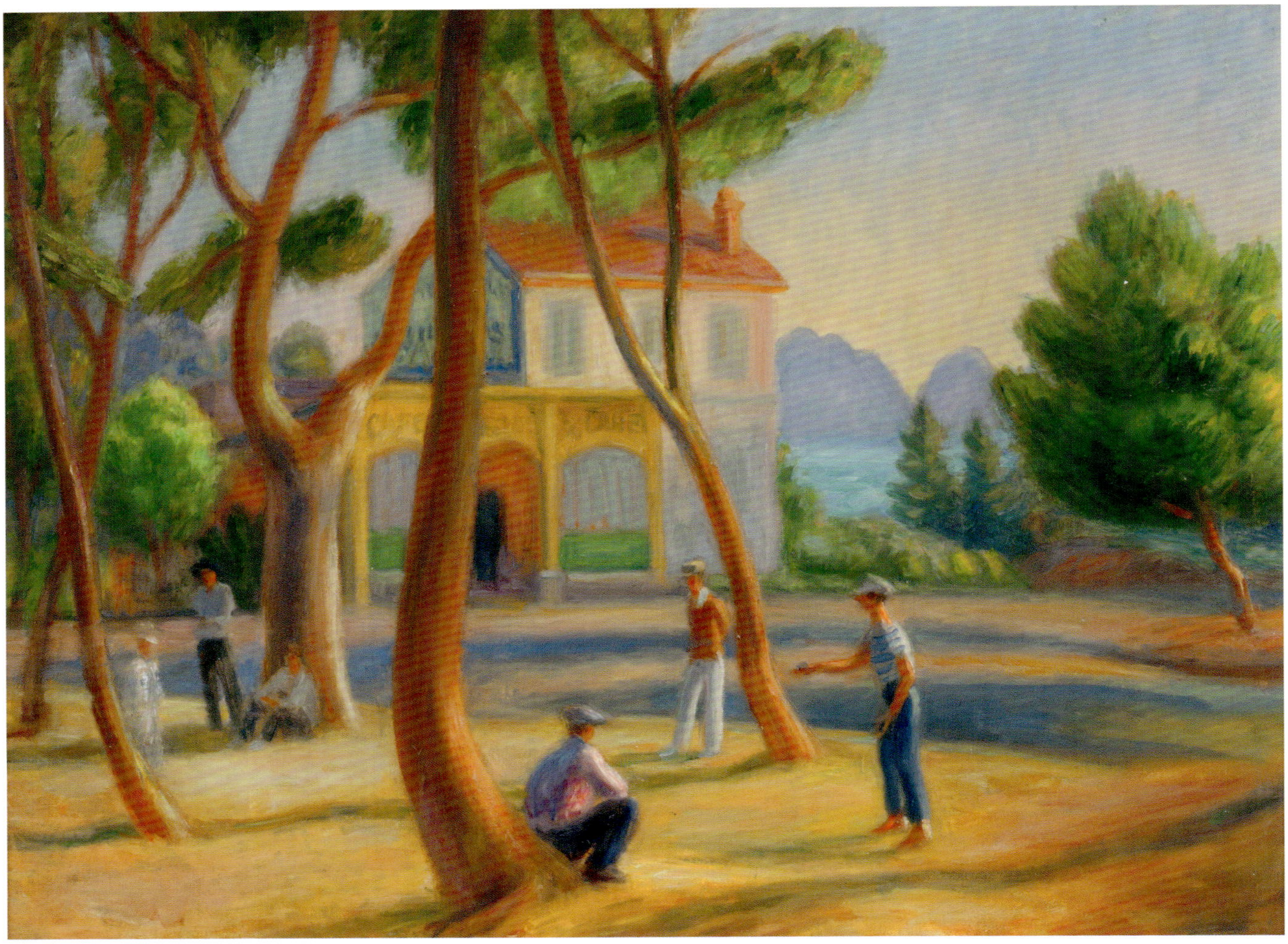

65. William J. Glackens
*St. Jean*, 1930
Oil on canvas
20 x 28 ⅞ in. (50.8 x 73.34 cm)

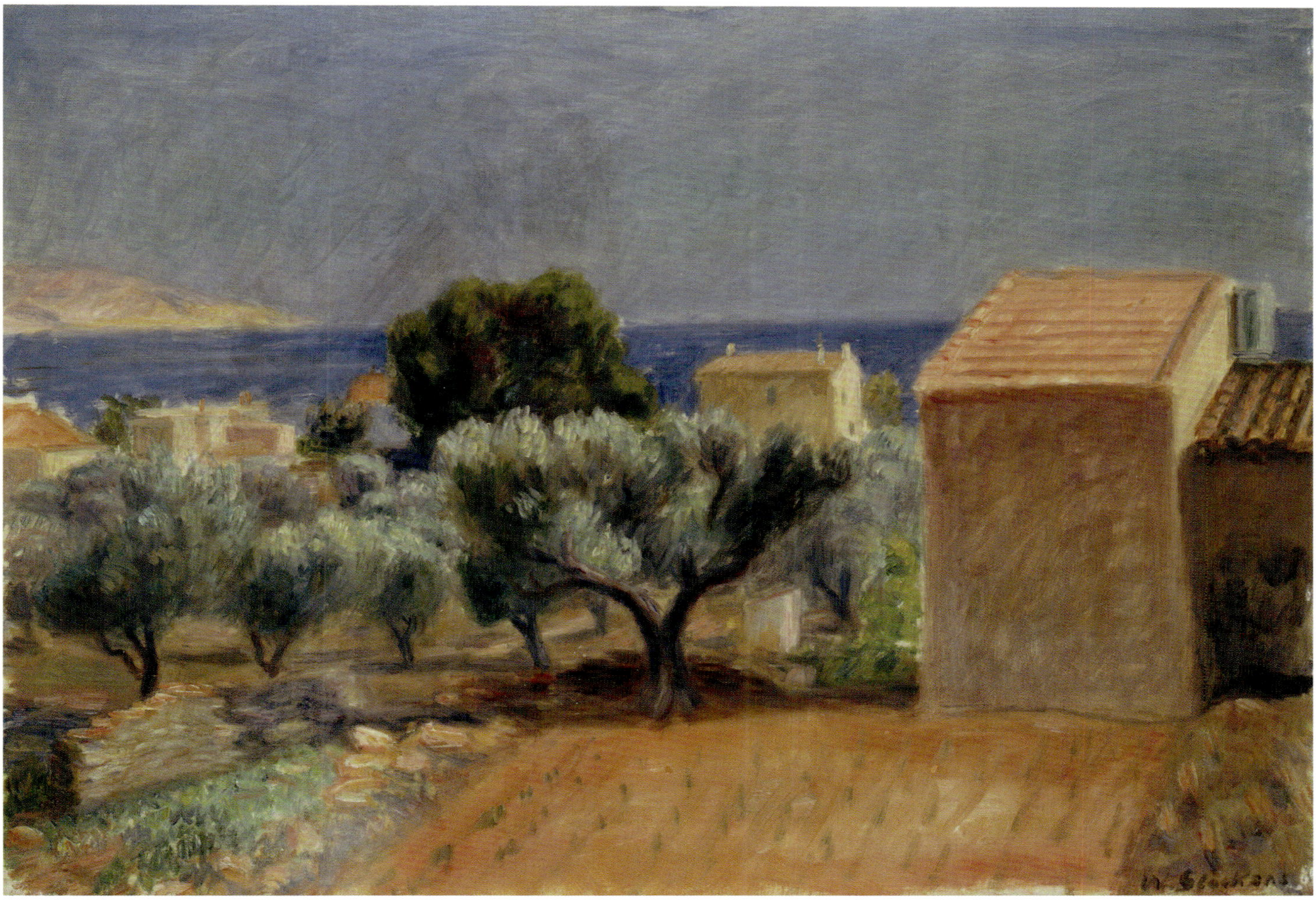

66. William J. Glackens
*Fruit and a White Rose*, c. 1930s
Oil on board
12 ¼ x 15 ¼ in. (31.11 x 38.73 cm)

67. William J. Glackens
*The Soda Fountain*, 1935
Oil on canvas
48 x 36 in. (121.92 x 91.44 cm)

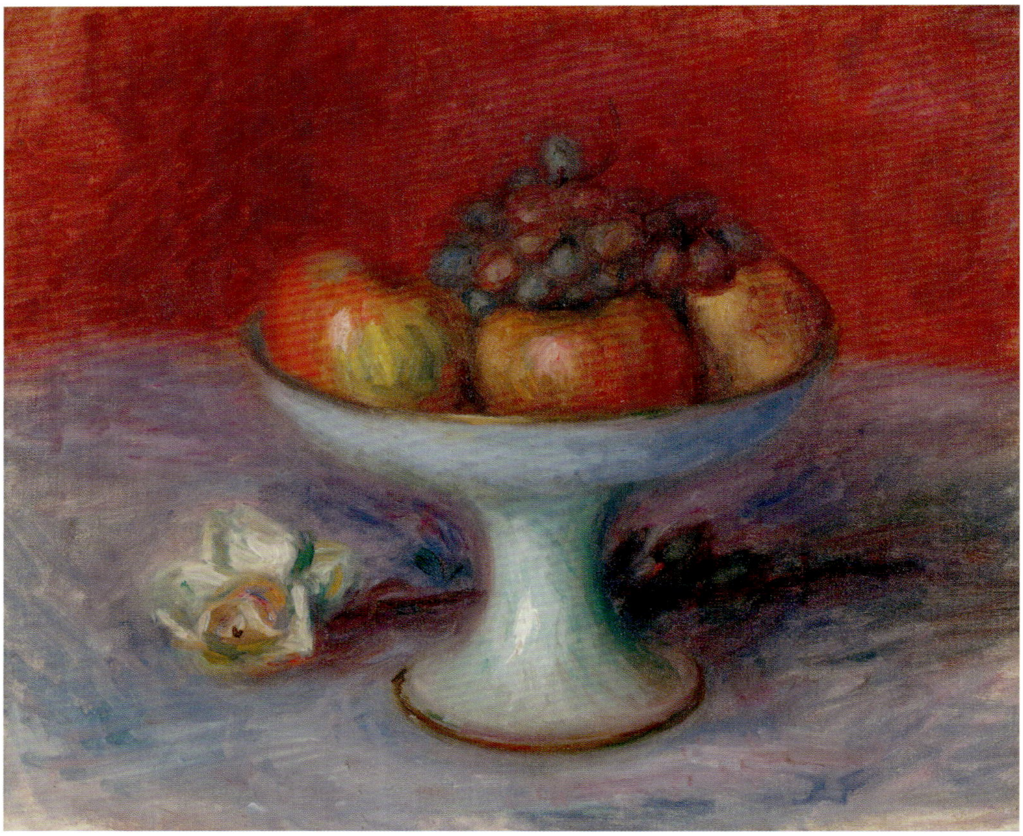

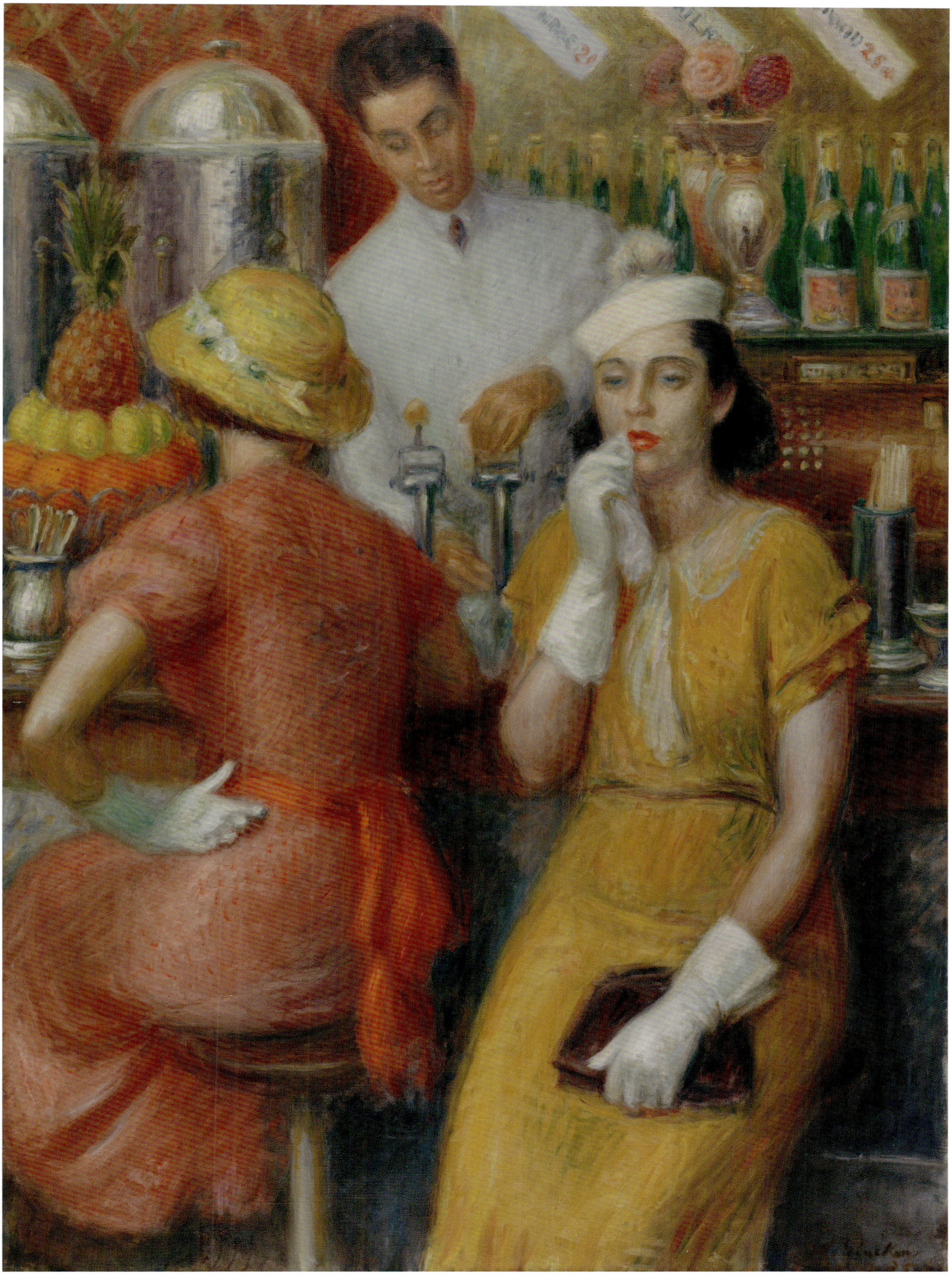

# Appendix

# List of Art Works

Sources provide various titles for some of the Renoir works in the exhibition. Those listed below were provided by owners. The catalogue raisonné numbers included in captions derive from Guy-Patrice and Michel Dauberville, *Renoir: Catalogue Raisonné of Paintings, Pastels, Drawings and Watercolors*, volumes I–V (Paris: Éditions Bernheim-Jeune, 2004–14): CR; or in Dr. Joseph G. Stella, *The Graphic Works of Renoir: Catalogue Raisonné* (Fort Lauderdale Museum of the Arts, 1975): CR/Stella. Other provenance provided by lending organizations. Not all works are on view at both venues.

**Pierre-Auguste Renoir**

Pierre-Auguste Renoir
*The Young Soldier* [*Le jeune militaire*], c. 1880
Oil on canvas
21 ⅝ x 13 in. (54.93 x 33.02 cm)
National Gallery of Art, Washington, D.C., Collection of Mr. and Mrs. Paul Mellon, 2014.18.46
Plate 1
(CR #520 vol. I)

Pierre-Auguste Renoir
*Moulin Huet Bay, Guernsey* [*La Baie du Moulin Huet, Guernesey*], c. 1883
Oil on canvas
11 ½ x 21 ¼ in. (29.2 x 54 cm)
The National Gallery, London. Bought, 1954
Plate 2
(CR #846 vol. II)

Pierre-Auguste Renoir
*Tamaris, France*, c. 1885
Oil on canvas
18 x 21 ⅝ in. (45.72 x 54.93 cm)
Minneapolis Institute of Art; Bequest of Mrs. Peter ffolliott, 2006.9.2
Plate 3
(CR #873 vol. II)

Pierre-Auguste Renoir
*Nude in a Chair* [*Nu au fauteuil*], c. 1885–90
Pastel on paper
24 3/16 x 20 ¼ in. (61.5 x 51.5 cm)
Private Collection, NY
Plate 5
(CR #04495 vol. V)

Pierre-Auguste Renoir
*Young Girls Styling Themselves* [*Jeunes filles se coiffant*], c. 1885–90
Pastel on paper
31 ⅛ x 24 ⅜ in. (79 x 62 cm)
Nahmad Collection, Monaco
Plate 4
(CR #1392 vol. II)

Pierre-Auguste Renoir
*Portrait of Edmond Renoir* [*Edmond Renoir, neveu du peintre*], 1888
Oil on canvas
14 x 10 ¾ in. (35.56 x 27.3 cm)
Denver Art Museum Collection, Funds from Helen Dill Bequest, 1937.4
Plate 7
(CR #1268 vol. II)

Pierre-Auguste Renoir
*Portrait of Pierre Renoir* [*Portrait de Pierre Renoir*], 1890
Oil on canvas
12 ⅞ x 9 ¾ in. (32 x 25 cm)
Collection of Nathan and Katharina Otto-Bernstein
Plate 6
(CR #1280 vol. II)

Pierre-Auguste Renoir
*Dancing in the Country* [*La danse à la campagne*], c. 1890·
Etching
8 11/16 x 5 7/16 in. (22 x 13.8 cm)
Courtesy of Drs. Walter and Mildred Padow
Plate 8
(CR/Stella #2)

Pierre-Auguste Renoir
*Still Life with Apples* [*Nature morte aux fruits*], c. 1890
Oil on canvas
7 ½ x 20 ¾ in. (19.05 x 52.70 cm)
High Museum of Art, Atlanta, GA; Gift of Micheline and Bob Gerson, 2008.166
Plate 9
(CR #1736 vol. III)

Pierre-Auguste Renoir
*Woman Arranging Her Hat* [*Femme arrangeant son chapeau*], c. 1890
Oil on canvas
10 ⅝ x 9 in. (27 x 22 cm)
High Museum of Art, Atlanta; Gift of Micheline and Bob Gerson, 2008.165
Plate 11
(CR #294 vol. I)

Pierre-Auguste Renoir
*Portrait of Jean* [*Portrait de Jean Renoir en rouge*], c. 1897
Oil on canvas
16 ⅜ x 13 ¼ in. (41.6 x 33.7 cm)
The Museum of Fine Arts, Houston; Gift of Isaac and Agnes Cullen Arnold, 68.55
Plate 12
(CR #2372 vol. III)

Pierre-Auguste Renoir
*Portrait of Jean Renoir* [*Portrait de Jean Renoir*], 1899
Oil on canvas
15 ¾ x 12 ¼ in. (40 x 32 cm)
Collection of Nathan and Katharina Otto-Bernstein
Plate 13
(CR #2381 vol. III)

Pierre-Auguste Renoir
*Head of a Young Woman* [*Tête d'une jeune femme*], late nineteenth century
Oil on canvas
16 3/8 x 12 3/4 in. (41.6 x 32.4 cm)
Minneapolis Institute of Art; Bequest of Margaret Washburn Hunt, 61.15
Plate 10

Pierre-Auguste Renoir
*Girl in a Straw Hat* [*Femme assise, Gabrielle au chapeau de paille*], 1900
Oil on canvas
45 x 39 in. (81.5 x 65.5 cm)
Nahmad Collection, Monaco
Plate 15
(CR #2181 vol. III)

Pierre-Auguste Renoir
*Children Playing Ball* [*Enfants jouant à la balle*], c. 1900
Lithograph
23 1/2 x 19 3/4 in. (60 x 51 cm)
Courtesy of Drs. Walter and Mildred Padow
Plate 14
(CR/Stella #32)

Pierre-Auguste Renoir
*Springtime in Essoyes* [*Printemps à Essoyes*], c. 1900
Oil on canvas
19 3/4 x 24 1/2 in. (50.16 x 62.23 cm)
Indianapolis Museum of Art at Newfields; Centennial gift of Mrs. Fisk Landers in memory of Caroline Marmon Fesler, 82.77, DiscoverNewfields.org
Plate 16

Pierre-Auguste Renoir
*Paul Cézanne*, c. 1902
Lithograph, second state
10 1/4 x 9 1/2 in. (26 x 24 cm)
Courtesy of Drs. Walter and Mildred Padow
Plate 17
(CR/Stella #34)

Pierre-Auguste Renoir
*Portrait of Claude Renoir* [*Buste d'enfant, Coco*], c. 1902
Oil on canvas
13 x 11 1/8 in. (32.5 x 28.5 cm)
Collection of Nathan and Katharina Otto-Bernstein
Plate 20
(CR #2398 vol. III)

Pierre-Auguste Renoir
*Claude Renoir, Head Lowered* [*Claude Renoir, la tête abaissée*], c. 1904
Lithograph, second state
8 1/2 x 7 3/8 in. (21.5 x 18.8 cm)
Courtesy of Drs. Walter and Mildred Padow
Plate 18
(CR/Stella #39)

Pierre-Auguste Renoir
*Coco*, 1905
Oil on canvas
10 7/8 x 14 3/16 in. (27.62 x 36 cm)
The Hyde Collection, Glens Falls, NY; Bequest of Charlotte Pruyn Hyde, 1971.38
Plate 19

Pierre-Auguste Renoir
*Reclining Nude* [*Femme nue couchée; Le modèle allongé*], c. 1906
Oil on canvas
12 3/4 x 11 in. (32.5 x 28.5 cm)
Nahmad Collection, Monaco
Plate 22
(CR #3507 vol. IV)

Pierre-Auguste Renoir
*Reclining Nude* [*Femme nue couchée, tournée à droite*], c. 1906
Etching
5 3/8 x 7 13/16 in. (13.6 x 19.8 cm)
Courtesy of Drs. Walter and Mildred Padow
Plate 21
(CR/Stella #13)

Pierre-Auguste Renoir
*Seated Nude* [*Femme nue assise*], c. 1906
Etching
7 3/8 x 5 7/8 in. (18.8 x 14.9 cm)
Courtesy of Drs. Walter and Mildred Padow
Plate 23
(CR/Stella #12)

Pierre-Auguste Renoir
*Woman in White Blouse* [*Femme en blouse blanche (Gabrielle)*], c. 1907
Oil on canvas
9 1/2 x 8 3/8 in. (24.2 x 21.4 cm)
Private Collection, Toronto
Courtesy of Hammer Galleries, New York
Plate 24
(CR #3314 vol. IV)

Pierre-Auguste Renoir
*Head of Coco* [*Tête de Coco*], 1908
Bronze
8 1/2 in. (21.59 cm) in diameter
Courtesy of Drs. Walter and Mildred Padow
Plate 27

Pierre-Auguste Renoir
*Seamstress at Window* [*Ravaudeuse à la fenêtre*], c. 1908–10
Oil on canvas
25 1/2 x 21 1/2 in. (64.77 x 54.61 cm)
New Orleans Museum of Art; Gift of Charles C. Henderson in memory of Margaret Henderson, 80.179
Plate 25
(CR #3267 vol. IV)

Pierre-Auguste Renoir
*Landscape at Cagnes* [*Paysage à Cagnes*], 1910
Oil on canvas
10 3/4 x 13 7/8 in. (27.3 x 35.24 cm)
Crocker Art Museum, Purchase, 2004.56
Plate 28

Pierre-Auguste Renoir
*Portrait of Mme. Thurneyssen and Her Daughter* [*Mère et enfant*], 1910
Oil on canvas
39 3/8 x 31 5/8 in. (100.01 x 80.33 cm)
Collection Albright-Knox Art Gallery, Buffalo, NY, General Purchase Funds, 1940:6
Plate 26
(CR #3139 vol. IV)

Pierre-Auguste Renoir
*Auguste Rodin*, c. 1910
Lithograph
15 3/4 x 15 3/8 in. (40 x 38.5 cm)
Courtesy of Drs. Walter and Mildred Padow
Plate 29
(CR/Stella #49)

Pierre-Auguste Renoir
*The Washers, 2nd State* [*Les laveuses, 2e Pensée*], c. 1910
Lithograph
18 1/2 x 23 13/16 in. (46.8 x 60.5 cm)
Courtesy of Drs. Walter and Mildred Padow
Plate 30
(CR/Stella #53)

Pierre-Auguste Renoir
*Bather* [*Baigneuse*], 1912
Oil on canvas
25 3/4 x 22 in. (65.4 x 55.9 cm)
Toledo Museum of Art; Gift of Mrs. C. Lockhart McKelvy, 1955.87
Plate 32

Pierre-Auguste Renoir
*Mlle. Estable*, 1912
Oil on canvas
16 5/16 x 12 3/8 in. (41.4 x 31.4 cm)
The Baltimore Museum of Art, The Cone Collection, formed by Dr. Claribel Cone and Miss Etta Cone of Baltimore, Maryland, BMA1950.287
Plate 33
(CR #4155 vol. V)

Pierre-Auguste Renoir
*Woman at the Corner Stove* [*Femme au coin du poêle*], 1912
Oil on canvas
18 1/8 x 19 3/4 in. (46 x 50 cm)
Nahmad Collection, Monaco
Plate 31
(CR #4137 vol. V)

Pierre-Auguste Renoir
*Flowers* [*Fleurs*], 1915–19
Oil on canvas
9 1/2 x 9 3/4 in. (24.13 x 24.77 cm)
Dallas Museum of Art; Gift of Mrs. Leslie Waggener in memory of Leslie Waggener, 1957.64
Plate 34

Pierre-Auguste Renoir
*Bare-breasted Sleeping Woman* [*Femme à la poitrine nue endormie*], 1919
Oil on canvas
15 3/4 x 20 1/8 in. (40 x 51 cm)
Nahmad Collection, Monaco
Plate 35
(CR #4409 vol. V)

**William J. Glackens**

William J. Glackens
*Outside the Guttenberg Race Track*, 1897
Oil on canvas
12 x 17 in. (30.48 x 43.18 cm)
NSU Art Museum Fort Lauderale;
Gift of the Sansom Foundation, 94.4
Plate 36

William J. Glackens
*Nude Dressing Her Hair*, 1909
Oil on canvas
30 x 25 in. (76.2 x 63.5 cm)
Courtesy of Lehigh University Art Galleries • Teaching Museum
Plate 37

William J. Glackens
*Semi-Nude with Hat*, c. 1909
Oil on canvas
32 x 25 in. (81.28 x 63.5 cm)
Courtesy of the Sansom Foundation and John H. Surovek Gallery, Palm Beach, FL
Plate 38

William J. Glackens
*Miss Olga D.*, 1910
Oil on canvas
32 x 26 in. (81.28 x 66.04 cm)
Hunter Museum of American Art, Chattanooga, TN; Gift of the Benwood Foundation, HMAA.1976.3.11
Plate 40

William J. Glackens
*Reclining Nude*, 1910
Oil on canvas
32 1/8 x 54 1/4 in. (81.6 x 137.8 cm)
Whitney Museum of American Art, New York; Gift of Charles Simon, 78.104
Plate 39

William J. Glackens
*Lenna at One Year*, 1914
Oil on canvas
14 3/4 x 11 1/2 in. (37.4 x 29.2 cm)
NSU Art Museum Fort Lauderdale;
Bequest of Ira D. Glackens, 92.35
Plate 41

William J. Glackens
*The Little Pier*, 1914
Oil on canvas
25 x 30 in. (63.5 x 76.2 cm)
Barnes Foundation, Merion and Philadelphia, PA, BF497
Plate 42

William J. Glackens
*Pier at Blue Point*, 1914
Oil on canvas
25 7/8 x 32 in. (65.72 x 81.28 cm)
Columbus Museum of Art, OH; Gift of Ferdinand Howald, 1931.171
Plate 43

William J. Glackens
*Summer*, 1914
Oil on canvas
26 x 32 in. (66.04 x 81.28 cm)
Private Collection, Virginia
Plate 44

William J. Glackens
*Indian Series (Flautist on Peacock)*, c. 1914–18
Oil on canvas
48 x 30 in. (121.92 x 76.2 cm)
NSU Art Museum Fort Lauderdale;
Gift of the Sansom Foundation, 94.5
Plate 47

William J. Glackens
*Julia's Sister*, c. 1915
Oil on canvas
32 1/8 x 26 1/8 in. (81.6 x 66.4 cm)
Terra Foundation for American Art, Daniel J. Terra Collection, 1999.58
Plate 45

William J. Glackens
*Girl in Red Dress Pinning on Hat*, c. 1915–16
Oil on canvas
31 3/4 x 26 in. (80.6 x 66 cm)
Barnes Foundation, Merion and Philadelphia, PA, BF174
Plate 46

William J. Glackens
*Artist's Daughter in Chinese Costume*, 1918
Oil on canvas
48 3/16 x 30 1/16 in. (122.39 x 76.35 cm)
NSU Art Museum Fort Lauderdale;
Gift of the Sansom Foundation, 92.28
Plate 48

William J. Glackens
*Beach Scene, New London*, 1918
Oil on canvas
26 x 31 7/8 in. (66.04 x 80.98 cm)
Columbus Museum of Art, OH;
Gift of Ferdinand Howald, 1931.170
Plate 49

William J. Glackens
*Boat Landing at Gloucester*, c. 1918
Oil on canvas
25 ¼ x 31 in. (64.14 x 78.74 cm)
Chrysler Museum of Art, Norfolk, VA;
Promised gift of Mr. and Mrs. Frank Batten
Plate 50

William J. Glackens
*Lenna Painting*, c. 1918
Oil on canvas
12 x 15 in. (30.48 x 38.1 cm)
NSU Art Museum Fort Lauderdale; Bequest
of Ira D. Glackens, 91.40.118
Plate 53

William J. Glackens
*Mixed Bouquet, Red Background*, c. 1918
Oil on canvas
21 ¾ x 15 ⅛ in. (55.24 x 38.41 cm)
Private Collection, Atlanta, GA
Plate 51

William J. Glackens
*Rose in a Glass*, c. 1918
Oil on canvas
11 ¼ x 8 ¼ in. (28.57 x 20.95 cm)
Kraushaar Galleries, New York
Plate 52

William J. Glackens
*Finnish Woman*, 1920
Oil on canvas
32 x 26 in. (81.28 x 66.04 cm)
Courtesy of the Pennsylvania Academy
of the Fine Arts; Gift of the Reverend Edward
M. DePaoli, Priest of the Archdiocese of
Philadelphia, on behalf of the Sansom
Foundation, 1996.6
Plate 54

William J. Glackens
*Hallie Knitting in Red Hat*, c. 1920
Oil on canvas
24 x 18 in. (60.96 x 45.72 cm)
London Family Collection
Plate 55

William J. Glackens
*Andalusian Woman,* c. 1920s
Oil on canvas
30 x 18 in. (76.2 x 45.72 cm)
Collection of the Meadows Museum
of Art, Centenary College of Louisiana;
Gift of Dr. David C. Kimball, 1999.2
Plate 58

William J. Glackens
*Turkish Lady Seated*, c. 1920s
Oil on canvas
24 x 17 in. (60.96 x 43.18 cm)
Courtesy of the Sansom Foundation and
John H. Surovek Gallery, Palm Beach, FL
Plate 59

William J. Glackens
*Lenna with Rabbit Hound*, c. 1922
Oil on canvas
35 ½ x 31 ¼ in. (90.17 x 79.37 cm)
NSU Art Museum Fort Lauderdale;
Bequest of Ira D. Glackens, 91.40.103
Plate 56

William J. Glackens
*Lenna Dressed as Toy Soldier*, c. 1923
Oil on canvas
25 ¼ x 12 ¾ in. (64.13 x 32.38 cm)
Private Collection, Gloucester, MA
Plate 57

William J. Glackens
*Negress in Oriental Costume*, c. 1923
Oil on canvas
32 x 26 in. (81.28 x 66.04 cm)
Myron Kunin Collection of American Art,
Minneapolis, MN
Plate 60

William J. Glackens
*Breakfast Porch*, 1925
Oil on canvas
31 x 25 in. (78.74 x 63.5 cm)
NSU Art Museum Fort Lauderdale; Gift
of the Sansom Foundation, 92.30
Plate 61

William J. Glackens
*The Promenade*, 1927
Oil on canvas
32 x 25 ¾ in. (81.3 x 65.4 cm)
Detroit Institute of Arts, City of Detroit
Purchase, 30.322
Plate 62

William J. Glackens
*Bowlers, La Ciotat*, 1930
Oil on canvas
22 ¼ x 31 in. (56.51 x 78.74 cm)
NSU Art Museum Fort Lauderdale; Gift
of the Sansom Foundation, 92.31
Plate 64

William J. Glackens
*St. Jean*, 1930
Oil on canvas
20 x 28 ⅞ in. (50.8 x 73.34 cm)
Addison Gallery of American Art, Phillips
Academy, Andover, MA, Museum Purchase,
1936.36
Plate 65

William J. Glackens
*Back of Nude*, c. 1930s
Oil on canvas
30 x 25 in. (76.2 x 63.5 cm)
NSU Art Museum Fort Lauderdale; Gift
of the Sansom Foundation, 92.34
Plate 63

William J. Glackens
*Fruit and a White Rose*, c. 1930s
Oil on board
12 ¼ x 15 ¼ in. (31.11 x 38.73 cm)
NSU Art Museum Fort Lauderdale; Bequest
of Ira D. Glackens, 91.40.26
Plate 66

William J. Glackens
*The Soda Fountain*, 1935
Oil on canvas
48 x 36 in. (121.92 x 91.44 cm)
Courtesy of the Pennsylvania Academy
of the Fine Arts, Joseph E. Temple Fund and
Henry D. Gilpin Fund, 1955.3
Plate 67

# List of Artists and Collectors

## Artists

Giovanni Bellini (Italian, c. 1431–1516)
Pierre Bonnard (French, 1867–1947)
François Boucher (French, 1703–1770)
Georges Braque (French, 1882–1963)
Mary Cassatt (American, 1844–1926)
Paul Cézanne (French, 1839–1906)
Robert Winthrop Chanler (American, 1872–1930)
William Cordova (American, b. 1971)
Gustave Courbet (French, 1819–1877)
Arthur B. Davies (American, 1862–1928)
Edgar Degas (French, 1834–1917)
Charles Demuth (American, 1883–1935)
Maurice Denis (French, 1870–1943)
André Derain (French, 1880–1954)
Marcel Duchamp (French 1887–1968)
Nicole Eisenman (American, b. 1965)
Henri Fantin-Latour (French, 1836–1904)
Jean-Honoré Fragonard (French, 1732–1806)
Paul Gauguin (French, 1848–1903)
Charles Dana Gibson (American, 1867–1944)
Giorgione (Italian, c. 1477–1510)
Giotto di Bondone (Italian, c. 1266–1337)
Edith Dimock Glackens (American, 1876–1955)
William J. Glackens (American, 1870–1938)
El Greco (Greek, 1541–1614)
Trenton Doyle Hancock (American, b. 1974)
Marsden Hartley (American, 1877–1943)
Robert Henri (American, 1865–1929)
William Kentridge (South African, b. 1955)
Martin Kippenberger (German, 1953–1997)
Willem de Kooning (American, 1904–1997)
Walt Kuhn (American, 1880–1949)
Ernest Lawson (American, 1873–1939)
Roy Lichtenstein (American, 1923–1997)
Claude Lorraine (French, 1604–1682)
Édouard Manet (French, 1832–1883)
Masaccio (Italian, 1401–1428)
Henri Matisse (French, 1869–1954)
Alfred Maurer (American, 1868–1932)
Amedeo Modigliani (Italian, 1884–1920)
Claude Monet (French, 1840–1926)
Berthe Morisot (French, 1841–1895)
Albert Oehlen (German, b. 1954)
Georgia O'Keeffe (American, 1887–1986)
Raymond Pettibon (American, b. 1957)
Francis Picabia (French, 1879–1953)
Pablo Picasso (Spanish, 1881–1973)
Camille Pissarro (French, 1831–1903)
Jackson Pollock (American, 1912–1956)
Charles Prendergast (American, 1863–1948)
Maurice Prendergast (American, 1858–1924)
Matthew Ritchie (English, b. 1964)
Norman Rockwell (American, 1894–1978)
Mark Rothko (American, 1903–1970)
Peter Paul Rubens (Flemish, 1577–1640)
David Salle (American, b. 1952)
Julian Schnabel (American, b. 1951)
Jim Shaw (American, b. 1952)
Charles Sheeler (American, 1883–1965)
Everett Shinn (American, 1876–1953)
John Sloan (American, 1871–1951)
Chaïm Soutine (Russian, 1893–1943)
Frank Stella (American, b. 1936)
Alfred Stieglitz (American, 1864–1946)
Domenico Tintoretto (Italian, 1560–1635)
Titian (Italian, c. 1488–1576)
Vincent van Gogh (Dutch, 1853–1890)
Jean-Antoine Watteau (French, 1684–1721)
Kehinde Wiley (American, b. 1977)

## Collectors

Albert C. Barnes (American, 1872–1951)
Lillie P. Bliss (American, 1864–1931)
Francine Clary Clark (French, 1876–1960)
Robert Sterling Clark (American, 1877–1956)
Alexander Cochrane (American, born in Scotland, 1840–1919)
Chester Dale (American, 1883–1962)
Maud Murray Dale (American, 1876–1953)
Paul Durand-Ruel (French, 1831–1922)
Arthur Brewster Emmons (American, 1850–1922)
Henry O. Havemeyer (American, 1847–1907)
Louisine Elder Havemeyer (American, 1855–1929)
Catholina Lambert (American, born in England, 1834–1923)
Adolph Lewisohn (American, born in Germany, 1849–1938)
Bertha Palmer (American, 1849–1918)
Duncan Phillips (American, 1886–1966)
John Quinn (American, 1870–1924)
Edward G. Robinson (American, born in Romania, 1893–1973)
Martin Ryerson (American, 1856–1932)
Josef Stransky (Czech, 1872–1936)
George Vanderbilt II (American, 1862–1914)

## Selected Bibliography


Anonymous. "Art Notes." *New York Times*, January 23, 1893.

Assouline, Pierre. *Discovering Impressionism: The Life of Paul Durand-Ruel*. New York: Vendome Press, 2014.

Bailey, Colin B. "The Origins of the Barnes Collection, 1912–15." In *The World of William Glackens: The C. Richard Hilker Art Lectures*, vol. 1. New York: D.A.P./Distributed Art Publishers, 2011.

___. *Renoir, Impressionism and Full-Length Painting*. New Haven: Yale University Press, 2012.

___, Christopher Riopelle, John House, Simon Kelly, and John Zarobell. *Renoir Landscapes 1865–1883*. London: The National Gallery, 2007.

Bénédite, Léonce. "*Madame Charpentier and Her Children*, by Auguste Renoir." *Burlington Magazine* 12, no. 57, December 1907.

Benjamin, Roger. "Why did Matisse Love Late Renoir." In Claudia Einecke and Roger Benjamin, *Renoir in the 20th Century*. Exhibition catalogue. Ostfildern: Hatje Cantz, 2010.

Brown, Milton W. *The Story of the Armory Show*, 2nd ed. New York: Abbeville Press, 1988.

Capps, Kristen. "Why Absolutely Everyone Hates Renoir." *The Atlantic*, October 13, 2015. https://www.theatlantic.com/entertainment/archive/2015/10/why-everyone-hates-renoir/410335/

Carbone, Teresa A. "All About Eve? William Glackens's Audacious *Girl with Apple*." In *The World of William Glackens*, vol. 2, edited by Judith A. Barter. New York: Sansom Foundation, Inc., 2017.

Clearwater, Bonnie. "The Mysterious Case of Richard Mutt." In *Some Aesthetic Decisions: A Centennial Celebration of Marcel Duchamp's "Fountain."* Exhibition catalogue. Milan: Skira, 2017.

____. *Richard Artschwager, Painting Then and Now*. Exhibition catalogue. North Miami: Museum of Contemporary Art, 2003.

Dawson, Anne E. *Pierre-Auguste Renoir and Modern Painting*. Exhibition catalogue. San Diego: San Diego Museum of Art, 2002.

Dolkart, Judith F. "William Glackens: 'Intensely Sincere and Intensely Brave.'" In *William Glackens*, edited by Avis Berman. Exhibition catalogue. New York and Philadelphia: Skira Rizzoli Publications, Inc. and The Barnes Foundation, 2014.

Downes, William Howe. "Boston Painters and Paintings: VI." *Atlantic Monthly* 62, no. 374, December 1888.

*Drawings, Lithographs, Watercolors, Etchings: Henri Matisse*. Exhibition catalogue. 291 Fifth Avenue Gallery of the Photo-Secession. New York, 1908.

Einecke, Claudia, and Roger Benjamin. *Renoir in the 20th Century*. Exhibition catalogue. Ostfildern: Hatje Cantz, 2010.

Farago, Jason. "Art Review: Like Impressionist, Like Filmmaker." *New York Times*, June 1, 2018.

Fitzgerald, Michael. *Making Moderism: Picasso and the Creation of the Market for Twentieth-Century Art*. Berkeley, Los Angeles, London: University of California Press, 1995. Paperback edition, 1996.

Fry, Roger. "The Charpentier Family by Renoir." *The Metropolitan Museum of Art Bulletin* 2, no. 6, June 1907.

____. "The Last Works of Renoir." *Arts & Decoration*, January 14, 1921.

Ganz, James A. "From Paris to Williamstown: Robert Sterling Clark's Life as a Collector." In Michael Conforti et al., *The Clarks Collect: Impressionist and Early Modern Paintings*. Williamstown, MA: Sterling and Francine Clark Art Institute, 2006.

Gerdts, William H. *William Glackens*. Fort Lauderdale: NSU Art Museum Fort Lauderdale and Abbeville Press, 1996.

Germer, Stefan. "Traditions and Trends: Taste Patterns in Chicago Collecting." In *The Old Guard and the Avant-Garde: Modernism in Chicago, 1910–1940*, edited by Sue Ann Prince. Chicago and London: University of Chicago Press, 1990.

Glackens, Ira. *William Glackens and the Ashcan Group*. New York: Crown Press, 1957.

___. *William Glackens and the Eight: The artists who freed American art*. New York: Horizon Press, 1983.

Glackens, William. "The American Section: The National Art, An Interview with the Chairman of the Domestic Committee, William J. Glackens." In the special exhibition issue, edited by Guy Pène du Bois. *Arts & Decoration* 3, no. 5, March 1913.

Glaves-Smith, John, and Ian Chilvers. *A Dictionary of Modern and Contemporary Art*. Oxford: OUP Oxford, 2009.

Grammont, Claudine. "Matisse in the Laboratory of Dr. Barnes: How and Why Barnes Collected Matisse." In *Matisse in the Barnes Foundation*, vol. 1, edited by Yve-Alain Bois. Merion and London: The Barnes Foundation and Thames & Hudson, 2015.

Greenberg, Clement. *Art and Culture: Critical Essays*. Boston: Beacon Press, 1961.

____. "Modernist Painting." In *Modern Art and Modernism: A Critical Anthology*, edited by Francis Frascina and Charles Harrison. New York: Harper & Row, 1982.

Gregorio, Vincent J. de. "The Life and Art of William J. Glackens." Ph.D. dissertation. Ann Arbor: University Microfilms, 1955.

*Henri Matisse Exhibition*. Exhibition catalogue. Montross Gallery. New York, 1915.

Hess, Thomas B. *Willem de Kooning*. New York: The Museum of Modern Art, 1968.

*Highly Valuable Paintings of Sterling Artistic Distinction Belong to Private Collectors and to Several Estates*. New York: American Art Association, 1920.

House, John. "Renoir: Between Modernist and Tradition." In Martha Lucy and John House, *Renoir in the Barnes Foundation*. New Haven: Yale University Press, in association with The Barnes Foundation, 2012.

Huneker, James G. "Eight Painters." *New York Sun*, February 10, 1908.

___. "Around the Galleries." *New York Sun*, April 7, 1910.

Jones, Kimberly A. "Cultivating the Chester Dale Collection." In Kimberly A. Jones and Maygene Daniels, *The Chester Dale Collection*. Washington, D.C.: National Gallery of Art, 2009.

Kern, Steven. "A Passion for Renoir." In Steven Kern et al., *A Passion for Renoir: Sterling and Francine Clark Collect, 1916–1951*. New York: Harry N. Abrams, in association with Sterling and Francine Clark Art Institute, 1996.

Kooning, Elaine de. "Renoir: As If By Magic," in *The Spirit of Abstract Expressionism: Selected Writings*, Essay by Rose Slivka. Preface by Marjorie Luyckx. New York: Braziller, 1994.

Kooning, Willem de. "The Renaissance and Order." Talk delivered at Studio 35, 8th Street, New York, autumn 1949. In Thomas B. Hess, *Willem de Kooning*. New York: The Museum of Modern Art, 1968. Reprinted from *Trans/formation* 1, no. 2, 1951.

Kopper, Philip. *America's National Gallery of Art*. Princeton, N.J.: Princeton University Press, 2016.

Kushner, Marilyn, and Kimberly Orcutt, Casey Blake et al. *The Armory Show at 100: Modernism and Revolution*. New York: Giles, 2015. http://armory.nyhistory.org/about/blogsit.

Kuspit, Donald. "A Note on Late Renoir." *Artnet.com*, 2010. http://www.artnet.com/magazineus/features/kuspit/pierre-auguste-renoir8-5-10.asp.

Leja, Michael. *Monet in the 20th Century*. New Haven: Yale University Press, 1998.

Loos, Ted. "Got a Few Million? Christie's May Have a Monet for You. Or Five." *New York Times*, April 17, 2018.

Lucy, Martha. "Glackens, French Art, and the Language of Modernism." In *William Glackens*, edited by Avis Berman. Exhibition catalogue. New York: Skira Rizzoli Publications, Inc., and The Barnes Foundation, 2014.

____. "Grappling with Renoir's Modernism in the Collection of Dr. Barnes." In Martha Lucy and John House, *Renoir in the Barnes Foundation*. New Haven: Yale University Press, in association with The Barnes Foundation, 2012.

____, and John House. *Renoir in the Barnes Foundation*. New Haven: Yale University Press, in association with The Barnes Foundation, 2012.

Madeline, Laurence. "Picasso 1917 to 1924: A 'Renoirian Crisis.'" In Claudia Einecke and Roger Benjamin, *Renoir in the 20th Century*. Exhibition catalogue. Ostfildern: Hatje Cantz, 2010.

Mathews, Nancy Mowll. "Maurice Prendergast and the Influence of European Modernism." In Nancy Mowll Mathews and Gwendolyn Owens, *Maurice Brazil Prendergast, Charles Prendergast, A Catalogue Raisonné*. Williamstown: Williams College Museum of Art; Munich: Prestel, 1990.

McBride, Henry. "The Renoirs in America: In Appreciation of the Metropolitan Museum of Art's Exhibition." *Art News* 35, no. 11, May 1, 1937.

Meier-Graefe, Julius. *Modern Art: Being a Contribution to a New System of Aesthetics*, vol. 1. Translated by Florence Simmonds and George W. Chrystal. New York: G. P. Putnam's Sons, 1908.

Molesworth, Charles. *The Capitalist and the Critic: J. P. Morgan, Roger Fry, and the Metropolitan Museum of Art*. Austin: University of Texas Press, 2016.

Pero, Linda Szekely. *Norman Rockwell: Pictures for the American People*. Exhibition catalogue. Atlanta and Stockbridge: High Museum of Art and Norman Rockwell Museum, 1999.

Phillips, Marjorie. *Duncan Phillips and His Collection*. Boston: Little, Brown and Co., 1970.

*Renoir 1841–1919: Artists in Guernsey.* Guernsey Museum and Art Gallery, 1988.

"Renior: A Symposium." *Art In America*, March 1986.

Robinson, Edward G., with Leonard Spigelgass. *All My Yesterdays: An Autobiography*. New York: Hawthorne Books, 1973.

Roob, Rona. "A Noble Legacy." *Art in America*, no. 11, November 2003.

Scott, David W. "The Evolution of a Critic: Changing Views in the Writings of Duncan Phillips." In *The Eye of Duncan Phillips: A Collection in the Making*, edited by Erika D. Passantino. New Haven and London: Phillips Collection, in association with Yale University Press, 1999.

Sharf, Frederic A. *Art of Collecting: The Spaulding Brothers and Their Legacy*. Boston: Museum of Fine Arts, 2007.

Stein, Leo. "Renoir and the Impressionists." *New Republic*, March 30, 1918.

Smith, Roberta. "The Beauty of the Everyday." *New York Times*, August 15, 2014.

___. "Hot Conceptualist Finds the Secret of Skin." *New York Times*, September 4, 2008.

Stella, Frank. Interview with William Rubin. New York: Museum of Modern Art, 1970. YouTube. https://www.youtube.com/watch?v=cN_rRCfRdmQ.

Thompson, Jennifer A. "Durand-Ruel and America." In Sylvie Patry et al., *Inventing Impressionism: Paul Durand-Ruel and the Modern Art Market*. London: National Gallery of Art, 2015.

Tinterow, Gary. "The Havemeyer Pictures." In Alice Cooney Frelinghuysen et al., *Splendid Legacy: The Havemeyer Collection*. New York: Metropolitan Museum of Art, 1993.

Wadley, Nicholas, and Michael Hoog. *Renoir un peintre, une vie, une œuvre*, edited by Nicholas Wadley, preface by Michael Hoog. Paris: Belfond, 1989.

Wattenmaker, Richard J. *American Paintings and Works on Paper in the Barnes Foundation*. Merion: The Barnes Foundation in association with Yale University Press, 2010.

Weitzenhoffer, Frances. *The Havemeyers: Impressionism Comes to America*. New York: Harry N. Abrams, 1986.

White, Barbara Ehrlich. *Renoir: An Intimate Biography*. London: Thames & Hudson, 2017.

Woodward, Richard B. "'Renoir: Father and Son: Painting and Cinema' Review: Creative Currents." In *The Wall Street Journal* online, May 5, 2018. https://www.wsj.com/articles/renoir-father-and-son-painting-and-cinema-review-creative-currents-1525518000.

Wouters, Gina. *Robert Winthrop Chanler: Discovering the Fantastic*. New York: The Monacelli Press, 2016.

# Photography Credits and Copyrights

### Plates

2: © The National Gallery, London
3, 10: Photo: Minneapolis Institute of Art
7: Photo courtesy Denver Art Museum
8, 14, 17, 18, 21, 23, 27, 29, 30, 38, 59: Photo by Ben Hayward Smith, Miami, FL
19: Photograph by Joseph Levy
24: Michael Cullen, Toronto, Canada
33: Photography By: Mitro Hood
42, 46: Image © 2018 The Barnes Foundation
45: Photography © Terra Foundation for American Art, Chicago
51, 55: Photo: Michael McKelvey Photography
57: Photo: Will Howcroft
62: Bridgeman Images
65: Addison Gallery of American Art, Phillips Academy, Andover, MA / Art Resource, NY

### Figures

1: Image © The Metropolitan Museum of Art. Image source: Art Resource, NY
3: Photograph by Steven Brooke
4: © Raymond Pettibon; Courtesy Regen Projects, Los Angeles
5: © Kehinde Wiley; Courtesy Sean Kelly, New York, Roberts Projects, Culver City, California, Rhona Hoffman Gallery, Chicago, and Galerie Daniel Templon, Paris
7: © Association Marcel Duchamp / ADAGP, Paris / Artists Rights Society (ARS), New York 2018
8: Image: © Durand-Ruel & Cie, rights reserved
9, 15–17: Image courtesy of the Clark Art Institute, Williamstown, Massachusetts
10, 11, 25: Image: The Art Institute of Chicago / Art Resource, NY
12: Photograph © 2018 Museum of Fine Arts, Boston
13: Photo: Imaging Department © President and Fellows of Harvard College
14: Image: Album / Art Resource, NY
19–23, 27, 29, 33, 34: Image © 2018 The Barnes Foundation
24: © Estate Pierre Matisse / Artists Rights Society (ARS), New York
30: Image: Glenn Castellano / New-York Historical Society
31: Photo: Jim Gipe - PIVOT Media and Stephen Petegorsky

# Authors' Biographies

**Avis Berman** is the author of *Rebels on Eighth Street: Juliana Force and the Whitney Museum of American Art* (Atheneum, 1990), *James McNeill Whistler* (Harry N. Abrams, 1993), and *Edward Hopper's New York* (Pomegranate, 2005), and co-author and editor of Katharine Kuh's memoir *My Love Affair with Modern Art: Behind the Scenes with a Legendary Curator* (Arcade, 2006), as well as hundreds of articles, essays, and reviews. In 2014, for NSU Art Museum Fort Lauderdale, she organized the first comprehensive survey of William Glackens's work in nearly 50 years.

**Bonnie Clearwater** is director and chief curator, NSU Art Museum Fort Lauderdale. She formerly was the curator of the Mark Rothko Foundation, New York, director of art programs of the Lannan Foundation, Los Angeles, and director and chief curator of the Museum of Contemporary Art North Miami. Among her publications are *Defining the Nineties: Consensus-making in New York, Miami and Los Angeles* (Museum of Contemporary Art North Miami, 1996), *Frank Stella at 2000: Changing the Rules* (Museum of Contemporary Art North Miami, 2000), *The Rothko Book* (Tate, 2006), *Mark Rothko: Works on Paper* (Hudson Hills, 2008), *Some Aesthetic Decisions: A Centennial Celebration of Duchamp's "Fountain,"* exhibition catalogue (Skira, 2017).

**Martha Lucy**, Ph.D., is deputy director for Research, Interpretation and Education at the Barnes Foundation. A specialist in nineteenth-century European art, she has published many articles and essays on topics ranging from evolutionary themes in the work of Odilon Redon to the motif of the mirror in Impressionist painting. She is the co-author of *Renoir in the Barnes Foundation* (Yale University Press, 2012), the first scholarly catalogue of the Barnes's enormous Renoir collection.

**Barbara Buhler Lynes**, Ph.D., is the Sunny Kaufman Senior Curator, NSU Art Museum Fort Lauderdale. She was formerly founding curator, Georgia O'Keeffe Museum, and founding director, Georgia O'Keeffe Museum Research Center. A specialist on the art and life of Georgia O'Keeffe, she is author of *O'Keeffe, Stieglitz and the Critics, 1916–1929* (Chicago University Press, 1989), *Georgia O'Keeffe: Catalogue Raisonné* (Yale University Press, 1999), *Georgia O'Keeffe* (Skira, 2011), and other books and numerous essays on O'Keeffe and her contemporaries.

# NSU Art Museum Fort Lauderdale
# Board of Governors and Staff List